To Set Before a Queen

To Set Before a Queen

Mrs McKee's royal cookery

edited by
Maureen Owen

GRACEWING

First published in 1963 by Arlington Books Ltd

This revised edition first published in 2003

Gracewing
2 Southern Avenue, Leominster
Herefordshire HR6 0QF

UK ISBN 0 85244 558 X

Typesetting by Action Publishing Technology Ltd,
Gloucester, GL1 5SR

Printed by Antony Rowe Ltd
Eastbourne BN23 6QT

Contents

Introduction

IN THE SHOWERY CHILL OF THE CLARENCE HOUSE GARDEN ON THE morning of 2nd June 1953 I felt the heartwarming glow of one at the centre of events, if not at the centre of fashion. Like thousands of others turning out for the great day, I was equipped with mac and umbrella. Plastic galoshes to go over the high heels considered essential, completed the post-war picture of would-be glamour combined with utility clothing. Most women, including the royals, wore lashings of lipstick.

Queen Elizabeth II's Coronation warmed the public heart, but according to records it was the coldest June of the century.

Together with other invited guests, I watched the procession from the specially erected stands overlooking the Mall and saw the Queen Mother smile and wave as she passed her home as if to say, 'Have a good time'. The new Queen also scanned the grounds of her old house nodding at familiar faces. Because of the rain guests soon made a beeline for the Clarence House private cinema where the proceedings on television were described in the emollient tones of Richard Dimblebly. But this was an occasion when getting wet was worth it to see the real thing. As the plumed and scarlet coated guardsmen flanking the royal coaches splashed past on horseback, the Coronation unfolded a transformation scene of blazing light and brilliance.

Set against the shortages, restrictions and all-pervading dreariness of the early Fifties, we suddenly felt life was on the up and up. And for those lucky enough to be inside royal walls on this colourful occasion, the magnificent cold buffet prepared by Mrs McKee the Queen Mother's cook – and presumably provided by the Queen Mother herself – seemed like Balshazzar's feast.

Mrs McKee was my friend at court. Like the rest of the visitors surging forward as the amazingly turbanned Queen Salote of Tonga rode by, I was a guest of a member of staff.

The guests were friends and relations of staff from Clarence House, Windsor and Sandringham with a sprinkling from

Balmoral; anyone in fact connected with royal service. I was the only journalist; someone who would normally be treated with caution by royal staff. But as a regular visitor to Clarence House, the elegant cream-coloured house on the Mall first occupied by Princess Elizabeth and her family in 1949 and then for the Coronation by the Queen Mother and Princess Margaret, I was a guest and, out of respect, my notebook stayed in my handbag.

All the same, as the day wore on, snatched fragments of conversation proved tantalizing .... At the last minute the Queen Mother decided to wear some of the Crown Jewels. A special car came down the sealed-off streets from the Tower – but nothing was right and the historic gems were returned. True or false? Possible I thought, but the newspaper I worked for, the left-leaning *News Chronicle*, disdained royal gossip. Moreover, I had already written my piece. In it, I described the new Queen as a modern career woman, a role model who would bring some sparkle and gaiety, to the dismal austerity of the time. I wrote a column called 'The Young Idea' but the youthquake of the Sixties was not in sight.

As one bent on having fun, my hopes were genuine. So was my admiration of the Princess. From what I had seen of Elizabeth she was bright, attractive and unaffected; a person who was generally good at things. This was an impression originally formed when taken as a child to play with the two Princesses in Hamilton Gardens, close to their house at 145 Piccadilly. Elizabeth's skill with the skipping rope had made a deep impression ... 'salt, mustard, vinegar, pepper –'. As the rope twirled in time to the rhyme, she performed the intricate steps with enviable precision, performing the difficult crossed arm manouevres with stylish grace. While I could only skip to ten and Princess Margaret tripped over the rope and sulked in the bushes, Elizabeth struck me as able and confident. First impressions die hard.

Later, as a royal watcher of the early Fifties, I had often noticed a twinkle of amusement in Elizabeth's eye. In fact I had a strong impression that she was longing for someone to do or say something to make her laugh. I noticed that those who did so were usually rewarded with a beaming smile. I think there was something in this as Prince Philip's Australian equerry, Michael Parker told me that he had been asked to tell a few jokes when on royal tours to keep up a happy smiley impression. In fact Parker, whom

I had first met sailing Philip's Dragon class yacht, was well known for his stock of outrageous jokes; some of Elizabeth's most radiant smiles being a direct result. I also had an uncle who was in the Crazy Gang (the Royal Family's favourite music hall turn), who said the King once remarked that the whole family adored people who made them laugh. Sadly most didn't, reacting stiffly in the royal presence.

One of my first newspaper jobs was to report on fashion, though hardly fashion as we know it today because of clothes rationing. Girls dressed like their mothers, their hair flattened under tight fitting hats. Royal fashion excited interest, it seems strange to recall, and junior reporters such as myself were all terribly correct about reporting it. Unlike today, no details of the royal wardrobe were released until the Queen or Princesses actually appeared in public. Our job was to stand outside the Palace gates in all weathers trying to peer through the car windows, jotting down notes on the style of hats and coats. This later had to be checked with royal couturiers such as Normal Hartnell or Hardy Amies.

Inside the Palace press office, Commander Richard Colville and his assistant Diana Lyttleton, (the joyless sister of Humphrey) regarded the press corps as a blot on the landscape. 'That is the Royal Family's own private business' was the standard response to most enquiries.

I had no sooner decided that the role of royal reporter was not for me, than matters took a surprising turn. It was Prince Charles' third birthday and despite their antipathy to royal minutiae my newspaper instructed me to find out what was happening behind the cream walls of Clarence House. My news editor, irritated by the usual brush off told me to adopt 'the public has a right to know' attitude.

This time an unimpressed Miss Lyttleton ended the familiar mantra by adding, 'If you are so frightfully interested why don't you call Clarence House?', before crashing down the phone. Since Clarence House had no press office and would only refer any queries back to the Palace, this was sarcasm at its most crushing. But as it was now lunchtime and I was stuck with what was clearly a hopeless story, I decided to take her advice. Explaining to the polite man on the switchboard that none other than Miss Lyttleton from Buckingham Palace had advised me to phone about the royal birthday arrangements, I held on while – guess what? – 'Enquiries were made'. Next came a courteous apology: Unfortunately everyone seemed to be at lunch, could I come round right away and talk to the Clarence House chef, Mrs McKee?

Poor Leslie Treby. It was his first day on the Clarence House switchboard and although I have no doubt he got a telling-off, I was glad to hear that he later found promotion at Buckingham Palace.

Meeting Mrs McKee in the dazzling new kitchen at Clarence House was, to compare it to a popular film of the era, like step-ping into a *Wizard of Oz* dream sequence. A time which coincided with the upbeat feeling of the Coronation and took me into the strange twin worlds of an upstairs-downstairs existence I could scarcely have imagined. Meeting Mrs McKee was a turning point in my perceptions. For a start I had visualized a male chef at Clarence House. Buckingham Palace had the half-French Monsieur Aubrey, Queen Mary over at Marlborough House had the Swiss-born Gabriel Tschumi. Both were fairly well known but no one had heard of Alma McKee. Over six foot tall and clad in snowy white overalls, with blue-grey eyes and rounded cheeks, Mrs McKee was the very picture of a revered and treasured family cook. A Swedish accent went with a charming manner and as I later found, a gloriously sweet-natured temperament: a sort of Guardian Angel of the table.

Except in American films or magazines, no one had ever seen anything like the Clarence House kitchen in run-down post-war Britain. All gleaming stainless steel with a central island for gas cooker and electric pastry oven, the units had been a wedding present from one of the Dominions and Elizabeth was so proud of her modern kitchen that she often brought guests downstairs to marvel at it. On this occasion, preparations were going ahead for the tea party: I remember banana sandwiches, egg and cress rolls, jelly, chocolate fingers and an amazing white and yellow birthday cake with pictures in icing which told the story of the Ugly Duckling from Hans Andersen. The era of crisps had not yet arrived.

After writing down the details and admiring the kitchen, I enquired into Mrs McKee's background. She was married to a Scottish butler and had trained in Sweden. Previously with ex-

King Peter and Queen Alexandra of Yugoslavia, she was indeed very happy at Clarence House. Before leaving I told her I was interested in cooking and asked if she would like to come out to lunch one day when less busy. In this rosy glow of enchantment, I was only slightly surprised when she accepted and gave me a number to ring.

Back in Fleet Street, I was finishing my story when the phone rang. It was General Sir Frederick Browning, Comptroller of Clarence House. He was sending a car into which I would get, bringing whatever I had written with me.

There were no 'ifs' or 'buts'.

I had a long wait in a downstairs room at Clarence House. The place was crammed with Grenadier Guardsmen. I later learned that the Grenadiers featured prominently in Clarence House life. The officers were often in evidence on social occasions and made up the numbers at parties. You could tell Grenadiers by the way they stood up in sections, unfolding their unusually long backs. Meanwhile they were doing what they were designed for – guarding.

General Sir Frederick Arthur Montague Browning, known as 'Boy' in the regiment, was six foot tall with penetrating grey eyes and dark moustache; very alert and energetic as he strode into the room with a confident bearing. Known as a ferocious disciplinarian who had set the highest standards for his men and himself in two world wars culminating in the battle of Arnhem, he was renowned for his smart appearance. The Yellow Brick Road from the *Wizard of Oz* had led to what appeared to be a dimly lit guardroom. My mouth went dry with fear.

The next half hour in which I could see myself in the Tower of London accused of treason, was extremely uncomfortable. I knew, General Browning told me, that as a journalist I was not allowed inside a royal residence; I had tricked my way in. It was a very serious offence ... my editor must be informed. What had I got to say for myself?

Deciding that under the circumstances attack was not just the best but the only form of defence, I told the General of the tedious and unnecessary rigmaroles which journalists endured in order to gain the tiniest crumb of information from Buckingham Palace. Did my newspaper for instance, mind if they never carried a royal report again? No. But did readers who admired the Princess and her family as I did, want to hear a few harmless human details? The answer was, yes. And I thought it was a shame that they couldn't. Pointing to my story lying on his desk I asked, 'What's wrong with a few banana sandwiches?'

After an unnerving silence, the General stood up and departed with my story through an inner door which had been left open during our interview. I was told to remain where I was. Imagining he had gone to get the guard, I was unprepared for his affable re-entry. I will never know what happened in the interval, but a vast difference seemed to have come over him. 'Well,' he said leaning back in his chair, 'full marks for initiative, I'll give you that.'

Mysteriously, I was given more than that. It was all right to visit Mrs McKee at Clarence House and to take her out to tea or lunch on her days off, 'as she so desired'. But anything I wrote as a result of my visits to Clarence House must first be submitted to him.

This entailed further visits to the Comptroller's office with whatever I'd written. 'What's this?' he would cry. 'More banana sandwiches?'

Getting to know the explosive General, I found him surprisingly moody. He admitted that at home he was known as 'Mopey'. Once he spent half an hour bemoaning the fact that on a beautiful day such as this he could be out on his yacht, the *Fanny Rosa*, moored in Cornwall near the house he shared with his wife Daphne du Maurier ... Why, I asked, don't you like your job? I found that a direct manner was the best way of talking to him. 'Good God,' he exploded, 'I was designed to be a soldier not a courtier.' On another occasion, I broached the fact that Elizabeth had been criticized for looking glum in photos.

'Good God,' he said, 'she isn't a bloody film star, grinning all over the shop.' It was the King, he once confided, that had noticed that the Royal Family's press cuttings were 'getting a bit thin' (apparently he checked them himself) and decided that a more relaxed attitude was needed in what was released to the press. What sort of thing, I asked?

'Well he's not going to tell the world what colour his bathroom is painted, but I suppose the sort of stuff you do is all right,' he said. 'You know, the lighter side.' In fact, even such faint and baffling praise as this presented some constraints. Although I was sent to Royal Ascot, Palace garden parties and premieres, thus observing the Royal Family at public level, no one at the *News Chronicle* except the Woman's editor, Gladys Boyd, took much interest in my visits to Clarence House. Another of General Browning's stipulations also prevented me from mentioning them in print ... 'Good God, we'd have the whole pack in here if they (the press) knew about you.'

The result of these conflicts was that although officially recognized by the policemen on the gate and the staff in the Comptroller's office, I never felt entirely relaxed on my visits to Clarence House. What was I doing there? It was a more deferential age and still partly traumatized by my first encounter with the General, I dreaded being suddenly apprehended as an interloper. Meanwhile I decided to concentrate on the cookery. At least I could learn how to be useful in the kitchen.

Continuing to see Mrs McKee, another world unfolded. She gave frequent dinner parties in a little room off the kitchen to which were invited notable chefs from hotels such as the Ritz and Savoy as well as her next-door neighbour, the philosophical Gabriel Tschumi, cook to Queen Mary. At Marlborough House, Queen Mary, Elizabeth's grandmother, ran an academy of excellence. No manufactured foods – not even a biscuit – were allowed on the premises. Tschumi made everything himself and spent hours discussing menus with the Queen. He held the view that to know what people liked (and didn't like) about food is half way to understanding them. Thus, Queen Mary's liking for the Black Hamburgh grapes sent from Windsor in the autumn were a happy reminder of her German background. According to Tschumi, all great dishes should have some special significance. No one was embarrassed when Mrs McKee announced that all her dishes were made with love. This was her abiding philosophy and a remark which could stand as her motto. Although ignorant of the difference between choux pastry and short, I came to see that through food a true chef expressed a relationship with the wider world where culinary talent was as individual as writing or painting. If only you could get the raw materials.

It had been true when I told Mrs McKee that I was interested in cookery. But I was interested in the way one might be about a distant country – I'd heard about it. In 1951 the Labour Government had cut the meat ration to its lowest level since rationing began: from 10*d* to 8*d* a week; the equivalent of 4ozs of steak per person per week. In order to qualify for a whole leg of lamb, you would need the coupons from thirteen different ration books.

I was always assured that the Royal Family stuck strictly to rationing and indeed Mrs McKee had been partly chosen for her resourcefulness. When Elizabeth and Philip visited their cousins ex-King Peter and Queen Alexandra of Yugoslavia at their rented house in Egham, they had greatly admired the ingenious way Mrs McKee had produced a delicious meal made almost entirely from vegetables cut from the garden. Apart from rationing, they were very hard-up though later they decamped to Monte Carlo to live in style after Alexandra sold her memoirs to *Woman's Own*.

If the roast beef of old England had become a fond memory, fresh vegetables were plentiful and there was a certain amount of fish available. Food experts, though, seemed to combine propaganda with oddly bizarre advice. Dr John Yudkin, a professor of nutrition, insisted that tinned vegetables were as good as fresh, launching the first post-war debate on food snobbery. Potato Pete, a popular Ministry of Food invention, advised, 'Save those orange rinds!' Grated and mixed with a little mashed potato, the potatoes will turn an exciting pink colour'. Dr Carrot was another Ministry of Food creation who despite the many delicious and varied uses for carrots later shown me by Mrs McKee, spent his time devising recipes for carrot jam and carrot marmalade (both disgusting) on the false premise that 'carrots help you to see in the dark!'

Attitudes of guilt lingered on. My mother's wartime recipe book, still in use, contained such gems as: 'Our sailors don't mind risking their lives to feed you and your family – but they do mind if you help the U-boats by wasting food'.

I was part of a generation which had been discouraged from experimenting with the rations. If waste was a sin, a burnt chop would be a crime. My mother presided over the stove and as result not only could I hardly cook at all, but was apprehensive about trying. Nor did cookery advice such as 'Six ways to stuff a potato' provide an inspirational start.

Shopping for anything involved queues. Things we take for granted today were considered exotic. For instance, olive oil, if ever used on its own, was only obtainable in small bottles from the chemist and Heinz Salad Cream, Spam and tinned soups were seen on the best tables. On the other hand, food was fresh and seasonal and even if people boiled the goodness out of a cabbage at home, produce had not been stored, frozen, packaged and driven up and down the country until it was tasteless like it is today. Presentation didn't matter and few people minded that English cooking was known as the worst in Europe. After all, we'd won the war.

Most people I knew regarded cooking as a chore, so not surprisingly Mrs McKee's attitude came as a revelation. I was taken by the look of her food long before I understood how to make it. Oddly, the first thing I remember were the vegetables which went with a main dish and which looked and tasted like no common or garden vegetables I had seen on a plate before. Hasselback potatoes; potatoes peeled, halved and sliced almost through to open out like crunchy fans in a high temperature oven, were a delicious Scandanavian idea which didn't waste anyone's rations. Carrot timbales – pureed carrots lightly steamed in ramekins to provide a dramatic splash of colour – were from French haute cuisine and as such had gone unrecommended by Dr Carrot at the Ministry of Food.

What I was seeing, smelling and tasting, now seems like a fore-runner of nouvelle cuisine with a Swedish angle. But despite the Scandanavian tag, there was never really a name for the unfettered variety of Mrs McKee's cooking. Her unique quality perhaps, was to 'bring out the flavour of those good ingredients' which coming from Home Farm, Windsor meant unmistakable freshness.

To this end, she would use herbs and – what surprised me – ginger, which I learned enhanced, rather than obscured the flavour of dishes such as pork, ham and duck. As herbs (except for a little crinkled parsley) were practically unobtainable at this stage in English history, much time was spent in a struggle for supplies. All but unheard of in Britain, dill was her particular favourite. She planted a root in the garden at Clarence House where it was dug up by the gardeners and would always bring some back from holidays in Sweden. Dill went with the fish which featured daily on the royal menus; particularly salmon from the Dee and the delicately flavoured Gravad Lax – then known as Salmon Dill – which she cured herself.

Sweet savory, an old English herb, difficult to find today unless you grow it, was used in soups and mixed with oil and lemon as a fragrant infusion for miniature broad beans. Parsley she seemed to use for colouring and flavour rather than for the stiff genteel sprigs then popular as decoration. The evocative smell of green pea and apple soup, its colour intensified by wringing a generous bunch of parsley into it before serving, was almost an aphrodisiac.

Although cooking smells, now mostly banished by extractor fans, are no longer much glorified, I certainly found that the scents floating from the Clarence House kitchen heightened my appreciation of good food. Is it a coincidence, for instance, that Prince Charles, who took a lively interest in food and who would always take a good sniff when entering the kitchen, is now known for keeping the best table in the Royal Family?

Speaking for myself, I will always remember the divinely aromatic strawberry juice which was sieved then striped over home-made ice cream – the original strawberry ripple. The Sandringham strawberries have a unique smell and flavour which to me is the best in the world. I once picked some with Mrs McKee in Edward VII's original walled garden at Sandringham. But sadly they do not travel well. Bedded in vine leaves, a short car journey was about enough for them. Then there was the delicious smell of one particular favourite: English applecake, slightly caramelized, tinged a glorious pink and served with cream from the Jersey herd ... 'Just a little', as the Queen Mother would say.

Learning to cook at Clarence House was not exactly a step by step experience. One day (during the Coronation period) I found Mrs McKee preparing a spectacular Grand Marnier soufflé decorated with spun sugar which was served on a block of ice filled with flowers. In its perfection, it looked deceptively easy to make. But to the ignorant, all things are possible – until of course you try it for yourself – which, with my mother guarding the rations as usual, was a doomed enterprise. On another visit, I watched the more humble stuffed cabbage in progress. A simple enough recipe but one which still required some finely judged processes to hold the texture together – reducing the sauce to go with it also needed care. As today's viewers of television cookery will realize, seeing a dish prepared is not the same as cooking it yourself. Mrs McKee did not use recipes – not even her own – and I had mostly been an onlooker until the day she collapsed with a migraine over the lunch preparations. The dish was pheasant with celery and, in fact, only needed finishing when I nervously tipped almost a whole pint of cream into the mixture which then curdled and had to be scraped off. I was visualizing the complaints when saved by the ubiquitous Clarence House butler, Ernest Bennett, who scraped off the cream, seized some redcurrant sauce from the fridge, heated it and poured it over the pheasants which he sliced with expert speed.

The importance of Ernest Bennett in the life of the present Queen remains publicly unsung. Few meeting him would be aware exactly what his role was; butler, major domo, page extra-ordinaire: his titles changed as time wore on but he was more like a master of ceremonies. Of all those who played a special part behind the scenes, Bennett was indispensible to the Queen and the indisputable doyen of Clarence House. The sort of man who knew where everything was and what anyone might need before they thought of it, he lived life with a flourish appearing to fly on winged feet between upstairs and downstairs while giving the impression that everything was done with the greatest of ease. Whenever Elizabeth went out, Bennett would be lurking, though not always in the background, with whatever might be needed for the occasion.

Bennett was extremely proud of the newly-reconditioned Clarence House. It had fallen into disrepair during the war and had never been properly modernized since it had been occupied by Queen Victoria's youngest son, the Duke of Connaught who died in 1942. Now it was probably the most beautifully appointed private house in Britain, simply decorated with sunshine stream-ing in at large windows and without the overfurnished finality of most historic homes.

Bennett loved showing people round. I remember him drawing the blue curtains in Prince Philip's study with the cry, 'What do you think of our drapes?' With its pale mushroom-carpeted corridors, hollyhock-patterned chintzes in the Princess's turquoise-coloured sitting room, the soft glisten of Waterford glass in the main reception rooms and fresh, contemporary atmosphere, Clarence House certainly compared favourably with the threadbare appearance of Buckingham Palace. I had been presented at court in 1948 and noticed that it was just as shabby as anywhere else in post-war Britain. With much of Europe still in ruins, rebuilding had been slow. Building licences – a fertile source of sharp practice, scandal and jealousy – were grudgingly issued for repairs. Only 46% of British householders had bath-rooms, so the fact that in 1947 Clarence House had no bathroom – only a copper bath that had to be pulled out of a cupboard – meant that the new owners had to apply for a licence and take their place in the queue for building permission. Current housing shortages also meant that not everyone was sympathetic to their problem.

Bennett was scornful of what he saw as jealous criticisms of the best Britain could do for its future Queen. He said that the King had been worn out by all the battles.

There had also been much argument about the sum of £50,000 voted by Parliament for the reconditioning of Clarence House. Records show that the equipment of kitchen, scullery and service quarters accounted for a large slice of expenditure and the instal-lation of light, power and heating left little over for embellishment. The finished result had a modern feel, not so much grand as a cheerful happy house. Bennett said that it was all the better for not being 'cluttered up with heavy stuff from Buckingham Palace'. Almost entirely furnished with wedding presents, there was room on the walls for more paintings: but apart from some portraits of the family of William IV found in the dining room, Elizabeth and Philip had mostly chosen contempo-rary artists such as Paul Nash, Edward Seago and Duncan Grant.

Elizabeth had stuck out the first storm of criticism and over the years was to see many others. As it turned out there were only to be a few short years in the one home furnished according to her own preferences. They were probably the happiest of her life.

In just over three years, it was back to the Palace. 'Dogs' pee all over the carpets again,' said Bennett. Although the corgis at Clarence House were house-trained, he had a horror of stains, strategically placing soda water siphons and blotting paper behind photographs and vases in case of a sudden lapse.

Bennett told me that none of the staff were keen on moving to the Palace. He said Mrs McKee was lucky she didn't have to go. Life there would be more bureaucratic. But move the Queen must. Meanwhile a complicated staff reshuffle took place overseen by General Browning who was going to the Palace as 'Treasurer' to Prince Philip. When I asked him what this entailed he said he'd no idea, but he expected he would find out.

If anything marked the royal households off as an Alice in

Wonderland world, it was their passion for arcane titles. Browning told me that they were regarded as a useful form of recognition and didn't cost anything. For instance, if the Royal Family wanted to bestow special recognition on a loyal servant, an archivist would unearth the fact that in the reign of Queen Anne or some other sovereign, there was once a Page of the Backstairs. The title would be revived and, 'Bingo,' he said, 'everyone was happy.'

Bennett, upset at leaving the house he had so scrupulously overseen, at least had the compensation of a more powerful position. He became the Queen's principal page at Buckingham Palace and was also give a grace and favour flat round the corner at Kensington Palace where he lived with his wife and a son who worked at Dunhill's in Piccadilly. I last saw him at a Buckingham Palace garden party putting the fear of God into some footmen who had failed to produce umbrellas for the royal party at a snap of his fingers. Never the discreet butler type, he was unafraid to use strong language when the occasion warranted and had a sergeant major wit which had long been the scourge of lowlier staff. 'I'll give 'em Any Umbrellas,' he said savagely humming the well-known tune and bustling into the garden. When something was wrong, Bennett didn't mind who heard his tirades. Elizabeth seemed to be used to it. Her closest servants were loyal but unlike the courtiers, never unduly deferential.

If Bennett was the Queen's most trusted servant, then Bobo MacDonald was her most loyal confidante. The Scottish sisters, Bobo and Ruby, had originally been taken on as nursery maids by the Queen Mother (then Duchess of York) when Elizabeth and Margaret were infants. Now Elizabeth's personal maid at Clarence House, Bobo preferred to be known as the Princess's 'Dresser'. She could easily have been one of those doughty theatrical dressers, a breed who are fully aware that without them the show will not go on. Always ironing, mending, brushing, steaming, matching accessories or packing, she was in total charge of the royal wardrobe. In the era of make-do and mend, Bobo spent her time taking up or letting down skirts and mending underwear. Where it all came from was a mystery. Thrifty by nature, I once saw her with a huge pile of baby clothes which she was altering for Princess Anne.

A small bird-like woman who when I saw her was usually

dressed in a tartan skirt and bright red twinset with matching lipstick, Bobo liked reading fashion magazines and could make her own clothes. As a cut above the other servants, she ate separately in her room upstairs, often with her sister, Ruby. With her strong Scottish accent, she would refer to Elizabeth as 'My little leddy' (meaning lady), and despite a reserved attitude, could be outspoken, 'My little leddy will never eat that!', she remarked once about a delicious but rather rich pudding. 'Think of her figure.' The dish came back scraped clean, but Mrs McKee declined to argue. Below stairs no one tangled with Bobo.

Both MacDonald sisters were totally dedicated to their own members of the Royal Family. Ruby had looked after Princess Margaret since childhood. But during the Coronation, she became the Queen Mother's dresser and would wait up until late at night in order to help her undress. However, after years of royal service, the MacDonald sisters were thinking of marriage. The close loyalty which bound them to the Royal Family could also have a limiting effect on outside relationships. Mrs McKee thought that Elizabeth's marriage had affected Bobo, making her more conscious of the future.

Mrs McKee believed she was psychic. One of her talents was to tell fortunes and after the dinner parties with fellow chefs palled, she would sometimes get the cards out for favoured guests. She correctly predicted the death of the King which caused a stir below stairs at the time although as Bennett rather sharply pointed out, anyone could see he was ill. But if Bennett wasn't interested, Bobo and Ruby came armed with questions about the future. Mrs McKee could not see any major changes in the cards for Bobo, but for Ruby, she predicted romance with a soldier. Some years afterwards, Ruby made a late marriage to a guardsman, while Bobo ended her days at Buckingham Palace. To the last she trusted no one else with the cleaning of the Queen's best known trademark, those gleaming white shoes.

Royal watchers who claim to have an intimate picture of the royals at home may like to know that at Buckingham Palace and other royal houses, life is so arranged that the majority of staff never set eyes on them. The exception was Clarence House where there was an open invitation for anyone who wanted to have a sort of private viewing when members of the Royal Family were going out on special occasions. The Queen Mother, who seemed to enjoy these previews which took place in the hall, would give a twirl in one of her crinolines, saying, 'Hasn't Mr Hartnell done well?' The thing to do was to wave her off and wish her a happy evening.

On the few occasions when I did see Elizabeth at home, I would copy Mrs McKee and give a half-curtsey. You would then wait to see if she wanted to talk. If she had the children with her, there would be no problem. Prince Charles adored Mrs McKee whom he called 'The Lady in White', and would chatter away about what he had been seeing and doing. At the 'Why?' and 'What for?' stage, he would ask innumerable questions – all of which were answered with thought, care and some jokes. In view of recent criticisms of her maternal role, I have to say that Elizabeth struck me as a warm and loving mother. She seemed proud of her children who could hardly be called repressed.

Shortly after becoming Queen, Elizabeth did have one go at correcting the image of herself as a cold and distant mother. It happened when a journalist from a Sunday newspaper reported that the royal children were made to behave with absurd formality in front of their mother. It turned out that a chambermaid who had never actually seen the Queen had been bribed into giving false reports. The journalist in question was sent for and the Queen made it clear that although the press could say whatever they liked about her, she would not accept invented stories about her children. But fifty years on it's strange to see history repeating itself with attacks on the Queen's maternal role when, if anything, the family had reacted strongly against Queen Mary's strict brand of domestic discipline.

I am not claiming that the relaxed and happy impression I had of the Queen with her family is anything but a personal snapshot. It was a different era; people were less cynical. But if after all these years the Queen is still cast as a frosty mother figure, I only hope she has given up worrying about it. And as Bennett once remarked, 'If she didn't laugh, she'd cry'. There can't be a working mother in the country who doesn't understand the difficulties of combining both roles, but unlike most of us, she didn't have the choice. I sometimes wonder what the reaction would have been if she had said, 'No, I don't want to be Queen yet. I want to stay at home with the children.' But with typical understatement, Elizabeth just went on record as saying that she would do the best job she could. I found that quite moving.

In the summer of 1952, I went to see my friend Mrs McKee who was enjoying a well-earned break at Royal Lodge Windsor. It had been a hectic period at Clarence House after the Accession. The number of visitors needing to be fed and watered had reached an all-time peak. Now the Queen Mother and Princess Margaret were coming to Clarence House. Only no one knew when. 'It's going to be a bit of a squeeze,' said the Queen Mother the last time she looked round. Her move was postponed three times. For the staff, waiting to resume their jobs, it was a time of uncertainty.

Meanwhile at the Palace, the Queen and Philip moved into the Belgian Suite, usually reserved for visiting foreign royals. The children were miles away in the old nurseries which hadn't been used for years. People began to wonder not when but if, the Queen Mother would move from the royal apartments.

Alma was overjoyed to have Poppet, her Siamese cat, with her at Royal Lodge. The Queen had originally given special permission for Poppet to live at Clarence House where he miraculously survived the corgis. Now she had personally arranged for Poppet to stay at Royal Lodge before returning to Clarence House with Mrs McKee. With everything else that was going on, Mrs McKee hadn't liked to ask whether the Queen Mother would let her keep Poppet at Clarence House. But Mrs McKee didn't have to ask. The Queen had already arranged it. She understood how much having her cat to care for meant to Mrs McKee. A small gesture perhaps, but I remembered it as an example of the thoughtful side of the Queen's character which Alma had always stressed. A sort of cat by Special Appointment, Poppet was having the time of his life chasing birds in the rhododendrons at Royal Lodge. Unfortunately, his days were to be numbered.

Less could be done about situations such as Alma's husband, Jimmy McKee, who was a butler to a titled lady and 'lived-in'. Jimmy would visit his wife on his days off and they would sometimes go out togther. In those days it was not unusual for a husband and wife in service to live separately. But pay was lowly – Mrs McKee was only paid £6 a week – and it meant that many could not afford their own homes until retirement, if then.

Getting to know the upstairs-downstairs world of royal service, I began to realize something of its hidden demands. General Browning sometimes spoke of the strains of separation. His wife Daphne du Maurier was based firmly in Cornwall. 'She can't stand London,' he barked. 'Hates dressing up.' But despite his obvious enjoyment of the social life (and the dressing up) which went with the job, he often admitted to feeling lonely.

Those like Bobo who had sacrificed their personal lives to royal service were made to feel Clarence House was their home and were encouraged to entertain their own friends; food and drink were on the house. According to General Browning, it was only as a friend of Mrs McKee that I had been given permission to visit Clarence House. It had always puzzled me as I had never met her before my first visit. However, once on the downstairs visitors' list you felt as welcome as any royal guest.

It was clear though, that for all its privileges, royal service combined uneasily with family life. Spouses didn't fit into the scene. Constantly on call, socially as well as officially, the ideal courtier would really be a bachelor. Both Michael Parker and Group Captain Peter Townsend who later replaced General Browning as Comptroller of Clarence House, were examples of the strains of court life which led to the breakdown of their marriages. Sacked, disgraced, and in Townsend's case banished after his romance with Princess Margaret, they paid the dangerous price of alienation from ordinary life. With his high voice and rather affected manner, Townsend reminded me of a courtier from the age of Elizabeth I; flattery and charm were his trademark. As regards efficiency, he was not rated as highly as General Browning (despite the moans and groans). Townsend was the father of two young sons and a wartime D.S.O. How much he had departed from reality was highlighted when staff noted that he could be seen at teatime going through the pages of Vogue with Princess Margaret and the Queen Mother. The easy-going Michael Parker, who would think nothing of inviting friends (myself among them) to cocktail parties on board *Britannia* had to leave his job as Philip's private secretary following his divorce in 1957. By then he had overstepped too many boundaries; in the artificial life of the courtier, doors that open as if by magic can close just as quickly.

Mrs McKee was usually too busy to think about the famous visitors she was cooking for, but among her favourites were the virtually unknown family of Prince Philip. To the British public, his mother Princess Alice of Greece was a mystery woman. Known as Ya-Ya (Greek for grandmother) to Princes Charles, the

Princess dressed in the austere robes of a nun, a nursing order she had founded herself.

Deaf from childhood, she had the knack of lip reading across a room, giving the uncanny impression that she was a mind reader when later repeating the conversation. No official mention was made of her visits and hearing that Alice had almost starved to death during the war in Greece, Mrs McKee didn't know whether to feed her up or cater for the ascetic tastes of a nun. Deciding on the latter course, she thought it prudent to serve simple but wholesome food in small quantities. Alice was appreciative of Mrs McKee's efforts, but it became clear when she paid a visit to the kitchen one day that she had a hearty appetite.

No one was more open in their enjoyment of good food than Princess Alice and no one showed fewer airs and graces. However, one un-nun like habit caused Bennett serious concern. She was a serious smoker and after noticing clouds of smoke coming from her room, he placed fire extinguishers outside.

Her four daughters, Prince Philip's elder sisters, had all married Germans, an inconvenient fact played down when World War II was still fresh in public memory. Because of it, Philip's sisters had not been invited to his wedding. But Philip's large extended family of nephews and nieces would often come to stay at Clarence House. Elizabeth was generous about offering hospitality and the Hesses, two young brothers and a sister, children of Philip's sister Cecile who had been killed in an air crash, said that they looked forward all year to these visits. Elizabeth arranged all sorts of things for them to do and gave them the freedom to invite their own guests. Mrs McKee described them as 'sparkling all over the place' whenever they came to stay – they even offered to help with the cooking.

But 'help' with the cooking was firmly discouraged. In this domain, Mrs McKee was queen. Mainly because naval officers were supposed to be good at making corned beef hash, a popular dish at the time, rumours got round that Prince Philip was in the habit of producing a nifty example during his informal visits to the kitchen. But Mrs McKee said rather tightly, 'No, never' and Bennett who liked a joke at the kitchen staff's expense added, 'Not on your Nelly'.

Most likely, even Philip wouldn't have dared to try his hand at cooking. The only time I heard indignant protests at Clarence House was after Princess Margaret cooked a late night supper for

some guests. Despite clearing up, she was said to have put everything back in the wrong cupboards. The Royal Family were
expected to know their place and as far as staff were concerned,
this did not include the kitchen. Had the Queen taken to cooking,
I sensed that there would have been trouble. In some ways, the
Royal Family were ruled by their staff.

Everything changed when the Queen Mother came to Clarence
House. The number of staff almost doubled, and with more
pictures than wall space, collections of china to be displayed and
lots of little tables everywhere, gone was the airy spaciousness of
what I thought of as the loveliest home in London. 'Clutter', as
Bennett called it, had taken over.

Luckily food rationing had been abolished in 1954 because
sometimes there would be a dinner party for the Queen Mother
followed an hour later by another for Princess Margaret. There
was a different set of dogs to be kept out of the kitchen and a
different set of people coming in at the front door – the Princess
Margaret set had arrived on the scene and, with the Princess bent
on enjoying a riotous time, Clarence House became a livelier –
and noisier – place.

In the swap-over between Clarence House and Buckingham
Palace many things, including pots and pans, were mislaid or
lost. One item that had been carefully preserved impressed me
particularly. This was the Queen Mother's butter pat which bore
her Scottish coat of arms. The pattern was solemnly stamped on
the butter that was taken up on her breakfast tray every morning.
It was thought of as quite normal, but if anything symbolized the
difference between a royal breakfast and anyone else's, I'd say
this was it.

Mrs McKee's last days at Clarence House were not to be the
happiest of her life.

The Queen Mother wanted her to stay on. 'We need good food,'
she told Mrs McKee. 'We need the stamina.' At the same time, she
said that she was used to a male chef. Mrs McKee herself believed
that a large kitchen was better controlled by a man. In fact, the
Clarence House kitchen was not large, comparatively speaking.
Yet with extra staff to be fed by day and two levels of royal
entertaining at night, the number of menus required proved in
time to be nothing less than a test of stamina. The only respite
came when the Queen Mother went to the Castle of Mey or joined

the usual rotation to Sandringham, Windsor and Balmoral. Overstaffing, especially among the footmen, did little to improve efficiency but at least provided some amusement. Once when the Queen Mother was due to go out for the evening, dressed in one of her fabulous crinolines, she changed her mind at the last minute about the tiara she was wearing. Another was sent for which was brought down by a footman who stepped out of the lift, wearing it. As some rather starchy members of the Household present looked shocked, the Queen Mother pretended to be cross but it was clear she could hardly stop laughing. Later I heard that it made her evening.

As time wore on Mrs McKee was usually either too busy or too tired to show me any more cooking.

Almost inevitably, when old staff are merged with the new and people work and live together within the same organization, petty jealousies begin to surface.

By 1953, Clarence House appeared to be no exception. Matters started to go wrong when the chocolate cake Mrs McKee made for the Queen Mother's birthday disappeared. It had been sent by car to Royal Lodge, Windsor where the Queen Mother was in residence, but all that arrived was an empty box. Hastily, making another cake, she took it to Windsor herself. The incident was disturbing. But worse was to come. One day she phoned me to say Poppet had disappeared. Her beloved Siamese had never strayed before and a search proved fruitless. Because she was the only staff member allowed to keep a pet, there had been whispers of favouritism and although Mrs McKee's first reaction was that he had been attacked by the corgis, no one had seen or heard anything. She now believed that like the chocolate cake, Poppet had been kidnapped – a victim of jealousy.

Farcical though these events may now sound, Mrs McKee was much distressed at the time. She was the sort of person who flourished in a positive and happy environment and although the Queen Mother was supportive, Mrs McKee felt that compliments on her cooking became a source of rivalry rather than encouragement. With rumours and gossip rustling through the household like a breeze in an orchard, gone were the golden days of a family atmosphere. Instead, staff jockeyed for position.

At Balmoral, where the staff could once look forward to the holiday atmosphere, the Queen now seemed more guarded and detached, rarely stopping to chat with familiar faces. If she did, it was interpreted as favouritism.

At Clarence House, which I continued to visit after the Coronation until Mrs McKee left in 1960, a more lavish lifestyle was detectable, while overstaffing gave footmen more opportunities for arguments.

Throughout the Coronation the Queen Mother continued to smile and wave as the public seemed to expect, but soon afterwards she had a reaction. Taking refuge in the remote Castle of Mey, she uncharacteristically wanted to be alone. Her husband was only fifty-seven when he died; they had withstood the Second World War together. The move to Clarence House had been difficult for her and for a time she seemed to assume that she would fade from the scene as her daughter took the limelight. The pattern had been set by the unsmiling Queen Mary after the death of George V. The Queen Mother's vivid creation of a new role did not come about immediately.

Meanwhile, Princess Margaret's romance with Peter Townsend was burgeoning. I saw them once at Windsor, hand in hand and clearly in love. Nor did they seek to hide their feelings from the staff at Clarence House. When my story appeared in the *News Chronicle*, cautiously headed 'Rumours of a Royal Romance', it was Ascot Week. There, rather to my surprise, I was rewarded with a beaming smile from Princess Margaret. She seemed happy for the world to know.

If this was a heyday for Princess Margaret, the strains on Mrs McKee were beginning to grow. The Princess kept late hours, sometimes returning from night clubs such as Ciro's or the 400 with friends after which they would have a party. From Mrs McKee's bedroom above the drawing room she could hear the Princess playing the piano and singing numbers from the current hit shows such as *South Pacific* or *Kiss Me Kate* until the early hours of the morning. The Queen Mother often remarked that she had no idea where her Civil List allowance went to. Periodically however, she would go round the house trying to think of economies saying, 'Do we really need all these light bulbs?' or to Mrs McKee, 'Can't we do without lemons, I hear they are terribly expensive?' She had little idea of how to economize and soon things would go back to the normality of a household budget which was almost twice as big as it had been when the Queen was at Clarence House. She put it down to 'the cost of living'.

By the mid-Fifties, the Queen Mother, back in public demand, was also leading an active social life. When she attended race meetings or the opera she would ask Mrs McKee to prepare hampers. Generally speaking there was nothing at all makeshift about these cold suppers which, if the evening was to be a late one, were followed by a further buffet at Clarence House.

It was no great surprise when Mrs McKee, then in her sixties and after ten hard working years at Clarence House, was eventually carried out on a stretcher. Ill health had always been her greatest fear and because of her own high standards, she decided she could no longer continue the job.

Fortunately Jimmy, her husband, had retired with a small nest egg and together they bought a house in Pinner for their retirement. It was one of the happiest periods in their lives. But it was not to be for long: they both died in the mid-1970s.

Alma knew that when the Queen asked her to write down her recipes, the results had been sketchy, if not indecipherable. But now at long last she had the time to get down to it, translating the inspiration she took for granted into practice. As she still thought in Swedish rather than English and had always measured everything by eye, she asked me to help with the recipes. It turned into a book, a copy of which was sent to the Queen.

By then married with children, my cooking had been picked up by osmosis; partly from watching Mrs McKee and partly from spur of the moment ideas from magazines or cookery books. Philip Harben had been my first stand-by, and when feeling ambitious, Constance Spry or Elizabeth David.

I only had to watch Mrs McKee at work to know that I was not a natural cook. The obvious difference was in the speed and confidence of her preparations, let alone her creative inspiration. There were certain things such as cakes and puddings which would take me all afternoon, and I hated sieving, chopping and boning. Like millions of enthusiastic amateurs, I was lost without recipes and had developed culinary faults; mine was a tendency to overcook.

They say it takes two for a recipe to work. Good advice and sound ideas from the one who creates it and hard work and the rigour of regular practice from the aspiring cook. Eventually, you develop an individual style.

I have no pretensions as a cook; the idea at the time was that if I could follow a particular recipe, so could anyone else. Maybe I had been of some use in the kitchen after all. At least I could explain to Mrs McKee that what was a doddle to her was not to me. I still think of her as Mrs McKee – de rigueur at Clarence House, although off-duty it was Alma.

It seemed like a footnote to the Clarence House era when my newspaper was forced to close down a few years after the Coronation. They hadn't changed with the times. It was typical of the *News Chronicle* that when Mrs McKee invited me to stay as her guest at Birkhall on the Balmoral estate, they refused to give me the time off. How I would have enjoyed that knees-up with the staff!

And how times have changed.

Maureen Owen
6 June 2002

Preface

HOW STRANGE IT IS TO LOOK BACK OVER FORTY YEARS AND REALIZE THAT you have devoted most of your life to food.

With cooking as my way of life, I have got into the habit of associating a particular event with a certain dish. For instance, I will always connect Sole Veronique with a lunch at Clarence House a few days before the Coronation of Queen Elizabeth II in 1953. When I think of Prince Charles, I remember him at the age of four asking for frikadeller – a Swedish dish I'll come to later.

I leave it to others to rhapsodize about the art of cooking. To me it is an expression of love and care. I enjoyed cooking as a child in Sweden because on a simple level, I had found that here was a way to please people and make them happy. Male chefs in the great houses I have known would produce amazing creations of haute cuisine. Is it or is it not a masterpiece, they would ask? Whether or not you actually enjoyed it, was another matter.

This I think is the essential difference between the male and female approach to cooking. A man cooks with his head, a woman with her heart.

When I first went to cook for Princess Elizabeth at Clarence House in 1950 I was told I was the only female chef in charge of a royal kitchen. I had previously cooked for ex-King Peter of Yugoslavia and his wife, then living over here in exile, but that was different. They were very young at the time and very informal.

After I had been there some time I developed pneumonia and had to leave in order to take a long convalesence. When I got back to health my agency offered me a choice of two jobs. One was with Isaac Wolfson the industrialist, the other at Clarence House with Princess Elizabeth and her young family.

I saw Mrs Wolfson first, who offered me £10 a week and a promise of being well looked after when I retired. 'If you come to us,' she told me, 'you'll never regret it.' When I went for my next interview with the Comptroller of Clarence House, General Sir

Frederick Browning, I had more or less decided to take Mrs Wolfson's offer, as at the time I was not sure I felt equal to the responsibility of a royal household.

But I had reckoned without the General's forceful charm.

He offered me £6 a week and said, 'You're just the person we've been looking for. When can you start?'

I said I would think it over and let him know.

'Think it over now and say yes,' said the General. He had been the wartime commander of the battle of Arnhem and was the handsome husband of the novelist Daphne du Maurier.

'All right,' I heard myself saying, and started the following Monday.

Like most Swedes, I was horribly shy, and on that first day at Clarence House, extremely nervous. I knew deep down that I could manage the job and that hundreds, if not thousands, of people had enjoyed my food. But occasionally you might meet someone who does not happen to enjoy it. There is nothing you can really do about that. Everbody has their own style of cooking, and at fifty-five it was too late to change mine. I prayed I would not have to try.

With my first meal came the first royal compliment. It was to be the forerunner of many, for Her Majesty is one of the most appreciative people I have ever worked for; frequently sending messages of congratulation or thanking me personally after a special dinner. There is something quite riveting about her smile, and I can assure you that when that smile is directed at you personally, there is nothing you would not do for her.

Perhaps because she is such a very inspiring person, I felt that my cooking was at its best during those carefree but numbered days at Clarence House when the Queen was Princess Elizabeth. I had never opened a recipe book, and I cooked as always by taste, adjusting the flavour and adding to the dish as I went along. Another quirk is that I always have to visualize the finished table in detail before I can start planning a meal.

People often ask me if I was made nervous by the illustrious names on the guest list when I was cooking at Clarence House.

Well, I would have been of course, had I always known who was to be there beforehand. But often the Comptroller's guest list, issued a fortnight in advance, simply stated the number of guests to a particular meal. Only later did I hear who was present, but fortified by royal encouragement, the ideas flowed and with them my confidence.

Things did not always go according to plan however, and I hadn't been at Clarence House long when I was told that there was to be a party for forty-five royal guests that very same night. There was nothing in the house as we had expected the family to be out that evening, and on looking round, I found that we had no really big dishes ... 'I'm sure you will manage beautifully Mrs McKee,' said the Comptroller serenely.

The dishes had to be borrowed from Buckingham Palace and what to put on them was quite a problem in those days of rationing.

Cooking for royalty is an honour, but it is no use pretending that the work is anything but demanding. It would be easy if all one had to do was to produce an inspired menu for the Royal Family and their guests and bask in the glory of it all. But real life in royal households is not like that. In my time at Clarence House there were between eight and a hundred unroyal mouths to feed as well. Numbers varied; just a few when members of the Royal Family were not in residence and full to overflowing around the hectic period of the Coronation.

At lunch there were usually about three different menus going at the same time. First the nursery, whose menus were simple but needed careful preparation. Then the royal lunch, normally with guests. Next the staff who ate substantially from a different menu and who could on occasions be critical – 'Not more game!' they would say when pheasants arrived from Sandringham. Then there were the ever-hungry policemen who ate after the staff and enjoyed whatever was going.

⁕

Sometimes it seemed that I was living in a grand hotel where all the guests were famous. But despite the trappings, the real core of the household where I now lived, was a happy and united family. Perhaps my best memories of Clarence House are of teatimes in the blue and white nursery, informal and cheerful, with Prince Charles chatting excitedly about the day's events. Even grand visitors like foreign kings and queens failed to make it anything but family tea, with everyone enjoying bread and butter with jam, gingerbread shapes and sponge cake.

Prince Charles was a little boy of two when I came to Clarence House and Princess Anne a tiny porcelain-skinned baby. As I always wore fresh white overalls every day, Prince Charles nicknamed me 'The Lady in White'. At that time he loved using the house telephone, much to the confusion of the office staff, and would often call me in the kitchen ... 'Is that the lady in white?' 'Yes, it's the lady in white. What would you like for lunch?' The answer was invariably meat balls, his description of the classic Swedish dish, frikadeller. Made from chicken, pork or veal, and sometimes off-the-ration rabbit as well, the recipe can be used in a variety of different ways and for a time Prince Charles developed a craze for it.

In playing back memories, I find that the small events such as these, rather than the grand occasions, are the ones stored in my memory. I remember too, Prince Philip's informal visits to the kitchen. He would look into saucepans, ask questions and crack some really good jokes. In times of stress and crisis, he was a real morale booster. I appreciated his relaxed style because usually a royal visit to the kitchen was preceded by a message from above which made us feel we were in for a sort of kit inspection. Prince Philip would just appear without warning and take us as we were.

Just before the Royal Family depart to Sandringham for Christmas, there is a staff party ...

At these parties the Princess would come round chatting quite naturally with everyone in turn, telling them of the things she had been doing and asking about their plans for Christmas, and so on.

One was encouraged to chat back and it all seemed very light-hearted and informal; but I noticed that almost as if she had a stopwatch, she spent just about the same amount of time with each person before moving on ... In those early days, Prince Philip was more inclined to get immersed in conversation with one particular person or group. Polite conversation is not so much for Prince Philip; he likes to thrash a subject out and will cross-question you until he gets the full story. When this went on for too long, the Princess had been known to give her husband a discreet sign to move on.

Married to a Scotsman, I had been in Britain long enough to know that family life always included dogs. The Royal Family were no exception; they take their dogs seriously.

Every day when the Princess was at home, she fed the corgis. A tray was sent up containing a jug of gravy, a bowl of meat and a bowl of dog biscuits. The Queen mixed and served the contents and when the dogs had finished, cleared the things up and returned them to the tray.

When the Queen Mother and Princess Margaret were together at Clarence House, feeding time was even more of a ritual. Mother and daugher took rather a formal tea together at a small table covered with a white cloth in one corner of the drawing room. Afterwards they laid another tablecloth on the floor on which the dogs were given their meal.

The royal corgis fully appreciated their privileged status and had the full run of the house. At night their favourite sleeping place was under the bed in Prince Charles' nursery. By day they conducted a private war on the policemen always on duty to guard the house. The corgis hated their patrolling habits or their uniforms or something about them, and in the kitchen (from which the dogs were banned), we were always sheltering enormous policemen who were pursued by these small but relentless animals.

❦

Until I was about thirty I had never bought a vegetable – I always picked them.

I was lucky in the way I learned about cooking. As a young girl I trained in one of the few remaining private castles in Sweden. The estate was almost entirely self-supporting. I snatched little beetroots from the earth, dashing the hopes of gardeners who wanted to grow them to exhibition size; pickled them to my own recipe or steamed them to preserve their rich colour and flavour and served them with herb butter.

The animals were slaughtered, salted and frozen and we learned how to use every part of a pig or a bullock. We celebrated a good harvest and prayed against drought and frost; we knew when the first fruits and vegetables were ripe for picking and bottling; and were able to cope with last-minute parties for fifty or more people. We were toasted in champagne (sometimes between courses) when our food was good and told to throw it away and start again when it was wrong. I learned the right way of using everything that came out of the earth, and with it, a deep respect for the order and rhythm of life. Horningshom Castle, where I first started, was the home of Count Bonde who lived in almost feudal magnificence, surrounded by water and with his own private prison! The Count's legendary crayfish parties would go on until the early hours with Jansson's Frestelses – a traditional savoury baked potato dish, served at midnight.

When I first came over from Sweden between the wars and married Jimmy McKee, people were still eating seven course meals in the grander houses. Now it is only on rare occasions that the Royal Family have five courses. Usually it is not more than three and the food is good but simple. The ingredients used are of the best and I was happy to find that the vegetables supplied had that fresh earthy smell which to me is at the heart of good cooking.

This is not say that everything was easy. In the days when I was in Clarence House, strict rationing was still in force and although we were supplemented by game, poultry and vegetables from the royal estates, we had problems just like everyone else. For instance, guests were supposed to bring their ration books with them, but seldom did. Unlike Lord Cromer, Governor of the Bank of England, who could be seen waiting patiently in the Comptroller's office as the required coupons were snipped from his book; Sir Winston Churchill, then Prime Minister, always forgot.

It would be naive to imagine that royalty always dine off rare delicacies, though people are sometimes surprised when I go to the trouble of describing how to cook a good kipper or haddock which the Royal Family certainly enjoyed. Stuffed cabbage was another great favourite. Having no need to impress, everything is judged on merit alone.

I had great recourse to fish, thankfully not on ration, although sometimes in short supply. Luckily the Royal Family like it and a fish course was always included in the dinner menu. Fish for the royal residences was delivered fresh from Billingsgate every morning as a wholesale order. I could not always get exactly what I wanted – Buckingham Palace came first. Milk, cream, chicken and vegetables were delivered twice a week in a little white van from Home Farm, Windsor. You couldn't order; they simply delivered what was available and I would build my menus around the produce provided. Game came from Sandringham and Balmoral, salmon was a treat from Deeside. Meat was supplied by a small butcher in Staines and groceries by Fortnum & Mason in Piccadilly. I also made regular trips to Soho for Continental groceries you could then only find in that district. I had a free hand with the housekeeping but had to make out the accounts in a double entry ledger every week.

Dinner at eight ... and you could set your clock by the Queen's appearance at the dinner table with guests. This punctuality, I am sure, was dictated by consideration for the people who worked for her. Dinner at eight meant that on a good day I could be finished in the kitchen by 10 pm. I always saw the dinner through, right down to the serving of coffee, although I did not, of course, have to wash up. Often after cooking a fine banquet, all I wanted was a light vegetable omelette. After this I would go to my room and write out the menus for the following day. Oddly enough, this was my greatest headache. The menus had to be in French and being no linguist I used to struggle for hours with the contortions of haute cuisine. As most dishes were very much my own creation, I sometimes had the nerve (or desperation) to call them after my own Christian names; Salade Veronica and Consommé à la Charlotte were two examples. Perhaps the Royal Family thought they referred to some distant ancestors of theirs. The menu cards would be placed on the dining room table in a holder for all to see and even after buying a very expensive book which contained all the terms I needed, I was still conscious of the odd mistake. However, the Princess, who speaks excellent French, was very kind about these shortcomings and tactfully ignored any errors.

Apart from being told to curtsey whenever I saw Her Royal Highness and to avoid the use of garlic, nobody told me how to behave or what to cook when I first joined the present Queen and her husband at Clarence House. Princess Elizabeth was the wife of a naval officer at the time and eagerly looked forward to their reunions. The routine ran smoothly, the domestic climate was calm and the newly-renovated house had a fresh, spring-like feeling. So natural and informal was the atmosphere, that often for weeks on end one would forget that this was a royal household known to the eyes of the world.

Towards the end of July, however, there is a great upheaval in the royal households. Preparations for the annual holiday at

Balmoral begin. Pots, pans, china and utensils, everything it seemed to me, except the Buckingham Palace stove, is packed up and sent ahead. On the appointed day the staff of Buckingham Palace and Clarence House meet on the station at King's Cross and wait for a special train that takes them to Ballater, the small station near Balmoral in Scotland.

On my first journey I remember being amazed that even Buckingham Palace could hold so many people until I realized that many were taking their wives, families and domestic animals as well. The scene reminded me of some king from ancient history moving camp.

The Scottish holiday is anything but dull. The Queen has a constant turnover of house guests. Almost every night there are film shows and frequent dances are given for the staff, including the famous Ghillies' Ball when everyone lets their hair down. On one occasion there was a 'Beatnik' dance with all the Royal Family turned out in appropriate costumes.

Out of all the palaces, castles, lodges and houses owned by the Royal Family, Birkhall, the private house on the Balmoral estate, seems to be the favourite. The charm of Birkhall is difficult to describe. It certainly is not beautiful, and it is far from luxurious. On the second occasion I went there, the kitchen range (dating from Edwardian days) blew up. But the Queen Mother preferred Birkhall to Balmoral Castle and it is certainly warmer.

At teatime when the shooting was over, everyone used to kick off their muddy shoes at the door and crowd into the not over-large drawing room, eagerly asking what there was for tea. The late King seemed to particularly enjoy these occasions. He was not at all shy and reserved as people seemed to imagine. Instead he had a great fund of funny stories which he told with roars of laughter, and he liked hearing others in exchange. He would also take a great delight in a friendly teasing of his daughters and would go on until threatened with cushions and even flying scones. These tea parties were in fact uproarious occasions and one had to fight one's way in with replenishments of tea.

At Birkhall, the holiday spirit was well in evidence in the servants' hall. Behind the baize door there was a piano which was played until all hours at night, with plenty of singing and dancing, too. Once at Birkhall, the normally quiet and discreet staff from Clarence House also joined in to the full. Perhaps it was something in the Scottish air, but I had never seen them like that before. There was no doubt that the noise percolated through to the royal quarters. But there were no complaints, Prince Philip merely remarking to the steward in charge of staff that he was jolly glad he didn't have to control them.

For the staff, Balmoral was rather like a working holiday camp. There was a private golf course at their disposal and tennis courts. Private bands were supplied for the dances and there was a canteen. Then there were the film shows to which everyone was invited. Sometimes the laughter and applause from the staff drowned the sound track, and the housekeeper, fearing that things were getting out of hand, subsequently apologized for the noise to the Queen Mother (then Queen).

'Not a bit of it,' said Queen Elizabeth, 'I like to know that everyone is happy and enjoying themselves.'

Looking back at my memories of Princess Elizabeth in the early Fifties, I realize that my view was a purely domestic one. I saw her at home; happy, relaxed and smiling. I remember the times when she would spend the afternoon playing on the lawn with her two small children, carefully packing up the toys when it was time for tea; Princess Anne just a baby in arms. An everyday scene, which seems to symbolize a simpler era.

In fact up to the day of her first Trooping of the Colour on Horse Guards Parade, I had never actually seen Princess Elizabeth in her official capacity. Because the King was too ill to take his part in this very public ceremony which according to tradition is performed by the monarch on horseback, the Princess had to deputize for him.

I was standing at the bottom of the stairs at Clarence House when the Princess came down in her uniform; dark blue riding skirt, scarlet jacket and tricorn hat. As always on official occasions, she was unhurried with time in hand for a few words with whoever happened to be about.

Turning to me, she indicated her hat and said, 'My father designed this for me. Do you like it?'

All at once, she looked different; the unfamiliar uniform, the tricorn hat and the grave, composed expression.

'Now,' she said with a slight smile, 'you see how I look on duty.'

Later, I watched the lone figure 'on duty' as she led the procession up the Mall on Winston, the police horse, with a mixture of pride and foreboding.

Everyone will remember, how soon afterwards, Princess Elizabeth flew from London Airport on a royal tour of Kenya only to return two days later as Queen of England.

Added to the shock of bereavement was the feeling that there should have been many more years for the Princess to develop her role. But as soon as the new Queen arrived home, staff who had gone on holiday hurriedly returned and we were plunged into hectic activity. Clarence House was permanently overflowing with ministers and officials, and in the rush there was no time to think of anything except feeding everybody.

At one point we all but ran out of food coupons for essentials such as sugar and meat. I had to tell General Browning who practically exploded. 'I know who owes us coupons,' he said and thankfully sorted the matter out.

Everyone was strained to the limit at that time particulary, of course, the new Queen. The closeness between her and the late King was well known. Maybe she dreaded the move from Clarence House to the Palace where there were so many sad associations because every time the subject of the changeover was broached we were told that the Queen wished to remain at Clarence House as long as possible.

Soon, however, with more affairs of State to be attended to and more officials crowding the small waiting room and spilling out into the corridors every day, it became clear that the Queen could no longer operate from Clarence House.

Sometime after the King's funeral, I offered her my sincere and humble condolences on her father's death.

I will never forget her reply, so simple and so moving.

'Yes,' she said quietly, 'he was a good man.'

A good man. From the Queen of England there is no higher praise.

Before the Queen left to move into the Belgian Suite, normally reserved for foreign visitors, at Buckingham Palace, (the Queen Mother moved over a year later), she said goodbye to all the staff who were not accompanying her. I received a white and gold enamel brooch with her initials. Everybody at that time was under six months' official notice and the new appointments would take months to sort out. There was certainly no place for a woman cook in the all-male stronghold at Buckingham Palace. Meanwhile I had been asked to go to Royal Lodge Windsor, which then belonged to the Queen Mother. The Queen and her family used to weekend there as guests, always saying, 'Thank you Mummy for a lovely time' when they left. Before she left Clarence House, the Queen had told me that she was glad she would be able to enjoy my cooking at weekends. 'I am sure you will like Royal Lodge,' she said and asked me if there was anything I was worried about.

I said I was happy to go to Windsor but didn't know what to do about Poppet, my Siamese cat, whom the Queen had kindly given me permission to keep at Clarence House.

The Queen smiled. 'Take him to Royal Lodge,' she said. 'There couldn't be a better place for a cat.'

So off we went – the Queen to her palace, and Poppet and myself to Windsor, where we were indeed very happy.

The Queen Mother had always been accustomed to a male chef so I was taken on under a temporary basis to see how we got along together. This was a point of view I perfectly understood as in England all the really big kitchens are run by men and the administrative work of a large kitchen with a big staff is a tough job, probably better done by a man.

Although the Queen and her family numbered more than her mother and sister, the Queen Mother had a far larger staff, most of whom had to be cooked for by me. Also, mother and daughter frequently gave separate dinner parties, usually with only an hour in between. If the Queen Mother was doubtful, I was certainly extremely apprehensive and at the last moment before she arrived at the newly-decorated Clarence House I discovered that in the chaos of the move between households, there were only two saucepans in the house. I had hardly met my new employer and my mind was blank of everything except where to find essential tools.

The Coronation was imminent and although the harassed Comptroller had not yet issued the programme, there was certain to be a huge amount of entertaining.

Into my mind came the soothing proportions of Cumberland sauce which if you are pushed for time as I was, requires no cooking; redcurrant jelly, orange marmalade, sherry and lemon juice are the basics, with a few little additions.

I do not remember what I served this sauce with, but it was a fortunate choice. The Queen Mother told me that she had not seen it since before the war and had almost despaired of finding it again.

Having established a rapport with the Queen Mother, I went on to find other sauces which would appeal to her – turbot with a creme citron sauce, for instance, or a Swedish dish; duck with a prune sauce. I was told that she had no particular dislikes but that I must take meticulous care about boning everything, particularly fish; she had a dread of choking on bones. I took care of this anyway, always boning everything from chicken to fish before serving.

The Queen Mother's dinner parties were quite cosmopolitan. At one the guest list went like this: The Duchess of Kent, Mr Billy Wallace, the Duke and Duchess of Norfolk, Mr Noel Coward, The Master of Elphinstone, Mr Peter Cazalet, Lord Salisbury, Mr Peter Ustinov, the Hon Mrs Wills and Norman Hackforth. The main dish was braised venison and the pudding a rich chestnut dish with cream and maraschino. But hot soufflés came off the menu when an old Scottish retainer came to stay. The dinner gong kept ringing as he told a string of stories all of which began, 'Do you remember when you were a wee girl at Glamis, Ma'am ...?'

One of my proudest and happiest days was when the late King Gustav of Sweden came to lunch. Knowing he had a delicate stomach, I prepared poached turbot, an easily digestible dish and to my surprise and pleasure, the Queen Mother sent for me upstairs so that the King of my country could congratulate me in person.

I would like to put in a word here about the Swedes. Hardly anyone ever does. To their great disadvantage with the rest of the world, the Swedes are two things; they are shy; and they are poor publicity men.

Their shyness earns them the reputation of being off-hand and gloomy. That song 'Wonderful, wonderful Copenhagen' got a lot of Swedes down, because although Stockholm is equally wonderful, none of them would think of saying so, far less singing about it.

Yet there is such a thing as Swedish cooking. We like our food. Above all we like to be able to taste the FLAVOUR of that good meat or fish, or whatever it is we are cooking. You will not find us flinging a glass of sherry or wine into a stew in the vague hope of making it more interesting. Instead, our cookery is based on scientific principles more concerned with drawing out the flavour of good basic ingredients than obscuring them.

People talk about the salt of the earth, but for many generations Swedes have known the value of its sugar too. In this book you will sometimes see a recipe for meat or savoury food which includes a pinch of sugar, or redcurrant jelly or even treacle. This is typically Swedish. It doesn't mean that the end result is going to taste sweet; it's there to bring out the flavour.

So what exactly is Scandanavian food? In a list of ingredients, fish comes high, and pork, poultry and venison are staples. Vegetables are imaginatively presented – sometimes as a splash of colour in carrot or spinach purees. In Swedish cookery there must be a hundred different uses for the humble potato, transforming it into a dish fit for a Queen. Fan-shaped Hasselback potatoes – roasted in a very hot oven until crisp – became a favourite, and I think I may have been the first cook to introduce the Royal Family to sweet potatoes – pureed with a slight kick of cayenne pepper – if I remember. Cucumbers, dill, parsley, horseradish and tarragon are personal standbys. So is anything that smacks of the sea or a freshwater lake or, like wild mushrooms, are born of the forest. Apples and almonds and cream can be used in a dozen different ways, and of course the freshest eggs you can find for that pale, creamy sauce, crowning glory of Swedish smorgasbord; home-made mayonnaise.

Strangely, it's not always the oldest traditions that die the hardest. When I first came to Clarence House, I was intrigued to find a well-known brand of bottled salad cream in the larder. I was told that the Royal Family like it with salads in the summer. Naturally, it was served in a silver sauce boat, not the famous bottle, but I could always tell it by its distinctive smell and flavour. I knew that this well-known brand is a national favourite, but I was also determined that the Royal Family should try my version of Swedish mayonnaise. Whisking it up with the little bunches of birch twigs I brought back from holidays in Stockholm, was second nature to me. Quite apart from a coating for salads, I regarded fresh mayonnaise as an essential sauce; versatile in the way it can be flavoured to enhance a number of different dishes. So henceforth, both the bottled and the home-made variety were sent to table – in silver sauce boats of course. But despite being told that my mayonnaise was much enjoyed and even once inventing a cooked salad cream which was similar to the bottled kind, I never really knew which they preferred.

And while I'm about it, here's another confession.

I frequently used garlic when cooking for royalty. This aversion to garlic which I was clearly told about when I first joined the present Queen in 1951 was also shared by Princess Margaret, though not by other members of the Royal Family.

It seemed understandable enough for obvious reasons, and to start with I kept to instructions. One day, however, when making a Provençal sauce with tomatoes and pimentoes, I 'forgot'. No complaints followed – in fact the reverse – kind messages followed – so thereafter I continued to use traces of garlic undetected.

'We never eat garlic,' I had been told. Well ...

I suppose you could say that my own cooking is a mixture of Swedish and English combined, of course, with many of the classics from French haute cuisine. But I have a great admiration for good English cooking and can think of nothing better than the English method of roasting meat; it is something that other nations admire and envy but seem incapable of imitating. I know this because when abroad I have been called upon in desperation by hungry British expatriates to produce that simple favourite so difficult to the Continental mind, roast beef.

When the Queen had to move to Buckingham Palace, she asked me to write down a selection of my recipes. As I was not accustomed to making notes of exact weights and measurements nor to describing my method of cooking in English (I still wrote in Swedish), the notes I gave her must have been decidedly sketchy. In fact, I felt sorry for the chef whose job it would be to decipher them.

The British Royal Family prefer all that is best in English cooking as a staple diet, but have an open mind on food and like trying new dishes providing they are good of their kind. I also learnt from the Queen Mother, knowledgeable about fish, who introduced me to red mullet, a delicious fish, which I cooked for her at Birkhall. Her appreciation of a really good home-made ice cream also spurred me on to try new variations, such as the Grand Marnier version in this book. Princess Margaret would come home with enthusiastic descriptions of a new dish she had tried at a restaurant, but alas, with little idea of what was in it.

For a time at Clarence House I was flattered to find that my name as a chef was getting around. By this I mean that it was known to the small circle of top-calibre chefs who are employed by the few remaining large private households, or who work for clubs and distinguished restaurants. These chefs, all men, invited me to dinner and in turn served me their masterpieces, generously giving me the recipes. Or some of them. I asked them back and gave of my best. It was all very jolly until they asked for my 'secrets'. Sooner than reveal that I had only the vaguest idea of how much of this or that I put into a dish, I had to preserve a mysterious silence which was interpreted as professional secrecy.

This was the end of the dinner parties.

After this, and the inadequate recipes I was forced to give to the Queen, I started studying myself at work, as it were, and for the first time began weighing things and analyzing my methods.

The recipes in this book, though only a fraction of the dishes I have cooked in a lifetime, are some of the ones I have been asked for most often, and I am happy I can at last supply the recipes. I must at this point thank Miss Maureen Owen for all her help in preparing them.

I am happy too, for the opportunity of setting out a few of the true principles of Swedish cookery – a sadly unknown branch of gastronomy.

Now in my late sixties, I spend a good deal of my time in the garden – a return to that most fulfilling of hobbies which I first learned to enjoy all those years ago in Sweden.

I started cooking because I enjoyed it and found it was a way in which I could please people and add to their well-being. I have tried never to lose sight of this simple theme, and all the nice exciting things that have happened to me in my life have sprung from this philosophy. Perhaps the best advice I can give for anyone who wants to make other people happy with their food, is to cook with love and trust your palate.

One more thing I should like to point out. I do not believe there is ever a time when a woman needs to feel bored or useless: many of the best things have happened to me late in life. I married late, I reached the peak of my career when I was over fifty. And it is only now in retirement that after years of living in even the grandest places, I can really enjoy the pleasures of my own house and garden. Even now, when I have discovered a new and useful phase in my life, I still get offers to cook for people who like my sort of food – so off I go – because I will always find the challenge of providing it irresistible.

And the root of all this happiness?

The humble art of cooking.

Alma McKee, writing in 1963

Soups

WHAT TO SERVE AS AN ORIGINAL FIRST COURSE CAN BE A PROBLEM, BUT the solution is very often simple: a thoroughly good soup.

The *good* soup is the one you make in your kitchen. Packets and tins are no substitute for the love and care you can put into a soup. It is a happy dish to make too; the low bubbling and delicious fragrance fills the kitchen with a warm atmosphere of contentment.

Soup is what you make it. It can be grand enough for a banquet, satisfying enough for a hard-working farmer, or creamy and sophisticated enough for the smart set. Soup nourishes the sick, gives strength to the active, and can be served hot or cold in winter or summer. One could hardly have a more versatile dish.

It would be sad if anyone thought of soup as dull, but it can certainly be disappointing if it does not receive its due measure of love and care in the preparation. To obtain the best from many soups it is necessary to let them simmer for several hours. But this should not dishearten anyone for they will simmer along quite happily on their own, and the gentle bubbling provides a cheerful background noise.

In Sweden we pay a lot of attention to soup garnishes as we think that a good soup deserves something rather special to mark the occasion. You will find some unusual garnishes in this chapter which will, I hope, arouse your interest and encourage you to think of other accompaniments to serve.

For the warmer weather, cold soups are very popular, and there can be no more soothing start to a meal on a hot summer's evening.

In writing this chapter I was reminded particularly of Princess Margaret, Prince Charles and ex-Queen Alexandra of Yugoslavia – all great soup people. Queen Alexandra was my chief soup patron, and for her I would rack my brains for a different soup each evening; the more adventurous they were, the more she liked them. With Princess Margaret I took great trouble to produce a classic, elegant sort of soup, and Prince Charles just thought that soup was great fun.

And I, for one, wholeheartedly agree with him.

The best of all good soups is the clear consommé. It does take time, admittedly, but in that time all the goodness from the meat and vegetables is extracted and you have a wonderful, nutritious soup at the end.

♛ CLEAR CONSOMMÉ

To make about 4 pints/2.5 litres:

3 lbs/1.5 kg shin of beef	½ stick of celery
1½ lbs/750 g shin of veal	1 onion
6 pints/3.5 litres water	1 bay leaf
2 teaspoons of salt	sprig of parsley
1 carrot	sprig of thyme
1 leek	4 or 5 peppercorns
½ beetroot	1 clove
1 parsnip	

Cut the meat up and break any bones. Rinse well and place in a saucepan. Cover with the water and allow to stand for one hour. Add the salt and bring to the boil over a low heat. Spoon any scum from the surface, then add the vegetables, cleaned and peeled but not cut. Add the herbs tied in a bundle, the peppercorns and the clove. Bring up to the boil again slowly and simmer for five or six hours on a low heat in an open pan.

When cooked, remove the meat and vegetables and strain the consommé through a colander lined with dampened muslin. Remove any remaining grease from the surface of the consommé with a paper towel. Serve hot or cold.

CLEAR CHICKEN CONSOMMÉ 👑

To make about 4 pints/2.5 litres:

1 large boiling fowl (about 5 lbs/2.5 kg)	1 onion
2 ozs/60 g butter	1 bay leaf
½ lb/250 g shin of veal	sprig of thyme
½ lb/250 g shin of beef	sprig of parsley
10 peppercorns	1 teaspoon of salt
1 clove	1 stick of celery
	1 leek

Remove the chicken breast and chop bones and legs in pieces. Remove skin and rinse well. Dry thoroughly. Brown the butter in a saucepan, add the chicken and brown over a low heat until golden. Pour in enough water to cover the chicken and bring slowly to the boil. Meanwhile, put the veal and beef, cut in large pieces, in a stock pot with water to cover and let stand for half an hour. Remove the scum from the chicken stock, add the stock and chicken pieces to the meat and bring to the boil very gently, skimming the surface from time to time. Add the peppercorns and the clove stuck into an onion, herbs and one teaspoon of salt. Add all the vegetables, peeled but uncut, and bring to the boil slowly. Simmer for at least three hours in an open pan.

Strain the consommé through a colander lined with dampened muslin. Serve hot or cold.

Once you have gone to the trouble of making these superlative consommés you will want to use them in a variety of different ways.

Now follow some very special soups with a consommé base, which will add enormous prestige to your reputation for keeping a good table.

🜲 CONSOMMÉ DE VOLAILLE AUX POINTS D'ASPERGES

To serve 6:

2 chicken breasts
2 pints/1.25 litres good chicken
   consommé (see previous
   recipe)
small tin of asparagus tips

1 glass of sherry
seasoning to taste
2 tablespoons of chopped fresh
   parsley

Cut the chicken breasts in small pieces and place them in a pan with enough water to cover them. Add salt and boil on a gentle heat, spooning off any scum that rises to the surface, until tender. Strain the stock from the chicken breasts and add it to the consommé. Add the chicken pieces and the asparagus tips with the juice from the tin. Add the sherry, season to taste and, just before serving, add the chopped parsley. Serve hot but do not boil.

🜲 CONSOMMÉ RIS DE VEAU AUX PETITS POIS VERT

To serve 6:

$\frac{1}{2}$ lb/250 g calves' sweetbreads
1$\frac{1}{2}$ pints/90 cl clear consommé
   (for recipe see page 2)
1 lb/500 g fresh or frozen peas
pinch of sugar

1 fresh or tinned truffle, peeled
   and finely chopped
1 glass of white wine
salt and pepper to taste

This consommé is definitely a tiara event, but one that you should enjoy even without the tiara. It will turn a lovely green colour.

Soak the sweetbreads in cold water, then blanch in boiling water for about two minutes. Peel off the surface membrane and any fat or gristle, and press under a board for about two hours to compact the flesh. Place the pressed sweetbreads in a pan, add enough water to cover and braise for about 30 to 40 minutes. Cut into small pieces and then add to the consommé. Cook the peas in salted water with a pinch of sugar for about five minutes, being careful not to overcook. Strain and add to the consommé. Add the wine, the chopped truffle and, if using a tinned truffle, the juice from the tin. Season with salt and pepper and serve hot.

PETITE MARMITE 👑

To serve 6:

2 pints/1.25 litres clear
  consommé (for recipe see
  page 2)

For the bread croutons:
3 slices of stale white bread

the cooked vegetables used in
  making the consommé
1 glass of sherry

2 ozs/60 g butter

Skim all fat from the cooled consommé and then press the cooked vegetables through a fine sieve to obtain a smooth purée. Add the purée to the soup with a glass of sherry. Heat the soup gently but do not boil. While the soup is heating make the bread croutons. Remove the crusts from the bread, and cut it into small cubes. Melt the butter in a sauté pan over a low heat and gently fry the bread cubes until they are crisp all the way through, and golden brown. Serve the hot croutons with the soup either separately or as a garnish.

Here are some consommés with unusual garnishes. They make exciting soups for special occasions.

GAME CONSOMMÉ WITH CREAM OF CHICKEN 👑 AND TRUFFLE

To serve 6:

game carcasses, for making
  the stock
3 pints/1.75 litres cold water
10 white peppercorns
1 tablespoon of salt

For the garnish:
2 chicken breasts
2 whites of eggs
½ pint/30 cl double cream
salt and pepper to taste

1 carrot
2 onions, peeled and cut
1 bay leaf
sprig of parsley

pinch of sugar
1 truffle, peeled and finely
  chopped
lettuce

Braise the game carcasses in the oven for half an hour. Place them in a saucepan and cover with about 3 pints/1.75 litres of cold water. Bring slowly to the boil and remove all scum. Add the seasoning, vegetables and herbs and simmer for four to five hours. Strain and remove all fat. Keep hot.

To make the garnish, mince the chicken breasts three times and mix with the raw whites of eggs. Stir in the cream gradually. Add salt, pepper and the sugar. Stir for fifteen minutes and add the truffle. Shape mixture into small balls with a teaspoon and boil in the consommé for a few minutes.

Pour the consommé into cups, add the chicken and truffle balls, and just before serving cut a lettuce into strips and use to garnish.

♛ CONSOMMÉ WITH BOUCHÉES MIMOSA

To serve 6:

For the consommé:
2 pints/1.25 litres game consommé (see previous recipe)

1 truffle, peeled and cut into strips (optional)
1 glass of port wine

For the bouchées mimosa:
8 small puff pastry cases
1 large tin of asparagus tips
1 tablespoon of plain flour
$\frac{1}{4}$ pint/15 cl double cream
1 oz/30 g butter

pepper, salt and a pinch of sugar to taste
4 hard-boiled eggs
1 oz/30 g Parmesan cheese, grated

This recipe is more than just soup; the garnish is more than just an ordinary garnish. Together they make a delicious first course.

Heat the consommé and add the wine and truffle. Put the *bouchée* cases into a low oven to heat. Strain the asparagus juice into a saucepan, add the flour and whisk until smooth. Bring to the boil stirring all the time and simmer for ten minutes. Add the cream and the butter and season to taste. Chop the white of the hard-boiled eggs coarsely and cut the asparagus tips each to about one inch in length. Add asparagus tips and chopped egg white to the sauce, then the Parmesan cheese. Heat, but do not boil.

Fill the *bouchées* with the mixture. Sieve the yolks of eggs over the *bouchées* and serve hot with the consommé.

CONSOMMÉ ROYAL ♔

Pre-heat oven to 150°C/300°F or gas mark 2
To serve 6:

2 pints/1.25 litres beef
   consommé

salt and a pinch of sugar

For the egg royal garnish:
1 egg
3 egg yolks
7 fl oz/20 cl single cream
pinch of nutmeg

1 red pepper, sliced thinly
2 tomatoes peeled, seeded
   and cut in strips

Here is a rather grand soup, made from the best beef consommé, that I often served at Clarence House on special occasions. The garnish melts in the mouth and is quite delicious. It looks very good too and always attracted favourable comment.

Gently heat the beef consommé, add seasoning and while it is heating make the garnish. Whisk the egg and egg yolks together with the cream, and add the nutmeg. Grease a soufflé dish or small metal moulds with butter and pour in the mixture. Place the custards on a rack set in a tin and pour in enough hot water to come halfway up the sides of the moulds. Cover the tin and poach in the oven pre-heated to 150°C/300°F or gas mark 2 for fifteen to twenty minutes, or until set. When cold, turn out and cut in small diamond shapes.

Garnish the hot soup with the egg royal, the red pepper and tomato.

♛ CONSOMMÉ CONTESSA

To serve 4:

> 1 tin of asparagus tips
> 4 ozs/125 g cooked ox tongue
> 1½ pints/90 cl clear chicken
>   consommé (for recipe see
>   page 3)
>
> 4 ozs/125 g tapioca
> 1 glass of sherry
> salt and pepper to taste

Cut the asparagus tips in half and cut the tongue into strips. Put the consommé in a saucepan and bring to a gentle boil. Add the tapioca and simmer for fifteen minutes. Add the asparagus tips together with the juice from the tin, the wine and the tongue. Make very hot, taste, season with the salt and pepper and serve.

♛ CONSOMMÉ EN GELÉE AU SHERRY

To serve 6:

> 2 pints/1.25 litres clear
>   consommé (for recipe see
>   page 2)
> 1 glass of sherry or white wine
>
> salt and pepper to taste
> chopped red or green
>   pepper or parsley for
>   decoration

Add to the consommé the glass of sherry or white wine and adjust seasoning to taste. Serve with chopped red or green pepper or parsley for decoration.

CONSOMMÉ BALMORAL AU HOMARD ♔

To serve 6:

*1 x 1 lb/500 g cooked lobster
or tinned lobster
½ lb/250 g cooked sweetbreads
1 oz/30 g butter
1 tablespoon of brandy
½ pint/30 cl of tomato purée
½ clove of garlic
3 ozs/90 g shallots
¼ pint/15 cl dry white wine
2 small sprigs of tarragon*

*salt and cayenne pepper, to
taste
2 pints/1.25 litres hot fish stock
(for recipe see page 212)
2 egg yolks
¼ pint/15 cl double cream
2 tablespoons of grated
Gruyère cheese*

Making a fish consommé is not the difficult task many people imagine it to be. A good fish stock is essential, however. The fish used for making the stock must be fresh and of good quality. You will find my recipe for fish stock on page 212.

Cut the cooked lobster in half lengthways and remove the meat, taking care not to use the little bag near the head. Cut the meat into small pieces leaving aside some for garnishing. Put the lobster into a saucepan with the cut, cooked sweetbreads and add the butter. Stir until hot, then add the brandy and set it alight. Pour in the tomato purée, the garlic, shallots, the wine, tarragon and seasoning, and bring to the boil. Cover the saucepan and simmer for ten minutes. Remove from the heat and allow to cool.

Press the mixture through a sieve with a wooden pestle. Discard the residual solids and place the liquid in a saucepan with the hot fish stock. Stir well and bring to the boil. Check the seasoning and strain the soup once more.

Heat, remove from cooker, beat up the egg yolks with the cream and then stir into the soup. Add the reserved pieces of lobster and the grated cheese. Stir and heat well, but do not boil. Serve immediately.

This soup is also delicious cold, but omit the cheese.

♔ OYSTER SOUP

To serve 6:

1 tablespoon of cornflour
3 pints/1.75 litres fish stock
  (for recipe see page 212)
12 live oysters
salt and pepper to taste
1 oz/30 g butter

2 egg yolks
$\frac{1}{4}$ pint/15 cl white wine
1 tablespoon grated Parmesan
  cheese
$\frac{1}{2}$ green pepper, finely chopped

For the garnish:
pork and chicken frikadellers
  (for recipe see page 81)

Mix the cornflour with a little fish stock, and stir until smooth. Bring the fish stock to the boil and thicken with the cornflour mixture, stir well and simmer for five minutes. Remove from heat.

Open the oysters by prising the shells apart with the blade of an oyster knife. Strain the juice from the oysters into a small saucepan and remove the oyster beards. Place the saucepan over a high heat, boil up and remove at once. Strain the oyster juice into the thickened fish stock, add the seasoning and the butter. Beat the egg yolks together with the wine in a cup of the hot soup. Add to the soup and whisk well. Keep hot, but do not boil.

Remove the oysters from their shells and add them to the pan. Put a lid on the pan and keep hot for five to ten minutes, but do not boil as this will toughen the oysters. Stir in the grated cheese. Pour into soup bowls and sprinkle a teaspoon of chopped pepper into each plate.

If adding the frikadellers, make the mixture according to the recipe and then poach them in boiling fish stock. Cover with a lid and simmer for five minutes. When cooked, add them to the soup with the cheese.

FISH SOUP À LA RUSSE 👑

To serve 4:

1 lb/500 g cod or haddock
1 onion
1 carrot
sprig of parsley
1 clove
1 teaspoon of Marmite
½ a bay leaf
1½ pints/90 cl water

salt and pepper
juice of ½ lemon
¼ pint/15 cl white wine
1 tablespoon of diced green
   pepper
24 oysters
2 tablespoons of chopped fresh
   parsley

For the cheese canapés:
white bread, sliced
butter
¼ lb/125 g grated Gruyère
   cheese

1 egg white, whipped
dash of Cayenne pepper

Clean and cut up the fish leaving in the bone and put in a saucepan with the onion, carrot, parsley, clove, salt and pepper, Marmite, the bay leaf and the water. Bring to the boil over a high heat and then simmer for about twenty-five minutes or until the fish is broken up. Strain off the stock through a dampened muslin cloth, replace the stock in the saucepan and add seasoning to taste. Heat and add the lemon juice, wine and the green pepper.

Remove the beards from the oysters and put them in a small saucepan with their juice. Bring to the boil quickly and remove at once. Strain the juice into the soup. Make the soup very hot, without actually boiling. It should have turned a golden brown colour. Remove the pan from the heat, add the oysters, cover with a lid and allow to stand for ten minutes. Add the chopped parsley.

For a splendid accompaniment to this soup, try cheese canapés.

Spread slices of white bread with butter and cut into fingers. Mix ¼ lb/125 g grated Gruyère cheese with whipped white of egg and a dash of cayenne pepper. Spread on the bread and bake in a hot over until golden brown. Salted biscuits or cream crackers can be used instead of bread.

👑 CREAM OF PEAS MONACO

To serve 4:

1 lb/500 g fresh green peas
2 pints/1.25 litres beef stock
½ pint/30 cl double cream
pepper, salt and pinch of
   sugar to season

1 oz/30 g butter
chopped mint
1 tablespoon of diced red
   pepper

This is a delicious creamy soup. First, cook the peas in salted water. Strain and sieve. Add the peas to the hot beef stock together with the cream, sugar and pepper and salt to taste. Heat thoroughly, but do not boil, then remove the pan from the heat and whisk in the butter. Garnish with chopped mint and red pepper.

👑 CREAM ALEXANDRA

To serve 4:

2 ozs/60 g butter
2 ozs/60 g plain flour
2 pints/1.25 litres chicken
   stock

the breast of a cooked chicken,
   minced and sieved

For the garnish:
¼ pint/15 cl single cream
½ teacup of petit pois cooked in
   salted water

1 carrot cut in fine strips and
   cooked in chicken stock

Here is another soup much liked by ex-Queen Alexandra of Yugoslavia – a great soup person. It is very smooth and creamy with quite an exciting flavour.

   Melt the butter and stir in the flour. Add the heated stock and stir until smooth. Bring to the boil, stirring all the time and boil for ten minutes. Add the minced chicken breast and simmer for a further ten minutes. Remove from the cooker. Heat, but do not boil the cream and add the peas and carrots. Pour into the soup, season to taste and serve.

ROSA'S COCK-A-LEEKIE 👑

To serve 6:

1 boiling fowl	*¼ lb/125 g cooked and stoned*
a little bacon	*prunes*
veal or beef bones (cooked)	*1½ lb/750 g chopped and partly*
salt and pepper	*cooked leeks*

For a good, warming winter supper there is nothing better than a dish of hearty soup. It is a complete meal.

Rosa's Cock-a-Leekie is a traditional Scottish recipe – good and hearty with a whole fowl which is left to simmer all day. The recipe was sent to me by a Scotswoman, who got it, she says, from Rosa Maltravers, cook to the noble Forbes family of Aberdeenshire for twenty-one years. Rosa, a fine Scottish cook, was famous for her Cock-a-Leekie, and one cannot do better than follow her version which is essentially a simple soup, calling for no special preparations.

First, cover the fowl, bones and bacon with water in a saucepan and leave to simmer all day. Season to taste. Strain the fowl and its stock through a sieve. Add the prunes and the leeks cut in half-inch squares to the stock. Return to the stove to heat thoroughly. Finally, add chopped meat from the fowl, if desired, and serve piping hot.

NETTLE SOUP WITH EGG BALLS (*Nessel Kal*) 👑

To serve 4:

1 pint/60 cl good stock made	*1 tablespoon of plain flour*
from veal and pork bones	*pepper, salt and a pinch of*
½ pint/30 cl nettle tops, cooked	*sugar to season*
and puréed through a fine	*½ tablespoon of finely-chopped*
sieve	*chives*
	1 tablespoon of cold butter

For the egg balls:	
2 hard-boiled eggs	*1 tablespoon of grated Gruyère*
½ oz/15 g butter	*cheese*

If you have a garden with a stinging nettle problem, don't despair – eat them. In Sweden, nettle soup is quite a delicacy. The nettle tops have a light, delicious taste rather like asparagus. They are said to help cure rheumatism too! Snip off tender nettle tops in April or early May, cook them for approximately five minutes and then sieve.

Bring the stock to the boil and thicken with the flour diluted in a little water. Simmer for ten minutes. Add the seasoning and sugar, the sieved nettles and the chives. Simmer for twenty minutes. Remove from heat, add the butter and stir with a whisk. Keep warm.

To make the egg balls, remove the yolks of the hard-boiled eggs and mix with the butter and cheese to form a smooth cream. Let the mixture harden a little in a cool place, then roll into small balls. The egg balls can be made while the soup is simmering so that they are ready to float in the soup just before serving.

In Sweden we sometimes make a meal of *nessel kal* by serving poached eggs sprinkled with Parmesan cheese instead of the egg balls.

♛ SWEDISH KOTTSOPPA

To serve 6–8:

2 lbs/1 kg chuck rib of beef	2 onions cut in halves
2 lbs/1 kg silverside of beef	2 carrots
6½ pints/4 litres water	1 parsnip
2 teaspoons of salt	1 stick of celery
10 white peppercorns	1 leek
a sprig of thyme	a sprig of parsley
1 bay leaf	

Kottsoppa is the Swedish version of pot au feu, and is served in Sweden as a substantial supper dish with boiled potatoes and horseradish sauce.

Put the meat in a deep saucepan with the water and bring to the boil slowly. Remove any scum, add salt, peppercorns, herbs, onions, one of the carrots and the parsnip. Cover the saucepan and simmer for three to four hours. When the meat is cooked, strain half the amount of stock into another saucepan and remove fat. Cut all the remaining vegetables into thin strips and add to the strained stock. Simmer until the vegetables are cooked. Add chopped parsley.

The meat should be sliced, and served with plain boiled potatoes, horseradish sauce and the vegetables from the stock.

POTAGE INTERLAKEN 👑

To serve 4:

2 chicken breasts	*¼ pint/15 cl double cream*
2 pints/1.25 litres good chicken	*1 oz/30 g grated Parmesan*
* stock*	* cheese*
4 ozs/125 g of noodles	*pepper and a pinch of sugar to*
1 egg	* taste*

This is a good, satisfying soup from Switzerland which I once enjoyed in Interlaken. You cut the chicken breasts into small pieces and boil them in enough salted water to cover them. Heat the chicken stock and cook the noodles. Beat the egg with the cream. Remove the stock from the heat and whisk in the egg and cream mixture. Add the chopped up chicken and the cooked noodles, season to taste and sprinkle in the cheese.

Serve hot, but do not boil once the egg mixture has been added.

MEAT SOUP WITH BARLEY 👑

To serve 6:

2 lbs/1 kg shin of beef with	*2 chicken stock cubes*
* bone*	*1 carrot*
1 parsnip	*salt and pepper*
1½ tablespoons of pearl barley	*½ lb/250 g small potatoes*
1 stick of celery	*parsley*
2 leeks cut in rings	

Cut the meat into squares and chop up the bones. Put into a saucepan together with enough water to cover, add salt and bring slowly to the boil. Remove scum and simmer for an hour. Dissolve chicken cubes in a little water and add to the meat stock together with the peeled and cut vegetables and barley. Season, cover the pan and bring to the boil. Simmer for two hours.

Fifteen minutes before cooking time is up, add the peeled potatoes. When ready, scoop out bones and fat and add freshly-chopped parsley.

♛ POTAGE ALEXANDRA

To serve 6:

2½ ozs/75 g butter
2 tablespoons of plain flour
2 pints/1.25 litres of chicken
    stock
salt, pepper and sugar to taste
2 ozs/60 g noodles, blanched

¾ pint/45 cl milk
20 prawns for garnishing
¼ pint/15 cl double cream
dash of cayenne pepper
2 tablespoons of Gruyère
    cheese

This soup was created for ex-Queen Alexandra of Yugoslavia, for whom I worked at one time. She adored it, but ex-King Peter only liked clear consommé and they used to eat different soups at dinner.

Melt 2 ozs/60 g of butter in a saucepan. Add the flour, mix well and stir in the heated stock a little at a time. Stir until smooth and creamy. Season. Bring to the boil and simmer over a gentle heat for ten minutes.

Meanwhile cut the blanched noodles into slices and simmer in the milk until tender, adding more milk if necessary. Add the cream, cayenne pepper, cheese and the rest of the butter. Do not boil.

ROSE HIP SOUP WITH CREAM ♔

To serve 4:

1 pint/500 g rose hips
3 pints/1.75 litres water
¼ lb/125 g sugar
small cup of sultanas
2 tablespoons of cornflour

1 tablespoon of blanched
* almonds*
½ pint/30 cl whipped double
* cream*

Rose hips are the orange-red, oval berries of the wild rose, found on the bushes between late August and November. They are not cultivated and are not available in the shops.

Boil the rose hips in water for one and a half hours, stirring frequently and mashing with a fork. When cooked, pass them through a fine sieve. Put the sieved rose hips and their liquor into a clean pan, add the sugar and the sultanas. Bring to the boil and remove any scum. Reduce the heat. Mix the cornflour with half a cup of cold water and whisk into the soup. Boil for two minutes. Remove from the heat and add the almonds cut into strips. Allow to cool.

Serve cold with a spoonful of whipped cream in each cup.

MELON EN GELÉE ♔

To serve 4:

½ pint/30 cl white wine
1 tablespoon of tomato purée
1½ pints/90 cl good beef
* consommé*

1 honeydew melon
5 ozs/150 g ham, cut in thin
* strips*

Mix the wine and tomato purée with the heated consommé, and then allow to cool almost to setting point. Cut the melon in half and remove seeds. Scoop out the melon flesh with a teaspoon so that it resembles small eggs and put in individual soup cups. Spoon the consommé over them and sprinkle the ham on top. Chill and serve cold.

♛ COLD CONSOMMÉ WITH OYSTERS

To serve 4:

> 1½ pints/90 cl reduced chicken
>   consommé (for recipe see
>   page 3)
> 1 glass of dry white wine
>
> 30 oysters
> shredded lettuce
> lemon slices, to garnish

Heat the consommé and mix in the white wine. Remove the beards from the oysters and put the oysters with their juice in a small saucepan and bring to the boil. Remove at once and add the oysters and juice to the consommé. Cool and allow to set to a jelly.

Serve in glasses with strips of lettuce in the bottom. Garnish with lemon twists.

♛ COLD TOMATO SOUP WITH CUCUMBER

To serve 4:

> 12 tomatoes
> 1 onion
> 1 oz/30 g butter
> 1½ pints/90 cl water
>
> seasoning
> 1 glass of Madeira
> 2 teaspoons of cornflour
> ½ cucumber

Rinse and slice the tomatoes in quarters. Chop the onion finely and braise lightly in the butter. Add the tomatoes, seasoning and the water. Bring to the boil and simmer for twenty minutes until the tomatoes are mushy. Pass through a fine sieve to remove seeds and skins, add the Madeira and bring to the boil.

Dissolve the cornflour in a little water and stir into the soup with a whisk. Boil for five minutes, then remove from heat and cool. Peel the cucumber and cut into pieces, removing the seeds. Add the cucumber to the tomato soup and serve chilled in soup cups.

To garnish, you could add some good cream cheese piped in the centre of each cup or serve cheese crisps separately.

GELÉE DE VOLAILLE AU TOMATES ♔

To serve 4:

½ lb/250 g raw minced shin of beef
2 onions, peeled and cut in rings
1 red pepper, seeded and cut in slices
2 whites of egg
8 tomatoes cut in quarters

salt and pepper to taste
10 white peppercorns
¼ teaspoon of garlic salt
½ teaspoon of celery salt
4 pints/2.5 litres good chicken consommé (for recipe see page 3)
1 hard-boiled egg, to garnish

Place the beef, vegetables, raw egg whites and tomatoes in a saucepan and add the seasoning. Mix over the heat and add the consommé. Bring slowly to the boil and then simmer for one and a quarter hours. Remove from heat and allow to stand for fifteen minutes. Strain through a dampened muslin cloth. The soup should be a clear ruby colour. Adjust seasoning to taste. Cool nearly to setting point and garnish with the hard-boiled egg white, finely chopped, and the sieved yolk. Chill and serve.

VELOUTÉ DE VOLAILLE FROID ♔

To serve 4:

1 pint/60 cl chicken consommé (for recipe see page 3)
1 pint/60 cl new green peas, puréed
1 egg yolk
¼ pint/15 cl double cream

1 tablespoon of finely chopped mint
pepper, salt and sugar to taste
4 ozs/125 g bacon cut in strips and fried until crisp, to garnish

Heat the consommé in a saucepan, add the purée of peas, stir and bring to the boil. Boil for five minutes, then remove from the heat but keep hot. Beat together the egg yolk and the cream and add to the soup with the mint. Mix well and season to taste. Pour into soup cups to cool. When set, garnish with bacon strips and serve.

♛ COLD CHERRY SOUP CHANTILLY

To serve 6:

2 ozs/60 g blanched almonds	1 tablespoon caster sugar
2¼ lbs/1 kg fresh cherries	4 teaspoons of cornflour
2 pints/1.25 litres water	½ pint/30 cl sweet white wine
1 stick of cinnamon	¼ pint/15 cl double cream

Skin the almonds, cut in strips and toast lightly. Wash and stem the cherries, reserving some to garnish the soup, and put in a saucepan with the water and cinnamon stick. Boil for twenty-five minutes. In the meantime, stone the remaining cherries and put aside for garnishing.

Strain the juice from the cooked cherries into a saucepan, add the sugar and bring to the boil. Add the reserved cherries. Mix the cornflour with half a cup of water and thicken the soup slightly. Mix well with a whisk to prevent lumps. Boil for about two minutes, then remove from heat and add the wine. Serve cold in soup cups with a spoonful of whipped cream on top of each, and sprinkle with the toasted almonds.

Fish

I AM A GREAT FISH-EATER. OF ALL THE RECIPES IN THIS BOOK, THOSE THAT I most enjoy preparing and eating are in this chapter.

I owe much to fish. Its rich source of Vitamin D has helped to sustain my energy and well-being throughout many hectic periods. Almost the first thing I did when moving house was to check that there was a good fishmonger in the area. My ideal place to live would, of course, be in a sea port so that I could buy the fish directly they came out of the sea!

I know that I have been spoilt as regards buying fish, for when I was at Clarence House all the fish came direct from London's Billingsgate Fish Market. Shopping without the Royal Warrant is rather a different matter, as I have subsequently found.

Use your eyes and – very important – your nose to ensure the fish is fresh. How can you be sure? With me it is instinct, but here is how I think I do it. First, look the fish in the eye. If the eyes are bright and clear with what I can only describe as that rather appealing look, it is all right. If you are not sure, cast an eye over the flesh which should be a bluish white, the gills scarlet. If you are still not sure, prod the fish, sniffing hard at the same time. If your finger leaves a dent and there is that unmistakable whiff, buy frozen fish instead.

With shellfish, be doubly careful. You will have to rely very much upon your fishmonger for fresh lobster and crab; frozen, peeled prawns are often preferable to the fresh prawns unless very fresh indeed, and when buying frozen shrimps, buy the larger packets as shrimps in small quantities rarely seem to freeze well.

There should be no snobbery about fish. Every fish possesses its own proud heritage. At the right time of year, salmon or trout are delicious and desirable to buy; at other times a fresh piece of cod is a dish fit for a queen. Indeed, I have often been proud to serve it to Her Majesty. My favourite dish is freshest haddock, dipped in melted butter, lightly floured and grilled.

Shellfish provides a rich variety of excellent dishes and with frozen prawns and shrimps readily available, you can always be sure the fish is fresh. A *good* prawn cocktail calls for judgement and artistry. Once at Clarence House I had an inspiration for a lunch-time party: I whipped the mayonnaise very stiff and coloured one half green and the other half red. I then swirled it around the inside of the glass so as to create a different-coloured ribbon effect before putting in the prawn mixture. Served with crushed ice, it made a cool-looking dish for a summer's afternoon. The luncheon party was most amused.

Mackerel is a fish which, ideally, should be caught and eaten on the same day, but this is not possible, of course, if you live some distance from the coast. I always think of it as a holiday fish because the Royal Family used particularly to like to eat it on holiday at Balmoral where it came straight from the Scottish ports. They were very fond of fish and would have it every day, usually in the evening when a fish course would be served at dinner.

♛ FILLETS OF CODFISH AU GRATIN

Pre-heat oven to 180 °C/350 °F or gas mark 4
To serve 3–4:

1 lb/500 g cod fillets	4 anchovy fillets
1 oz/30 g butter	¼ pint/15 cl creamy milk
½ pint/30 cl egg sauce	½ cup grated Parmesan cheese
(for recipe see page 203)	

Rinse the cod fillets, remove skin and bone and dry thoroughly. Cut into fingers about 1 inch thick. Butter an ovenproof dish and cover the bottom with a little of the egg sauce. Place the fillets in the dish, cut the anchovies in pieces and place them on top of the fish. Cover with the rest of the sauce and smooth over with a knife. Dot knobs of butter on top. Pour on the milk and sprinkle with the cheese. Bake in the oven at 180 °C/350 °F or gas mark 4 for twenty minutes.

CODFISH PIE ♔

Pre-heat oven to 180°C/350°F or gas mark 4
To serve 4:

2½ ozs/75 g butter   *seasoning*
3 anchovy fillets   *1 pint/60 cl egg sauce*
2 tablespoons of tomato purée   *(for recipe see page 203)*
2 lbs/1 kg potatoes, peeled   *1 lb/500g cod fillets*
2 oz/60 g butter   *1 tablespoon of double cream*
3 fl ozs/8 cl boiled milk   *1 tablespoon of Parmesan*
1 egg yolk   *cheese, grated*

Melt 1½ ozs/40 g of the butter over a low heat, add the anchovies and the tomato purée. Mix well together.

Boil the potatoes in salted water, strain and mash with the remaining butter and then pour in the hot milk gradually. Beat well, then add the egg yolk and seasoning.

Butter an ovenproof dish, pour a layer of egg sauce on the bottom, add the cod fillets and spread the tomato and anchovy mixture on top. Pour over the rest of the egg sauce. Spread the cream on top. Pipe the creamed potatoes in a pretty pattern on top and sprinkle with cheese.

Bake in the oven at 180°C/350°F or gas mark 4 for twenty minutes until the potato is golden-brown.

FISH CAKES ♔

To make 12 fish cakes:

½ lb/250 g cooked cod or   *1 egg, beaten*
   haddock   *3 ozs/90 g butter*
salt, pepper and pinch of sugar   *plain flour*
½ lb/250 g potatoes, mashed

Flake and bone the fish and mix with the seasoning, potato, egg and 1 oz/30 g of the butter. It does not matter if the butter is a bit lumpy. Shape into cakes and roll in flour. Fry slowly in remaining butter until golden-brown. This will take quite a long time, as fish cakes need gentle treatment. Dish up and pour butter over the fish cakes.

Delicious served for breakfast with a slice of crisp bacon.

♔ POACHED FRESH HADDOCK IN BUTTER SAUCE

Pre-heat oven to 220 °C/425 °F or gas mark 7
To serve 3–4:

1 lb/500 g fillet of haddock, fresh or frozen	½ pint/30 cl English butter sauce (for recipe see page 207)
1 teaspoon of salt	1 tablespoon of mayonnaise or salad cream
1 oz/30 g butter	
½ pint/30 cl milk	chopped parsley and red or green pepper, to garnish

Rinse and dry the haddock, remove skin and bones. Cut the fillets in portions, sprinkle with the salt, and place in a buttered oven-proof dish. Cover with greaseproof paper and poach in milk in the oven at 220 °C/425 °F or gas mark 7 for twelve–fifteen minutes. If the fillets are frozen they will take nearer twenty minutes.

When cooked, remove to a serving dish. Strain the remains of the juice from the poaching into the butter sauce and add the mayonnaise or salad cream. Heat the sauce, but do not boil. Cover the fish with the sauce and sprinkle with chopped parsley and pepper.

Serve with plain boiled potatoes and spinach.

♔ HADDOCK AU GRATIN

Pre-heat oven to 180 °C/350 °F or gas mark 4
To serve 3–4:

½ lb/250 g mushrooms	1 oz/30 g butter
½ pint/30 cl milk	¼ pint/15 cl double cream
dash of cayenne pepper	1 egg white
1 teaspoon of salt	¼ lb/125 g grated Parmesan cheese
1 lb/500 g filleted haddock	

Peel and slice the mushrooms, boil in the milk with a little of the butter and add a pinch of salt and pepper. Boil for two or three minutes. Strain off the milk and reserve.

Rinse and skin the fish, remove bones and dry thoroughly. Place the fish in a buttered ovenproof dish, pour the milk over it with a pinch of cayenne pepper, cover with greaseproof paper and poach for fifteen minutes in the oven at 180°C/350°F or gas mark 4. Mix the cream and the mushrooms and pour over the fish. Beat the egg white to a froth and spread over the fish fillets and sprinkle with cheese. Raise the oven temperature to 220°C/425°F or gas mark 7 and bake until light brown.

OVEN-BAKED HADDOCK 👑

Pre-heat oven to 180°C/350°F or gas mark 4
To serve 6:

1 haddock, 2–3 lbs/1–1.5 kg in weight	1 tablespoon tomato purée
1 teaspoon of salt	½ pint/30 cl creamy milk
fish farce (for recipe see page 214)	6 ozs shrimps
flour	½ lb/250 g small button mushrooms
egg	1 tablespoon of grated Parmesan cheese
breadcrumbs	1 tablespoon of chopped fresh parsley, to garnish
2 ozs/60 g butter	

Clean the fish, keep the head but remove eyes and backbone. Rub the fish inside and out with salt and stuff with the fish farcie. Then close the fish and dip in flour, beaten egg and breadcrumbs. Place in a baking tin with melted butter, mixed with tomato purée. Bake in the oven at 180°C/350°F or gas mark 4 for ten minutes. Baste the fish with the butter, then add the milk and cook for fifteen minutes, basting with the sauce at intervals.

Add the mushrooms and shrimps and cook for a further ten minutes. Place the fish on a serving dish and garnish with the shrimps and the mushrooms. Add the Parmesan cheese to the sauce left in the pan, mix well and pour over the fish. Garnish with fresh parsley.

Serve with plain boiled new potatoes and peas.

♔ BUCKLING AU GRATIN

Pre-heat oven to 220 °C/425 °F or gas mark 7
To serve 6:

> 3 tomatoes, skinned,
>   de-seeded and cut in strips
> ½ onion, finely chopped and
>   lightly fried in butter
> 6 buckling

> 1 oz/30 g butter
> ½ pint/30 cl creamy milk
> 1 oz/30 g grated Gruyère
>   cheese

Buckling, a form of smoked herring, is a popular dish in Sweden, but not so well-known here. This is a way of cooking buckling that you are sure to enjoy.

Place the tomatoes with the fried onions in a gratin dish and put the buckling fillets on top. Dot over the butter, pour the milk and cheese on top, sprinkle with breadcrumbs and place in the oven set at 220 °C/425 °F or gas mark 7 to bake for ten to fifteen minutes until golden-brown.

♔ BAKED HERRING IN TOMATO SAUCE

Pre-heat oven to 220 °C/425 °F or gas mark 7
To serve 6:

> 6 medium-sized herrings
> 1 teaspoon of salt
> 1 oz/30 g butter

> 1 teaspoon of anchovy essence
> 1 tablespoon of tomato sauce
> 2 tablespoons of breadcrumbs

Clean and bone the herrings, sprinkle with salt inside and out and leave them for five minutes. Melt the butter and stir in the anchovy essence and tomato sauce.

Butter a 2-inch/50-mm deep ovenproof dish, roll the herrings, place in the dish and sprinkle with breadcrumbs. Cover with the tomato sauce mixture and place in the oven at 220 °C/425 °F or gas mark 7 to bake for ten minutes until golden-brown.

Sprats are delicious prepared in the same way, but bake for five to six minutes only.

STUFFED MACKEREL 👑

Pre-heat oven to 180°C/350°F or gas mark 4
To serve 4:

4 mackerel
½ lemon
salt and pepper
½ lb/250 g breadcrumbs
2 tablespoons of cold butter

1 egg, beaten
2 tablespoons of chopped fresh
   parsley
2 tablespoons of melted butter

Rinse fish and leave the heads on. Slit and remove back-bones. Rub with lemon, salt and pepper. Mix the breadcrumbs, cold butter, egg and half the parsley to a paste and stuff the fish. Roll the mackerel in flour and then dip in the melted butter. Bake in the oven at 180°C/350°F or gas mark 4 for twenty minutes, basting once or twice with the butter.

Serve, glazed with butter and sprinkled with the remaining chopped parsley.

SOUSED MACKEREL 👑

Pre-heat oven to 180°C/350°F or gas mark 4
To serve 4–6:

1 mackerel per person

For the marinade:
½ pint/30 cl water
¼ pint/15 cl vinegar
6 white peppercorns, crushed
½ onion, sliced

2 sprigs of dill
½ teaspoon of salt
sugar to taste

Mix all the ingredients for the marinade together in a saucepan and boil. Put the fish in an ovenproof dish and pour over the marinade. Place in the oven at 180°C/350°F or gas mark 4 and cook for fifteen minutes. Remove, allow to cool and eat cold with horseradish sauce in mayonnaise, and creamed potatoes.

♛ MACKEREL MARNIES

Pre-heat oven to 220 °C / 425 °F or gas mark 7
To serve 4:

4 medium-sized mackerel   *10 black peppercorns*
¼ pint/15 cl dry white wine   *½ teaspoon of mustard-seed*
¼ pint/15 cl water   *1 large onion, sliced*
2 tablespoons of vinegar   *1 dried red chilli, crushed*
1 bay leaf

For the garnish:
lettuce   *1 sprig of parsley*
hard-boiled eggs   *1 sprig of dill*

Place the mackerel in an ovenproof dish. Put all the other ingredients in a saucepan and bring to the boil. Pour over the mackerel, cover with greaseproof paper and place in the oven at 220 °C/ 425 °F or gas mark 7, to cook for fifteen to twenty minutes.

Allow to cool in the stock, then remove the mackerel and place on a bed of lettuce. The stock should settle into a jelly. Glaze the fish with the jellied stock and garnish with sliced, hard-boiled eggs, parsley and dill.

Serve with vinaigrette salad sauce (for recipe see page 206) and boiled potatoes. This dish can also be made with herring instead of mackerel.

♛ SCOTCH KIPPERS

It gives me much pleasure to include in this chapter the humble kipper, which I consider to be a very special fish. If you buy the best quality kipper and cook it properly, it makes the most delicious dish.

This is the only way to cook a kipper.

First, you must use real Scotch kippers, properly cured, not, horror of horrors, *painted*. Cut off the head and tail of the kippers. Place them in an ovenproof dish and rinse in boiling water. Leave about a tablespoon of hot water in the dish. Place a knob of butter on each kipper. Leave them under a hot grill for about four or five minutes, basting once or twice. When cooked, transfer to a serving plate and glaze with the melted butter.

Perform the whole operation as fast as you can and enjoy the benefits of one of the few really special dishes that require the minimum of preparation.

PRAWN COCKTAIL WITH EGGS ♔

To serve 2:

2 eggs
2 anchovy fillets
¼ pint/15 cl mayonnaise mixed with 2 tablespoons of whipped cream
1 teaspoon of chopped chives
1 tablespoon of tomato sauce

dash of cayenne pepper
1 lettuce
4 ozs/125 g peeled prawns, fresh or frozen
1 tablespoon of chopped radishes

Boil the eggs for six minutes (but do not hard-boil them), then shell in cold water. Chop the anchovies and blend with half the amount of mayonnaise mixture, add the chives, tomato sauce and cayenne pepper. Rinse and dry the lettuce thoroughly, cut in strips and put in the bottom of two glasses. Stand the eggs up in the middle, arrange the prawns around them and pour over the sauce. Cover with the rest of the mayonnaise mixture and decorate with chopped radishes.

Serve with melba toast.

SPICY PRAWN COCKTAIL ♔

To serve 6:

2 lettuce hearts
¾ lb/350 g peeled prawns
4 tablespoons of mayonnaise
1 tablespoon of tomato sauce
1 teaspoon of brandy
dash of cayenne pepper

½ cucumber, thinly cut into strips
2 tablespoons of double cream
1 teaspoon of lemon juice
1 tablespoon of oil
salt, pepper and sugar to taste

This is a piquant prawn cocktail with a certain kick to it.

Rinse, dry, and cut lettuce into strips. Put a bed of lettuce in each individual glass, mix the rest of the ingredients together and pile into the glasses.

☖ PRAWNS AU GRATIN

To serve 4 as a first course:

$1\frac{1}{2}$ *ozs/40 g butter*
1 oz/30 g plain flour
1 teaspoon of curry powder
salt
dash of cayenne pepper
2 tablespoons of tomato purée

$\frac{1}{2}$ *pint/30 cl creamy milk*
   (heated)
1 lb/500g peeled prawns
1 tablespoon of brandy or
   sherry
1 oz/30 g grated cheese

Melt 1 oz/30 g of butter and add the flour, curry powder, seasoning and tomato purée. Stir and add the heated milk a little at a time. Stir until smooth, then simmer for ten minutes. Add the prawns and brandy or sherry. Bring to the boil and add the remaining butter. Dish up in an ovenproof dish, sprinkle with cheese and brown under the grill.

☖ PRAWNS PIQUANT

To serve 6:

$\frac{1}{2}$ *pint/30 cl white sauce*
$\frac{1}{2}$ *glass of sherry or white wine*
1 tablespoon of tomato sauce
1 tablespoon of mayonnaise
$\frac{1}{2}$ *teaspoon of salt*

pinch of cayenne pepper
pinch of sugar
$1\frac{1}{2}$ *lb/750 g peeled Dublin Bay*
   prawns
parsley, to garnish

To the white sauce add the sherry, tomato sauce, mayonnaise, salt, cayenne pepper and sugar. Blend well and simmer for two or three minutes. Pour over the prawns and garnish with parsley.

CASSOULET DE CREVETTES ♔

To serve 6:

1 lb/450 g peeled shrimps
1½ ozs/40 g butter
1 oz/30 g plain flour
½ pint/30 cl fish stock (for
   recipe see page 212)

1 teaspoon of salt
pinch of cayenne pepper
2 tablespoons of double cream
2 tablespoons of dry white
   wine

You can serve this dish either as the fish course of a dinner party menu or as the main course of a light luncheon. It is the pinch of cayenne pepper that gives the extra kick to these delicious little shellfish.

Make the sauce by melting the butter and then adding the flour. Once the flour is absorbed pour in the fish stock and seasoning and mix over a low heat. Add cream, and stir until the mixture thickens. Stir in the wine and then pour the sauce over the shrimps.

Serve in a pretty dish with melba toast.

SHRIMPS WITH RICE ♔

To serve 2:

¼ lb/125 g rice
2 ozs/60 g butter
2 tablespoons of plain flour
1 large tin of asparagus tips
¼ pint/15 cl creamy milk
pepper, salt and sugar to taste

pinch of nutmeg
10 oz/300g peeled shrimps
1 oz/30 g grated Gruyère
   cheese
1 red or green pepper, finely
   sliced

Melt the butter, add the flour and mix in the juice from the tin of asparagus tips. Stir until smooth, then simmer for five or six minutes. Add the milk and seasoning, the nutmeg and the shrimps, leaving aside a few for decoration. Simmer for five minutes.

Meanwhile, boil the rice in salted water for ten to twelve minutes and place in a border round the serving dish. Scoop the shrimp mixture into the centre. Decorate the rice with the remainder of the shrimps and the asparagus tips. Sprinkle with the grated Gruyère cheese and pepper strips.

👑 SCAMPI

To serve 4:

Dublin Bay prawns (4–6 per person)	*6 ozs/175 g breadcrumbs*
2 eggs, beaten	*1 pint/60 cl cooking oil*
	chopped fresh parsley

Dip the prawns in the beaten egg and then in the breadcrumbs. Deep-fry in boiling oil until golden. Drain and place in a napkin. Using a straining spoon, dip the parsley in the oil for a couple of seconds and then sprinkle over the scampi.

Serve with green tartare sauce (for recipe see page 205).

👑 COQUILLES ST JACQUES BALMORAL

To serve 4:

4–6 scallops	*1 tablespoon of butter*
½ pint/30 cl milk	*1 oz/30 g plain flour*
6 peppercorns	*1 oz/30 g grated Parmesan*
bay leaf	*cheese*
salt and pepper	*1 oz/30 g breadcrumbs*

Remove the meat from the shells and cut it into piecs. Put in a saucepan with the milk, peppercorns and bay leaf, and season to taste. Bring to the boil and simmer for five minutes. Strain, but reserve the milk. Remove the peppercorns and bay leaf from the meat.

Put the butter into a saucepan, add the flour and strained milk. Simmer for five or six minutes, then add the cheese. Put half the sauce into the cleaned and buttered scallop shells and put the meat on top. Cover with the rest of the sauce, sprinkle bread-crumbs on top and brown under a hot grill.

OYSTERS IN WINE SAUCE 👑

Pre-heat oven to 220 °C/425 °F or gas mark 7
To serve 4:

24 oysters
2 shallots, finely chopped
½ oz/15 g butter
4 or 5 mushrooms, peeled and
  sliced
½ tablespoon of chopped fresh
  parsley

2 tablespoons of breadcrumbs
½ glass of dry white wine
¼ pint/15 cl of double cream
2 tablespoons of grated
  Gruyère cheese
pepper and sugar, to taste

Remove the oysters from their shells and steam in their own juice for half a minute. Strain and save the juice for the sauce. Remove the beards and put the oysters into china scallop shells or small ramekin dishes.

To make the sauce, fry the shallots in a little butter over a gentle heat, add the mushrooms, parsley, half the breadcrumbs and the wine. Stir and cook for one minute. Add the cream and the oyster juice. Remove from heat and add half the cheese. Season with pepper and a pinch of sugar. Cover the oysters with the mixture. Sprinkle the oysters with the remaining cheese and breadcrumbs, add a knob of butter and bake in the oven at 220 °C/425 °F or gas mark 7 for ten minutes until light brown.

ROULADES DE SAUMON FUMÉ 👑

To serve 6–8:

½ pint/30 cl double cream
1 tablespoon of grated
  horseradish
juice of ½ lemon
½ lb/250 g peeled prawns,
  fresh or frozen

½ lb/250 g smoked salmon,
  thinly sliced
French lettuce
lemon slices, to garnish

There cannot be a more luxurious first course than this for a special dinner party.

Whip the cream, add the horseradish and lemon juice. Peel and rinse the fresh prawns in salted water or defrost frozen prawns. Add the prawns to the cream, put a spoonful of the mixture on the slices of smoked salmon and roll up lightly. Serve on a bed of French lettuce. Garnish with twisted slices of lemon, and serve with brown bread and butter, thinly sliced.

BALMORAL SALMON

One of the pleasantest interludes when I worked for the Royal Family was a stay at Balmoral while the Queen Mother was there with Prince Charles and Princess Anne, who were then still children. This was virtually in the nature of a holiday for me as the Buckingham Palace staff were there, and such was the below stairs protocol that I would not have dared bake so much as a cake without a formal request from the chef.

Preparations for the annual holiday at Balmoral would start towards the end of July. Pots, pans, china and utensils, everything in fact except the Buckingham Palace stove, would be packed up and sent ahead. After the Coronation, I cooked for the Queen Mother at Birkhall, a Jacobean mansion which had a very old-fashioned kitchen.

On my first journey I remember being amazed that even Buckingham Palace could hold so many people, until I realized that many took their families.

Whenever the Queen went to Balmoral, Windsor or Sandringham, her chief chef, his four principal assistants and a staff that varied from fifty to two hundred, according to the length of the stay, would go with her. The remaining staff at Buckingham Palace would then go on a system known as board wages. Board wages is an old-fashioned system whereby the staff can either eat in the palace or take the money to buy their own food. At the palace there were six male chefs and a staff of about five hundred, all of whom had to be fed. It would have been impossible to keep all the royal palaces fully staffed, so every now and again there was this great move.

At Balmoral all the Royal Family would lead an outdoor life, but of the ladies, it was the Queen Mother who was the most energetic. Her great passion was for salmon fishing, and this she did with intense concentration for hours on end. She would put on waders and old clothes and attempt to catch the biggest salmon she could find. She liked no interruption and took with her only the simplest of cold picnics.

Once, after two whole days of concentrated fishing, the Queen Mother presented me with two salmon, one of which must have weighed about 20 lbs. 'Do what you like with them,' she said. 'Why not give the staff a treat?'

As there was only one rather small, and very old-fashioned refrigerator at Birkhall, I sent the large salmon to Clarence House to be put in the deep freeze to await my return, and cooked the smaller one according to this recipe.

To serve 4–6:

1 salmon	2 teaspoons of salt
1 carrot, sliced	1 dessertspoon of vinegar
1 small onion, sliced	parsley, chopped
10 white peppercorns	

For the lemon sauce:

$\frac{1}{2}$ pint/30 cl double cream	pinch of sugar
$\frac{3}{4}$ pint/40 cl mayonnaise	juice of $\frac{1}{2}$ lemon
$\frac{1}{2}$ teaspoon of mustard	

Rinse salmon and drain and place in a large saucepan with the sliced carrot, onion, peppercorns, salt and vinegar. Add water to cover and bring to the boil. Reduce heat and keep hot for five minutes. When dishing up, remove skin and bone without breaking the flesh and drain well.

To make the sauce, whip cream, stir in mayonnaise, gradually add mustard, sugar and lemon juice. Serve the cold salmon garnished with the chopped parsley and accompanied by small boiled potatoes and cucumber salad.

♕ SAUMON COURT BOUILLON

To serve 4:

4 slices of salmon	bunch of parsley
pinch of sugar, salt and pepper	1 carrot
10 white peppercorns	1 large onion

Rinse the salmon slices and place in a flat, shallow pan. Add water to cover, seasoning, peppercorns, parsley and sliced vegetables. Cover with greaseproof paper. Place pan over heat and bring to the boil. Lower the heat and simmer for five or six minutes. Remove and keep hot. Remove skin and bones without breaking the fish.

Place on a serving dish and cover with some hollandaise sauce (for recipe see page 203). Serve the rest of the sauce separately.

Serve boiled new potatoes with butter and dill.

♕ TRUITE EN BLEU ROYALE

To serve 6:

6 blue trout weighing	1 oz/30 g plain flour
6 ozs/175 g each	salt and pepper
½ lb/250 g butter	

For the tarragon sauce:

½ lb/250 g butter	1 tablespoon of dry tarragon
½ tablespoon of tarragon	leaves
vinegar	pinch each of salt, pepper,
juice of ½ lemon	cayenne and sugar

This is a dish of the utmost simplicity, but one which repays careful attention to detail. The boning of the fish is easily done if a nice, clean slit is made in the stomach and the backbone removed from the tail end.

The flesh of the blue trout should be a firm whitish pink. Remove scales, fins and the backbone but not the head. Remove as many small bones as possible. Rinse well and drain on a towel for ten minutes. Open and season, then close. Melt butter in a frying pan. Dip the trout in the flour and cook gently in the butter until golden-brown, about five minutes each side. When cooked, place in a dish with a little butter and cover with greaseproof paper before serving.

To make the tarragon sauce, cream the butter in a basin and gradually work in the vinegar and lemon juice. Stirring all the time, add the tarragon leaves, salt, pepper, cayenne and small pinch of sugar. The texture should be light and creamy.

This dish is delicious with cucumber salad and piped creamed potatoes.

SALMON TROUT FARCIE IN ASPIC ♔

Pre-heat oven to 170 °C/325 °F or gas mark 3
To serve 4–6:

1 salmon trout, about 2½ lbs/1 kg

For the stuffing:
½ lb/250 g lemon sole, filleted   *1 oz/30 g plain flour*
2 ozs/60 g butter   *2 eggs, separated*
½ lb/250 g peeled prawns   *pepper, salt and sugar to taste*
¼ pint/15 cl creamy milk

For the poaching liquid:
juice from a tin of asparagus   *parsley*
* tips*   *4 slices of onion*
¼ pint/15 cl dry white wine   *6 white peppercorns*

For the garnish:
prawns   *tomato purée*
rings of green pepper   *asparagus tips*
hard-boiled eggs

For the aspic:
½ oz/15 g gelatine   *1 pint/60 cl clear fish stock*
*   (for recipe see page 212)*

This is a party dish which always looks immensely graceful and is as good to eat. To me it epitomizes the British table at its best. How I would love to do it again for a summer dance, perhaps, with the guests in gauzy dresses drifting around as they do in a Jean Anouilh play, or as cool refreshment after an elegant race meeting. It is a dish to bring out a sense of occasion.

Get your fishmonger to remove the backbone and gills of the fish but leave the head intact. When you get it home wash and dry the fish and sprinkle some salt inside.

Make the stuffing by scraping the fillets of lemon sole from the skin, making sure there are no bones, then putting through the mincer with the butter and prawns. Mince three times and put in a bowl. In another bowl make a liquid mixture of the milk, flour, two egg yolks, pepper, salt and sugar to taste. Mix really smooth and then gradually add it a little at a time to the fish cream, stirring continuously. Whip egg whites to a stiff froth and fold into the fish cream.

Place the salmon trout in a flat pan and stuff it with the fish cream. Pour the asparagus juice and the wine into the pan. Add the parsley, onion rings and peppercorns. Cover with greaseproof paper before putting on the lid. Heat to just below boiling point, then transfer to the oven which has been pre-heated to 170°C/ 325°F or gas mark 3, to poach for twenty minutes. When cooked, remove covering and let it cool. When cold, remove skin very gently so as not to break the flesh. Place the fish carefully on a dish and garnish with prawns down the centre, alternating with green pepper rings.

To make the aspic, dissolve the gelatine in a little water and add to the heated fish stock. When mixed let the aspic cool until it is nearly, but not quite, set. Then spoon the aspic over the fish until it is well covered.

Decorate round the dish with hard-boiled egg whites stuffed with the sieved yolks mixed with tomato purée. Place bunches of asparagus tips between the eggs.

Serve with a mild-flavoured mayonnaise and lettuce and cucumber salad.

LOBSTER IN ASPIC 👑

To serve 8–10:

2 cooked lobsters, about
   1¾ lbs/850 g each
1 pint/60 cl fish aspic (see
   previous recipe), coloured
   green

2 hard-boiled eggs
1 red pepper

For the stuffed tomatoes:
½ pint/30 cl mayonnaise
2 tablespoons of chopped fresh
   parsley
¼ pint/15 cl double cream

6 tomatoes
salt and pepper
2 hard-boiled eggs

For the garnish:
lettuce
cucumber

lemon slices

Like the previous recipe (salmon trout farcie in aspic), this is a dish that always looks elegant and is suitable for any special occasion.

Cut the lobsters in half lengthwise, break the claws gently and remove the meat from claws and tail. Remove all shell and bones, but retain the creamy green portion for the stuffed tomatoes.

Make the aspic according to the previous recipe and colour it green. This is done by blanching, then draining 1 lb/500 g of spinach and squeezing it through muslin to obtain a green liquid which is then added to the aspic. Alternatively, you can add 1 or 2 drops of green vegetable colouring, bought in bottles. Fill the bottom of a mould with the green aspic, and leave it to cool. Decorate the mould with slices of hard-boiled egg and the red pepper cut in strips. Sprinkle a little aspic on top to keep the decorations in place.

Cut the lobster meat into neat pieces and place the best of them down the sides and the bottom of the mould. Then fill the mould with the cooled but still liquid, aspic. Place in a refrigerator to set for two hours. When solid, loosen the aspic round the edges of the mould carefully with a knife, then dip the mould quickly in hot water. Place a cold dish on top of the mould and turn quickly upside down. Decorate the dish with cubes of cut aspic.

To make the stuffed tomatoes, sieve the soft creamy part of the lobster and mix this with a little warm aspic. Let it cool and, when nearly set, stir in some seasoned mayonnaise mixed with parsley and a little cream. Skin and cut the tomatoes in half, remove seeds, season and pipe in the lobster cream. Top with the sieved hard-boiled egg yolks and place the tomatoes round the lobster.

Serve with lettuce and cucumber garnished with lemon twists.

👑 LOBSTER THERMIDOR

Pre-heat oven to 220°C/425°F or gas mark 7
To serve 2:

1 large cooked lobster	*1 tablespoon of tomato purée*
1 oz/30 g butter	*3 fl oz/8 cl double cream*
2 tablespoons of plain flour	*1 tablespoon of brandy*
½ pint/30 cl milk, heated	*1 oz/30 g grated Gruyère*
salt and sugar	*cheese*
pinch of cayenne pepper	*watercress, to garnish*
dash of Tabasco sauce	

Cut lobster in half lengthways, remove claws and tail, crack the claws and remove the meat. Cut the meat into pieces.

Melt the butter and flour and add the heated milk. Mix until smooth and thick, season and add tomato purée. Simmer for five minutes. Stir in the cream and add the lobster meat and brandy. Keep hot. Trim the lobster shell, leaving the legs, and fill with the thermidor mixture. Sprinkle cheese on top and place in the oven at 220°C/425°F or gas mark 7 for ten minutes to brown.

Serve on a bed of watercress.

FRIED OYSTERS 👑

To serve 2:

> 1 dozen oysters
> 1 tablespoon of double cream
> plain flour

> lemon quarters and parsley, to
> garnish

This makes for a really first-class hors d'oeuvre.

Remove the oysters from their shells and steam for half a minute in their own juice. Put them in a basin with the juice. Add the cream and leave to stand for ten minutes. Remove from the liquid and roll in flour, then fry in hot oil until golden-brown. Cut if necessary and garnish with lemon quarters and parsley.

CRAB VOL-AU-VENT 👑

To serve 4:

> 1 large puff-pastry case
> 1 tablespoon of fish farce
>   (for recipe see page 214)
> ¾ pint/40 cl creamy milk
> salt, pepper and sugar to taste
> 1 tin of crab meat

> 2 tablespoons of plain flour
> 3 fl ozs/8 cl white wine
> 2 ozs/60 g butter
> ¼ lb/125 g frozen, peeled prawns
> watercress, to garnish

The following is an 'easy-way-out' dish in that almost all the ingredients are canned, frozen or ready-made. All you have to do is buy them and then mix them all together – and very good it is, too.

Warm the vol-au-vent case and keep until required. Cook the fish farce in half the amount of milk. Add seasoning and steam over a gentle heat until set. Strain and cool. Cut the crab meat in bits. Add the flour to the strained milk and cook over a gentle heat, stir until thick and smooth. Add the rest of the milk and the wine. Simmer for five or six minutes and lastly add the butter.

Put in the crab meat and the prawns, leaving some aside for garnishing, taste for flavour and bring to the boil over a gentle heat. Remove at once and fill the pastry case with the mixture.

This dish looks its best served on a silver plate, garnished with watercress and a few whole prawns.

♛ STUFFED PANCAKES WITH CREAM OF FISH AND SHRIMPS

Pre-heat oven to 180°C/350°F or gas mark 4
To make 8 thin pancakes:

¼ lb/125 g plain flour	½ pint/30 cl milk
1 egg	sunflower oil for frying
1 egg yolk	scant butter
pinch of salt	parsley sprigs, to garnish

For the filling:
½ pint/30 cl fish cream	½ lb/250 g peeled frozen
(for recipe see page 214)	shrimps, defrosted

Place the flour in a basin, break in the whole eggs and the egg yolk, mix together and add the salt. Add the milk little by little. Put enough oil in a small frying pan to coat the bottom and heat gently. When hot pour in enough batter to make a thin pancake. Fry on both sides.

Mix the fish cream with the shrimps and fill the pancakes with the mixture. Roll up and place on a well-buttered baking sheet, cover with buttered greaseproof paper and place in the oven set at 180°C/350°F or gas mark 4 for five minutes. Dish up and glaze the pancakes with a little butter.

Decorate with parsley and serve hot or cold.

CUTLETS OF HALIBUT GRATINÉE 👑

To serve 4–6:

2 lbs/1 kg middle cut of halibut	flour
salt	breadcrumbs
2 eggs	3 ozs/90 g butter
2 tablespoons of milk	$\frac{1}{2}$ lemon

For the sauce:

4 tablespoons of mayonnaise	juice of $\frac{1}{2}$ lemon
$\frac{3}{4}$ pint/40 cl double cream	1 teaspoon of mustard

For the garnish:

4 slices of lemon	anchovy fillets
chopped capers	

Cut the fish into one-inch thick cutlets, remove skin and bone, rinse and dry on a cloth and sprinkle with salt. Beat a couple of eggs with the milk. Turn the fish in flour, coat in the egg mixture and then breadcrumbs. Melt the butter in a frying pan over a gentle heat and fry the fish cutlets golden-brown on both sides for ten to fifteen minutes. Make sure the fish is well cooked in the middle. Squeeze lemon juice over the cutlets.

For the sauce, mix the mayonnaise, cream, lemon and mustard together and serve separately.

Garnish the cutlets with the lemon slices, the anchovies in rings on top, and the chopped capers in the middle.

CUTLETS OF PLAICE IN BUTTER 👑

To serve 2:

4 fillets of plaice	2 eggs, beaten
salt and pepper	lemon slices and fresh parsley,
plain flour	to garnish
2 ozs/60 g butter	

This is a very simple but delicious dish. Skin, rinse and dry the fillets. Season with salt and pepper. Spread some flour on grease-proof paper. Fold the fillets in half so that the inside is on the outside, turn them in the flour and dip in the beaten egg. Put the butter in a frying pan and place over a low heat. Heat gradually but do not let the butter turn brown. Drop the fish in the hot butter and fry about three minutes on each side until golden-brown.

Dish up and garnish with lemon slices and fresh parsley. Serve with peas or spinach.

♔ FILET DE SOLE MEUNIÈRE

To serve 6:

6 fillets of Dover sole	1 teaspoon of salt
3 ozs/90 g butter	chopped parsley and lemon
2 tablespoons of plain flour	slices, to garnish

Rinse and skin the fillets of sole, place on a cloth to dry. Toss the fillets in seasoned flour and then toss in the butter which has been melted in a frying pan. Place in an ovenproof dish and grill to a golden colour.

Dish up and sprinkle a line of finely chopped parsley on top. Garnish with slices of lemon.

SOLE À LA SAUCE RÉMOULADE 👑

Pre-heat oven to 180°C/350°F or gas mark 4
To serve 4:

2 filleted Dover sole
seasoning
½ pint/30 cl good fish stock
 (for recipe see page 212)

1 lb/500 g of potatoes, mashed
 and creamed
½ pint/30 cl peeled shrimps
parsley

For the rémoulade sauce:
4 hard-boiled eggs
3 egg yolks
¼ pint/15 cl olive oil
¼ pint/15 cl tarragon vinegar

1 tablespoon of French or
 English mustard
1 tablespoon of capers
4 anchovies
½ pint/30 cl whipped cream

Rinse fillets and dry well. Season and place in a tin with the stock. Cover with greaseproof paper and poach in the oven, set at 180°C/350°F or gas mark 4 for fifteen minutes.

To make the sauce, put the yolks of the hard-boiled eggs through a sieve, stir in the raw yolks and mix to a smooth paste. Add the oil and vinegar gradually, mixing all the time, then the mustard, capers and anchovies. Lastly, stir in the whipped cream.

Border a dish with the creamed potatoes, drain the fish and arrange in the middle. Coat with the rémoulade sauce and decorate with shrimps and parsley.

♛ FILLET OF DOVER SOLE REGINA

Pre-heat oven to 220 °C/425 °F or gas mark 7
To serve 6:

6 Dover sole
1 lb/500 g lemon sole fillets
½ bottle of champagne or dry
  white wine
6 ozs/175 g butter
½ pint/30 cl double cream

¼ pint/15 cl milk
3 eggs, separated
2 cooked lobster, about
  1½ lb/750 g each
parsley, to garnish

For the sauce:
1 oz/30 g plain flour
3 ozs/90 g butter

1 pint/60 cl fish stock
  (for recipe see page 212)

Skin and fillet the Dover sole. Cover some of the bones and heads with half the wine and ½ pint/30 cl water, bring to the boil and simmer for half an hour. Make a forcemeat with the lemon sole and 3 ozs/90 g of the butter by passing through the mincer three times. In another bowl mix the cream, milk and three egg yolks and stir into the forcemeat. Dissect the lobsters and add any small bits and pieces of lobster to the fish cream.

Rinse and dry the filleted Dover sole and season well. Keeping the underside on the inside, roll and stuff the fillets with the force-meat. Place in a buttered ovenproof dish with the rest of the wine and cover with greaseproof paper. Poach in the oven at 220 °C/ 425 °F or gas mark 7 for twenty minutes.

Remove the fillets and drain. Reduce the liquid by simmering. Make a sauce with the flour, 1 oz/30 g of butter, and the fish stock. Cook until it thickens. Lower heat and while simmering add the reduced liquid from the fillets. Remove from heat and strain the sauce. Stir in the remaining butter. Put the dissected lobster on top of each fillet and place on a serving dish. Coat with the sauce.

Garnish the border of the serving dish with the meat from the lobster claws and some parsley. Serve with button mushrooms steamed in butter, and new potatoes.

SOLE VALEOSKA 👑

To serve 4–6:

For the sauce:
1 cooked lobster, about
   1¾ lbs/850 g in weight
½ pint/30 cl béchamel sauce
   (for recipe see page 201)
1 tablespoon of tomato purée

salt and sugar
dash of cayenne pepper
¼ pint/15 cl sherry
¼ pint/15 cl double cream

For the sole:
2 lbs/1 kg fillet Dover sole
salt
juice of 1 lemon
beaten egg

flour
breadcrumbs
parsley and lemon slices, to
   garnish

To make the sauce, cut the lobster in half lengthways, remove meat and cut into fairly large pieces, not forgetting the meat from the claws. Put the béchamel sauce in a pan, add the tomato purée, a pinch of sugar, salt, cayenne pepper and the sherry. Bring to the boil, reduce heat, add the lobster meat, and then stir in the cream. Simmer for five to ten minutes.

Cut the fillets of sole in half lengthways, and sprinkle with salt and lemon. Dip in flour, beaten egg and then coat in breadcrumbs. Twist the fillets and fry in deep oil. Drain on absorbent paper.

Pour the sauce onto a serving dish and pile the sole in the middle. Garnish with parsley and slices of lemon.

RED MULLET POACHED IN WINE 👑

Pre-heat oven to 220°C/425°F or gas mark 7
To serve 2:

2 red mullet weighing about
   ¾ lb/350 g each
lemon
salt
2 ozs/60 g butter

plain flour
pepper
¼ pint/15 cl dry white wine
pinch of cinnamon

It was the Queen Mother, who had a very wide knowledge of fish, who introduced me to red mullet. I am grateful to her, as it is really a very lovely fish. This is the way I cooked it for her at Birkhall.

Leave on the heads of the red mullet. Rinse and rub the fish inside with lemon and salt. Melt the butter in an ovenproof dish and dip the fish first in butter, then in flour and again in butter. Pour half the amount of wine over the mullet and sprinkle them with a very little cinnamon. Place in the oven set at 220°C/425°F or gas mark 7. After five minutes, add the rest of the wine and then poach for a further ten minutes.

Serve plain.

👑 POACHED TURBOT IN BUTTER SAUCE

Pre-heat oven to 170°C/325°F or gas mark 3
To serve 4:

4 *fillets of turbot*	1 *tablespoon of plain flour*
1 *glass of dry white wine*	*juice of ½ lemon*
1 *glass of fish stock (for*	*salt and pepper*
recipe see page 212)	*chopped parsley to garnish*
2 *ozs/60 g butter*	

The day the King of Sweden, the late King Gustav VI, came to lunch was the only time I paid more attention to the tastes of the guest than of the host. I knew, though of course I had not been officially informed, that the King had a delicate stomach, so I planned accordingly. The dishes would have to be mild and bland but of the very best quality.

Afterwards, the King of my country asked to see me upstairs and said some very wonderful things about my cooking. It was a proud and happy day. It was this dish he liked particularly.

Poach the fillets in wine and stock in the oven set at 170°C/325°F or gas mark 3, for fifteen minutes. Dish up the fish and keep warm.

Melt 1 oz/30 g of the butter and add the flour. Mix well then strain the juice from the poached fillets into the pan. Stir over the heat and simmer gently for ten minutes. Mix in the lemon juice and stir in the remaining butter. Season with salt and pepper. Glaze the fish with the sauce and garnish with parsley.

TURBOT CAFÉ DE PARIS 👑

To serve 6:

2 lbs/1 kg middle-cut of
 turbot
1 pint/60 cl fish stock, heated
 (for recipe see page 212)
¼ pint/15 cl dry white wine
juice of ½ lemon
2 sprigs of parsley
salt and pepper

½ pint/30 cl mornay sauce
 (for recipe see page 202)
4 ozs/125 g frozen, peeled
 prawns, defrosted
grated Parmesan cheese
watercress and twists of
 lemon, to garnish

Cut the turbot into one-inch thick slices. Put them flat in the bottom of a shallow saucepan. Cover with hot fish stock and add the wine, lemon juice and the parsley. Season to taste. Cover the saucepan and bring to the boil. Lower the heat and simmer for five or six minutes.

When the fish is cooked, remove from the stock, take off the skin and bones, being careful not to break the fillets. Pour a little of the mornay sauce onto the serving dish and place the fish fillets on top. Put the prawns on top of the fillets and cover with the rest of the sauce. Sprinkle Parmesan cheese over the top, place under the grill or in a hot oven for a few minutes, to turn a golden colour.

Before serving, place a bunch of watercress in the middle of the dish and decorate with one or two lemon twists.

TURBOT WITH HORSERADISH SAUCE 👑

To serve 4:

2 lbs/1 kg of middle-cut of
 turbot
1 pint/60 cl of boiling water
1 dessertspoon of salt

8 peppercorns
1 tablespoon of plain flour
1½ ozs/40 g cold butter
½ teaspoon of grated horseradish

Turbot is a good rich fish and served according to this recipe as a main course, would need only a clear soup beforehand and perhaps a savoury afterwards to make a fine dinner party menu.

Cut the turbot into cutlets about two inches thick without removing the bone. Place the cutlets in boiling water, and add seasoning. Cover with greaseproof paper and steam for ten to fifteen minutes. Strain the fish stock and thicken with the flour to form a thick sauce. Add more seasoning to taste and then simmer for five minutes. Remove from heat and whisk in the cold butter little by little. Keep hot. Carefully remove skin and bones from the fish and place the cutlets on a dish. Cover the fish with some of the sauce. Serve the rest separately with the grated horseradish stirred in.

Serve with plain boiled potatoes in a white napkin.

Meat

THE MOST IMPORTANT PART OF EVERY MEAL IS THE MAIN DISH, AND IF you decide to serve meat, there is no likelihood of your being stuck for choice. All you have to do is make four main subdivisions – beef, lamb, veal and pork – which gives you about fifty different cuts from which to choose. After that you must consider whether you want to roast, grill, fry, braise, stew, poach or boil the meat. Then, of course, there are a million other little tricks from marinading to mincing that will provide a distinctive touch or two, plus a wide variety of suitable sauces and garnishes.

The recipes in this chapter pay tribute to the excellent quality of British meat, and the treatment accorded it is designed to enhance rather than disguise its fine flavour. With this in mind, I have included some traditional recipes like boiled leg of mutton with caper sauce and glazed saddle of veal, popular dishes which combine the best in British meat and cooking. The other recipes will, I hope, provide ideas for those days when inspiration and the sight of so much raw meat in your butcher's shop do not seem to march hand in hand.

Despite the fact that the quality of meat in this country is usually excellent, be ever vigilant. Treat your butcher as an ally and bear the following in mind. Lamb and mutton must be light red, with the fat creamy-white; beef should not be too dark; pork should be pale pink with the fat shining white; veal should be very pale. Never accept veal that is blue and blistered or, even worse, a mottled red colour.

♔ BOILED BRISKET OF BEEF

To serve 6–8:

3 lbs/1.5 kg rolled and boned brisket of beef	3 onions
4 pints/2 litres water	1 stick of celery
1 tablespoon of salt	1 leek
10 white peppercorns	1 tablespoon of chopped fresh parsley
2 carrots	

Place the beef in a saucepan with enough water to cover. Bring to the boil and remove any scum. Add the salt and peppercorns, then cover and cook over a low heat for two and a half hours. Add the cut vegetables and a sprig of parsley, bring to the boil and simmer for another hour.

When the meat is cooked, cut some slices and place on a serving dish. Arrange the vegetables round the beef and moisten with a little stock. Sprinkle with chopped parsley on top. Serve with creamed potatoes and horseradish sauce.

The remaining stock is excellent for soup.

♔ SALT SILVERSIDE WITH SUET DUMPLINGS

To serve 6–8:

3 lbs/1.5 kg salt silverside	2 carrots
4 pints/2 litres water	3 onions
10 peppercorns	1 tablespoon of chopped fresh parsley
1 leek	
1 swede	

For the suet dumplings:

1 lb/500 g plain flour	4 ozs/125 g beef suet
1 teaspoon of baking powder	$\frac{1}{4}$–$\frac{1}{2}$ pint/8–15 cl water
$\frac{1}{4}$ teaspoon of salt	

Place the silverside in a saucepan of cold water and bring to the boil. Remove scum and simmer for two hours. Peel and chop the vegetables, add to the pan and bring to the boil. Cook on a low heat for one hour.

Meanwhile, to make the dumplings mix the ingredients together in a bowl. Make into small balls and drop these into boiling stock in a separate saucepan and cover. Boil gently for ten to twelve minutes and serve immediately with the silverside, which should be sliced and arranged on a serving dish. Place the vegetables around the meat, moisten with stock and sprinkle some chopped parsley on top.

CHATEAUBRIAND À LA ROSENBAD 👑

To serve 4:

3 ozs/90 g butter	*4 slices thickly cut fillet steak*
½ tablespoon of oil	*(Chateaubriand) in all*
	about 12 ozs/350 g in weight
	and 1½ inches/4 cm thick

For the sauce:

1 tablespoon of brandy	*1 oz/30 g butter*
3 fl ozs/8 cl sherry	*dash of Worcestershire sauce*
¼ pint/15 cl beef gravy	*4 truffles, sliced, and the juice*
2 tablespoons of liver paté	*from the tin*

I served this dish to the late King Frederik of Denmark when he paid a State visit in 1951. He was such a charming man that everyone was anxious to see he enjoyed his visit in every possible way. I can remember Prince Philip coming into the kitchen before his visit and discussing the food. I always enjoyed Prince Philip's informal visits. He would look into the saucepans, ask questions and crack some very good jokes. In times of stress and kitchen crises, he was a real morale booster. I appreciated the informality of these visits because normally a royal visit to the kitchen was preceded by a warning from above which made us feel we were in for a sort of kit inspection. Prince Philip, however, would appear without warning and take us as we were.

First, put the butter and the oil in a frying pan. When hot and golden-brown add the steaks and fry on both sides, basting a little. Cook for four to five minutes (underdone) or seven to eight minutes (medium), basting when necessary. Remove from the pan, reserving the juices for the sauce, and keep hot.

To make the sauce, pour the brandy into a clean pan. Heat and set alight, then pour in the sherry to extinguish the flame. Add beef gravy and the gravy from the steaks and boil for a few minutes. Add the liver paté, the butter, Worcestershire sauce and the juice from the truffles. Season to taste. Stir well, bring to the boil and strain the sauce over the Chateaubriand.

Garnish each steak with a slice of truffle. Serve with crisp fried potatoes and salad.

👑 ENTRECÔTE GRILL

To serve 2:

2 sirloin, porterhouse or T-bone steaks	salt and pepper
1 tablespoon of oil	$\frac{1}{2}$ lb/250 g mushrooms
1 clove of garlic, put through a garlic press	$\frac{1}{4}$ pint/15 cl red wine
	$\frac{1}{4}$ pint/15 cl beef stock
	1 tablespoon of chopped fresh parsley

Trim unwanted fat from the steaks, brush with the oil and place on a grill pan. Grill for ten or fifteen minutes and place on a serving dish. Season to taste with salt and pepper and keep hot. Add butter and garlic to the pan and toss the mushrooms. Arrange with the steaks. Add the wine and stock to the pan and stir well. Reduce the sauce until thick and then strain over the steaks. Sprinkle with chopped parsley and serve with vegetable salad (for recipe see page 145).

FILET DE BOEUF WITH SAUCE PIQUANT 👑

Pre-heat oven to 220 °C/425 °F or gas mark 7
To serve 6–8:

*3 lb/1.5 kg undercut fillet of
   beef
salt and pepper*

*garlic salt
$\frac{1}{4}$ lb/125 g bacon fat*

For the sauce:
*$\frac{1}{2}$ pint/30 cl beef stock
1 tablespoon of tomato sauce
$\frac{1}{4}$ pint/15 cl of sherry*

*$\frac{1}{2}$ tablespoon of Worcestershire
   sauce
2 anchovy fillets*

Rub the fillet with salt and pepper and sprinkle over a little garlic salt. Tie the bacon fat round the beef and cook in the oven at 220 °C/425 °F or gas mark 7. When brown on the outside, lower the heat, to 190 °C/375 °F or gas mark 5, baste and roast for a further forty-five minutes. Baste every fifteen minutes with the meat juices. When cooked, untie the bacon, remove the meat from the pan, cut in thin slices and place in the middle of the serving dish. To make the piquant sauce, add all the ingredients to the pan juices. Boil for one or two minutes until thickened. Then strain and serve with the beef.

SWEDISH HAMBURGER STEAKS 👑

To serve 6:

*1 lb/500 g rump steak, minced
2 ozs/60 g butter
$\frac{1}{2}$ pint/30 cl beef stock*

*1 teaspoon of Worcestershire
   sauce
1 tablespoon of tomato purée
6 poached eggs, to garnish*

Cut the meat into pieces and remove unwanted skin and fat. Put through the mincer twice. Roll meat into a firm loaf and divide into six portions. Flatten them to one inch thick and criss-cross with a knife on top. Heat the butter in a frying pan and when the butter has turned light brown, put in the steaks and fry for three or four minutes on each side, basting all the time. Regulate the heat to prevent burning. Place the hamburgers on a serving dish and keep hot. Add the stock to the pan together with the Worcestershire sauce, a knob of butter, tomato purée and seasoning. Boil and reduce until thickened. Pour over the hamburgers. Place a poached egg on top of each and serve.

♛ FILET MIGNON ARENBURG

To serve 6:

> 2 lbs/1 kg fillet beef (the undercut)
> 6 slices of bread and butter
> 2 ozs/60 g butter
> 1 tablespoon of sunflower oil
> 1 teaspoon of garlic salt
> salt and pepper to taste
>
> ½ pint/30 cl clear consommé (for recipe see page 2)
> 1 glass of Madeira wine or sherry
> ½ pint/30 cl béarnaise sauce (for recipe see page 204)
> watercress, to garnish

Cut six small round steaks about one inch thick. Fry six rounds of bread and butter. Fry the steaks in butter and oil for two minutes on both sides, basting all the time. Dish up on the bread croûtons. Sprinkle with salt, pepper and garlic salt. Whisk out the pan with the consommé, a knob of butter and the Madeira wine or sherry. Place over a high heat and reduce to a glaze. Pour over the steaks.

Just before serving, cover each steak with a tablespoon of bearnaise sauce and garnish with watercress.

♛ ENTRECÔTE STEAK WITH WINE SAUCE

To serve 6:

> 2 ozs/60 g fat bacon
> salt and pepper to taste
> 1 clove garlic
> 2 lbs/1 kg fillet of entrecôte steak
> ¼ pint/15 cl Madeira wine
>
> 1 tablespoon of sunflower oil
> 2 ozs/60 g butter
> 1 pint/60 cl heated beef stock
> 1 tablespoon of plain flour
> ¼ lb/125 g braised button mushrooms, to garnish

First, bully your butcher to see that the meat is well hung. Cut the bacon into long strips the same length as the steak and about half an inch wide. Season the strips with salt and pepper and rub with the garlic clove. Leave in a cold place to harden for half an hour. Trim the steak of fat, gristle and skin, and rub with a couple of tablespoons of the Madeira wine and a tablespoon of oil mixed together. Leave to soak for one or two hours, turning the steak once.

Insert the bacon strips with a larding needle, or with a sharp skewer, along the grain of the steak. Rub with salt and pepper and tie up with string making the fillet into a nice neat shape. Put an ounce of butter (25 g) and half a tablespoon of oil into an iron saucepan. The pan should be just big enough for the steak. When the butter and oil have turned golden-brown over the heat, put in the meat and braise it all round, using two wooden spoons to turn.

When the steak is brown all over, add half the amount of hot stock and half the wine. Cover the saucepan and braise for two or three hours, turning the fillet every half hour. Add some more stock after one hour and the rest of the wine half an hour before the end of the cooking time. When cooked, remove the fillet to a hot dish. Cut the fillet into thin slices and glaze with some of the gravy.

Put a tablespoon of flour into the rest of the sauce and stir well until absorbed. Skim the fat. Add the rest of the beef stock and stir until smooth. Simmer for ten to fifteen minutes. Strain and season to taste. Garnish the entrecôte with braised button mushrooms.

COLLOPS OF BEEF 👑

To serve 6:

2 tablespoons of plain flour	2 lbs/1 kg braising steak, cut
$\frac{1}{4}$ teaspoon of pepper	in slices
$\frac{1}{2}$ tablespoon of salt	6 peppercorns
2 ozs/60 g butter	1 bay leaf
$\frac{1}{2}$ tablespoon of corn oil	1 teaspoon of gravy browning
2 or 3 onions, chopped	

Mix the flour with the pepper and salt. Pound the steaks on both sides and dip them in the seasoned flour. Heat the saucepan (preferably an iron one) and put in the butter and oil. Add the chopped onion and braise a little. Add the meat and turn in the saucepan with a spoon. Put in the peppercorns and the bay leaf. Mix the gravy browning with a little hot water and add. Turn the meat once, add water and bring to the boil on a high heat, then cover the saucepan and simmer for two or three hours.

When cooked, serve in a casserole or deep dish. Skim fat from gravy and add more hot water if it is too thick. Heat and pour the sauce over the meat.

Serve with plain boiled potatoes.

👑 MARINADED BEEF ROULADES

Pre-heat oven to 170 °C/325 °F or gas mark 3
To serve 6:

> 2 lbs/1 kg rump beef or topside

For the marinade:
$\frac{1}{2}$ tablespoon of oil
1 tablespoon of red wine or
   wine vinegar

$\frac{1}{2}$ teaspoon of salt
pinch of white pepper and
   pinch of garlic salt

For the stuffing:
$\frac{1}{2}$ lb/250 g minced smoked
   gammon
1 small onion, finely chopped
1 tablespoon of chopped fresh
   parsley

1 tablespoon of tomato purée
1 oz/30 g chopped anchovy
   fillets
1 oz/30 g butter

For the sauce:
2 ozs/60 g butter
1 tablespoon of plain flour

$\frac{3}{4}$ pint/40 cl of beef stock or
   water
$\frac{1}{4}$ pint/15 cl of red wine

Cut the meat into two-inch slices, then flatten by pounding. Spread flat on a dish. Mix the ingredients for the marinade and pour over the meat. Let it stand for one hour, turning the meat once.

Mix the minced smoked gammon, onion, parsley, tomato purée, anchovies and butter well together. Remove the beef slices from the marinade, and spread the stuffing on the middle of each slice. Roll them up and fasten with a wooden skewer or tie with fine string.

To make the sauce, heat 2 ozs/60 g butter in a frying pan and brown the roulades all round. When brown put in a saucepan or casserole dish. Add the flour to the butter in the frying pan, stir until browned, then add the hot stock or water and stir until smooth. Simmer for five minutes. Strain the sauce into another pan, add the wine and bring to the boil. Pour over the roulades, cover with a lid and cook in the oven at 170°C/325°F or gas mark 3 or on top of the stove on a gentle heat for about two hours.

Serve in the casserole accompanied by plain boiled rice or creamed potatoes. Or for a special occasion, serve in a flat dish with a border of rice or pipe the creamed potatoes round the roulades. Garnish the border with quartered tomatoes, skinned and seeded, and place a sprig of parsley on each side.

BEEF STEAK AND KIDNEY PUDDING 👑

To serve 4:

> suet pastry (for recipe see
>   page 216)
> 1 lb/500 g stewing steak
> 6 ozs/175 g ox kidney
> 2 ozs/60 g chopped onions or a
>   small clove of garlic,
>   chopped

> salt and pepper
> 1 tablespoon of plain flour
> ½ pint/30 cl water
> 1 glass of sherry

Grease a pudding basin and line with the suet pastry. Make enough to cover and overlap the rim of the basin. Cut the stewing steak and kidney into small pieces, and remove unwanted fat and skin. Put in a bowl, add the onion or garlic, pepper and salt, and the flour. Mix together and spoon into the suet-lined basin. Add the water and sherry. Cover with the pastry overlapping the rim of the basin. Cover with greaseproof paper and tie a napkin over the top. Put the basin in a steamer containing boiling water which reaches three-quarters of the way up the basin. Boil for six or seven hours, topping up the boiling water when necessary.

To serve, undo the wrappings and fold a clean white napkin round the basin.

VAMPIRE STEAK

To serve 4:

1 lb/500 g rump or sirloin steak	1 onion, finely chopped
4 egg yolks	1 beetroot, chopped
2 tablespoons of capers	

Scrape the steak very finely with a grater (mincing is not quite good enough) and roll into one long loaf. Cut into four portions and flatten so that each steak is half an inch thick. Make a dent in the centre of each steak, into which you put an unbroken egg yolk. Chop the capers and sprinkle them round the yolks, then add the chopped onion and beetroot.

Serve with horseradish sauce and mayonnaise.

SAILOR BEEF

Pre-heat oven to 170°C/325°F or gas mark 3
To serve 4–6:

2 lbs/1 kg rump steak	butter
1 oz/30 g plain flour mixed	$\frac{3}{4}$ pint/45 cl stock
with 1 teaspoon of salt	$\frac{1}{2}$ teaspoon gravy browning
2 lbs/1 kg potatoes	$\frac{1}{4}$ pint/15 cl claret
2 large onions	salt
$\frac{1}{2}$ lb/250 g mushrooms	

When Prince Philip returned from his spell of duty in Malta as a naval officer there was, of course, great rejoicing at Clarence House. All sailors seem to enjoy their food with extra zest, and the standard of cooking is higher in the navy than in the other services. Sailors know good food when they see it, and Prince Philip was no exception. I can remember how much I enjoyed cooking for him on his return and how, with the staff, I plotted and planned in the kitchen for our welcome-home dishes. This was one of them.

Cut the meat into individual steaks half an inch thick, then pound them well. Turn the steaks in seasoned flour. Peel and cut the potatoes and onions in thick slices. Peel and slice the mushrooms and fry in butter. Mix the stock with the gravy browning and claret. Grease a casserole dish with 1 oz/30 g of butter. Place the potatoes on the bottom of the dish, cover with a layer of onions and place the beef steaks and mushrooms on top. Finish with another layer of potatoes and sprinkle with salt and pepper. Dot with knobs of butter and pour over the mixed wine and stock. Cover with a lid and braise on top of the cooker or in the oven at 170°C/325°F or gas mark 3 for two and a half hours.

FILLET OF BEEF WITH MUSHROOMS AND 👑 YORKSHIRE PUDDING

Pre-heat oven to 220°C/425°F or gas mark 7
To serve 8:

3 lbs/1.5 kg fillet of beef from the undercut	1 lb/500 g mushrooms
1 clove of garlic	½ pint/30 cl beef stock (heated)
2 tablespoons of sunflower oil	1 tablespoon of tomato purée
butter	dash of Worcestershire sauce

Batter for Yorkshire puddings:

4 ozs/125 g plain flour	10 fl ozs/30 cl creamy milk
pinch of salt	lard
1 egg	

There is no better meat in the world, in my opinion, than the undercut of British beef, sitting pinkly on a dish and bathed in its own glorious juices. It is a privilege to cook such marvellous meat and, remember, no-one knows quite how to cook it like the

British. This was the first dish I set about learning when I came to this country and often, when living abroad since, I have been called upon by desperate British ex-patriates to show their cooks the right way of cooking beef. Roast beef is only really properly understood in Britain.

This is how I served it on one occasion to Lord Cromer, then Governor of the Bank of England. A dish, I thought, as solid and traditional as the Bank itself with, perhaps, that little extra touch of distinction such as possessed only by British bankers.

Trim the fillet and remove all skin, gristle and fat. Crush the garlic and add to the oil. Sprinkle pepper on the beef and smear all over with the garlic oil. Allow to stand for one hour.

Remove the pieces of garlic and tie the fillet with fine string to keep a neat shape. Place it in a roasting tin with the oil and 1 oz/30 g butter, and put in the oven preheated to 220°C/425°F or gas mark 7. Baste after fifteen minutes and reduce the heat a little. Roast for thirty-five minutes, basting occasionally.

Meanwhile, make individual Yorkshire puddings. Sift the flour with the salt. Beat the eggs with the water and make a well in the centre of the flour. Pour in the eggs, mixing in the flour little by little. Add the milk and beat for four or five minutes. Allow to rest for half an hour. Add half a teaspoon of lard to individual moulds and warm the tins. Beat the batter once more and then fill each tin half full with the mixture. Bake for fifteen minutes at the top of the oven or until crispy.

Ten minutes before the meat and Yorkshire puddings have finished cooking, braise the mushrooms in butter and keep hot until you are ready to serve.

When the meat is cooked, remove from the oven and keep warm while making the gravy. Skim off the oil from the roasting tin, add the heated stock and stir. Boil over a high heat, add the tomato purée, Worcestershire sauce and 1 oz/30 g of butter, and season to taste. Reduce to a glazed sauce. Remove the string from the beef, slice thinly and put together again, then glaze with a little of the sauce.

Surround the meat with the braised mushrooms and Yorkshire pudding. Pour over a little of the glazed sauce. Serve with crisp roast potatoes and broccoli, or petis pois and a fresh salad.

PINK BEEF 👑

Pre-heat oven to 220°C/425°F or gas mark 7
To serve 12–16:

*4 lbs/2 kg sirloin or undercut
    of beef
1 tablespoon of sunflower oil
½ teaspoon of garlic salt
½ oz/15 g gelatine
½ pint/30 cl of beef stock*

*20 pickling onions
1 tablespoon of tomato juice
dash of Worcestershire sauce
grated horseradish and
    shredded lettuce, to garnish*

Smear the beef with oil and sprinkle over some garlic salt. Roast at 220°C/425°F or gas mark 7 for fifteen minutes to seal the juices; baste, lower heat to 190°C/375°F or gas mark 5 and cook for one hour. Dish up the beef, add the gelatine to the warm stock and pour into the pan used for cooking the beef. Boil the liquid so that it is reduced to a glaze and coat the beef with the gravy.

Cover the onions with water and cook with the lid off until the water evaporates. Add the tomato juice and Worcestershire sauce and simmer slowly.

When the beef has cooled on the dish, cut into thin slices. Arrange the glazed onions round the beef. Make horseradish ribbons by using the large holes on the grater and decorate the dish with shredded lettuce and horseradish strips.

Mutton is the meat from a sheep that is over a year old, and in this country is now a rarity. It has more flavour than lamb and is firmer in texture. If you are unable to buy mutton you may substitute lamb for the following three dishes and reduce the cooking time slightly.

♛ BOILED LEG OF MUTTON (OR LAMB) WITH CAPER SAUCE

To serve 6–8:

4 lbs/2 kg leg of mutton (or lamb, but see note above)	sprig of parsley
	10 peppercorns
2 carrots	salt and pepper
1 onion	

For the caper sauce:

2 ozs/60 g plain flour	2 tablespoons of roughly-chopped capers
$\frac{1}{2}$ pint/30 cl mutton (or lamb) stock	
juice of a lemon	salt, pepper and sugar to taste
$\frac{1}{4}$ pint/15 cl creamy milk	2 egg yolks
	a little milk or water
	1 tablespoon of butter

Rinse the meat in scalding water, place it in a pan and cover with boiling water. Add the whole vegetables, parsley, peppercorns, salt and pepper. Bring to the boil and simmer slowly for one and a half hours. When cooked remove from the stock and place on a dish to keep hot.

To make the sauce, blend the flour and a little stock together in a saucepan, to make a smooth paste. Add the rest of the half pint of stock slowly, to avoid lumps, and whisk till smooth. Add the lemon juice. Place over a low heat and bring to the boil, whisking all the time until thick. Add the milk gradually and boil over a low heat for five minutes. Add the capers and the seasoning. Beat the egg yolks with a little milk or water and add to the sauce. Remove from heat and stir in the butter.

Serve with Brussels sprouts and creamed potatoes.

NAVARIN OF MUTTON (OR LAMB) ♔

To serve 6:

2 lbs/1 kg leg of mutton (or lamb, but see note on page 64)
1 lb/500 g mushrooms
2 carrots
¼ pint/15 cl stock
3 fl ozs/8 cl red wine
1 teaspoon of sugar

2 lambs kidneys
1 tablespoon of plain flour
3 ozs/90 g butter
salt and pepper to taste
12 small onions
1 tablespoon of chopped fresh parsley

Remove unnecessary fat from meat and cut the meat into two-inch squares. Cut the mushrooms in half, dice the carrots and cut the kidneys into slices. Sprinkle the meat with flour and braise in butter until light brown. Season to taste and place in a pan with the carrots. Braise the onions and mushrooms quickly in butter and add to the pan.

Pour the stock into the frying pan, heat and stir. Strain over the meat, add the wine and sugar and bring to the boil. Cover and cook on a low heat for one and a half hours. Stir once or twice during cooking.

Serve with sprinkled parsley on top.

RAGOÛT OF MUTTON (OR LAMB) ♔

Pre-heat oven to 180°C/350°F or gas mark 4
To serve 6:

1 shoulder of mutton (or lamb, but see note on page 64) about 3 lbs/1.5 kg
2 onions
2 carrots
2 pints/1.25 litres of water
salt and pepper

small bunch of parsley
10 peppercorns
1 oz/30 g plain flour
2 eggs
4 ozs/125 g breadcrumbs
2 ozs/60 g melted butter

Ask your butcher to chop the shoulder in ½ lb/250 g portions and remove the top skin. Trim off any unnecessary fat and put in a pan with the vegetables and water to cover. Bring to the boil and remove any scum. Add salt, pepper, parsley and peppercorns and boil for one hour. Remove the meat, allow to cool a little and dip portions into flour, beaten egg and then breadcrumbs. Place in a roasting tin, moisten with 2 ozs/60 g melted butter and cook in the oven at 180°C/350°F or gas mark 4 for one hour. Turn the meat once during cooking and baste with the fat.

When cooked the meat should be tender, crisp and brown on top. Serve with creamed potatoes, Brussels sprouts and puréed onion sauce.

The remaining stock will be an excellent basis for soups or sauces.

♔ ROAST BREAST OF LAMB

To serve 4:

1 breast of lamb	1 small swede, halved
salt to taste	10 white peppercorns
2 onions, halved	

Place the breast of lamb in a saucepan and cover with hot water. Add salt, the halved onions, the halved swede and peppercorns. Bring to the boil and simmer for twenty minutes. Remove from water, place in a roasting tin and grill for twenty-five minutes, basting every ten minutes. Or put on a spit and cook for half an hour.

Serve with boiled new potatoes and mint jelly.

LAMB CUTLETS 👑

To serve 6:

12 *fillets of lamb*	4 *ozs/125 g breadcrumbs*
2 *tablespoons of chopped*	1 *tablespoon of oil*
fresh parsley	6 *slices of pickled cucumber*
2 *ozs/60 g butter*	*redcurrant jelly*
salt and pepper	1 *tablespoon of mushroom*
1 *oz/30 g plain flour*	*ketchup*
2 *eggs*	$\frac{1}{2}$ *pint/30 cl stock*

Beat and flatten the fillets. Mix the chopped parsley and 1 oz/ 30 g of butter together and place a dollop on top of six of the steaks. Sprinkle with salt and pepper, then place the other six steaks on top like a sandwich.

Turn them carefully in flour, beaten egg and then breadcrumbs and fry in remaining butter and oil over a gentle heat for ten or fifteen minutes until golden-brown. Place on a serving dish.

Put the mushroom ketchup in the frying pan, add the stock and boil to reduce a little. Strain over the cutlets. Place a slice of cucumber on top of each and serve with redcurrant jelly.

MINCED LAMB CUTLETS 👑

To serve 4:

$\frac{1}{2}$ *lb/250 g mushrooms*	1 *tablespoon of oil*
1 *tablespoon of finely-*	$\frac{1}{4}$ *pint/15 cl stock*
chopped onion	1 *oz/30 g butter*
1$\frac{1}{2}$ *lbs/750 g lamb, minced*	*dash of Worcestershire sauce*
salt and pepper to taste	

Mince the mushrooms and lightly fry the chopped onion in the oil. Mix together with the minced lamb and salt and pepper. Form into small cutlets about half an inch thick and fry in the oil on a gentle heat for six minutes on each side.

Swirl out the pan with the stock, add butter and a dash of Worcestershire sauce. Bring to the boil and strain over the cutlets.

♛ SADDLE OF LAMB AU GRATIN

Pre-heat oven to 220 °C/425 °F or gas mark 7
To serve 8:

4 lbs/2 kg saddle of spring lamb	1 teaspoon of salt
	$\frac{1}{4}$ teaspoon of white pepper

For the sauce:

$\frac{1}{2}$ lb/250 g mushrooms	1 tablespoon of Madeira wine
1 onion	1 tablespoon of double cream
$1\frac{1}{2}$ ozs/40 g butter	2 ozs/60 g grated Gruyère cheese
1 tablespoon of plain flour	
salt and pepper to taste	2 ozs/60 g toasted white breadcrumbs
$\frac{1}{4}$ pint/15 cl good beef or mutton stock	1 tablespoon of oil

Wring out a cloth in hot water and wipe the saddle. Remove top skin and unwanted fat and trim. Season with salt and pepper. Tie the saddle at both ends with string to keep in shape. Roast in the oven at 220 °C/425 °F or gas mark 7 for $1\frac{1}{4}$ hours, basting frequently.

While the saddle is cooking make the gratin mixture. Peel the mushrooms and chop into small pieces, peel the onion and chop finely. Put the butter in a pan to brown and braise the mushrooms and onion lightly. Sprinkle over flour and cook for two minutes, stirring all the time. Season to taste and add the hot stock. Stir well and cook for five or six minutes. Reduce heat and add the Madeira wine, cream and half the cheese. Stir well, remove from heat and keep hot.

When the saddle is cooked, remove the string and slice the two fillets from the top. Remove the two small under fillets and cut them into one-inch thick slices diagonally. Spread the cheese and mushroom sauce on top of the meat. Sprinkle the remaining cheese over the top and cover with breadcrumbs mixed with butter. Moisten with the oil and place in the oven to brown for ten or fifteen minutes.

Dish up and garnish with spring peas and small potatoes braised in butter. Serve with plain salad and redcurrant jelly.

GIGOT D'AGNEAU AU FOUR 👑

Pre-heat oven to 220°C/425°F or gas mark 7
To serve 4:

*4 lamb steaks cut from the
    middle of the leg
    (about ½ lb/250 g each)*
salt and pepper
2 tablespoons of plain flour
3 ozs/90 g butter
2 carrots

*½ lb/250 g potatoes, peeled and
    sliced*
10 small onions
½ pint/30 cl stock
1 tablespoon of tomato purée
*1 tablespoon of chopped fresh
    parsley*

Pound the steaks a little, sprinkle with pepper and salt and toss in flour. Melt 1 oz/30 g of the butter in a roasting tin. Put in the carrots (cut lengthways), the potatoes and the onions and brown over a low heat. Bring the hot stock mixed with the tomato purée to the boil and pour over the vegetables. Place in the oven pre-heated to 220°C/425°F or gas mark 7 and cook for half an hour.

Braise the meat in the remaining butter on both sides until brown and add to the vegetables in the roasting tin. Add the potatoes and bake in the oven for three-quarters of an hour, or until the meat is tender. Dish up and serve the meat on a bed of vegetables. Garnish with parsley.

HARICOT LAMB 👑

To serve 4:

*2 lbs/250 g best end of spring
    lamb*
1 oz/30 g butter
1 tablespoon of plain flour
salt and pepper, to taste
½ lb/250 g mushrooms
½ clove of crushed garlic

½ pint/30 cl good stock
½ glass of sherry
*1 tablespoon of redcurrant
    jelly*
½ pint/15 cl double cream
gravy browning (optional)

Ask the butcher to chine the backbone, remove the top skin and cut the best end of lamb into double cutlets. Trim the cutlets and brown in butter, sprinkle over with flour and braise. Season and add the mushrooms, peeled and cut into slices, the garlic, hot stock, sherry and the redcurrant jelly. Mix gently, cover the pan and cook for one hour and fifteen minutes. Stir once or twice very gently to prevent any sticking at the bottom of the pan.

When ready, remove the cutlets and place in a deep dish. Add the cream to the sauce and a little gravy browning if necessary. The sauce should be a creamy, golden colour. Pour the sauce over the cutlets and serve with haricot beans.

♔ GRILLED LAMB CUTLETS WITH PARSLEY BUTTER AND PURÉE OF GREEN PEAS

To serve 6:

6 double lamb cutlets, one per person	juice of $\frac{1}{2}$ lemon
salt and pepper	dash of Worcestershire sauce
$\frac{1}{4}$ lb/125 g butter	$1\frac{1}{2}$ lbs/750 g peas
1 tablespoon of chopped fresh parsley	1 tablespoon of double cream
	$\frac{1}{2}$ lb/250 g rice
	1 green pepper

Grill lamb cutlets for four to five minutes on each side and season with salt and pepper when cooked. Keep at low temperature. Soften but don't melt the butter in a separate pan, mix in chopped parsley, lemon juice and Worcestershire sauce. Refrigerate this mixture for half an hour and, just before serving, slice and place on each lamb cutlet.

Cook the peas, and sieve. Add a knob of butter, a tablespoon of cream, some salt and mix together. Keep hot.

Boil the rice for twenty minutes. Chop the pepper finely and mix in with the rice.

MINCED LAMB CUTLETS WITH REDCURRANT SAUCE 👑

To serve 4:

$\frac{1}{4}$ *lb/125 g rice*
8 fl oz/225 cl stock
1 large onion, chopped
1 lb/500 g meat from
  under-done roast lamb

1 egg
salt, pepper and sugar, to taste
plain flour
butter or bacon fat for frying

For the sauce:
1 tablespoon of plain flour
$\frac{1}{2}$ *pint/30 cl good stock*
$\frac{1}{4}$ *lb/125 g redcurrants, washed*
  and topped and tailed

$\frac{1}{4}$ *pint/15 cl red wine*
salt and pepper
1 tablespoon of brown sugar
$\frac{1}{2}$ *tablespoon of butter*

Boil the rice in the stock with the chopped onion for twenty minutes. Strain and cool. Mince the meat and add the rice, the egg, salt, pepper and a little sugar. Mix well. Make into rissoles, dip in flour and fry to a golden brown in the butter or bacon fat over a slow heat. Dish up and keep hot.

To make the sauce, mix flour and stock in a saucepan and bring to the boil over a low heat, stirring until smooth. Add the currants, wine, salt, pepper and brown sugar. Simmer for fifteen minutes, then stir in the butter.

Serve with the minced lamb cutlets and vegetables in season.

LAMB NOISETTES 👑

To serve 4:

8 lamb noisettes
salt and pepper
4 ozs/125 g butter
Worcestershire sauce
$\frac{1}{2}$ *pint/30 cl stock*
1 tablespoon of tomato purée

1 teaspoon of Bovril
1 glass of Madeira wine
$1\frac{1}{2}$ *lbs/750 g mushrooms*
1 lb/500 g petits pois
watercress, to garnish

Ask your butcher to prepare the noisettes by cutting out the fillets from a loin of lamb, and cutting the fillets into 1½ inch slices. The noisettes should have a ribbon of fat fastened round them with a wooden stick.

Season the noisettes with salt and pepper. Place 2 ozs/60 g of the butter on top and grill for five or six minutes on both sides, basting once or twice, so that they are browned on the outside and a light pink inside.

While the noisettes are grilling, braise the mushrooms in the remaining butter and cook the petit pois. When the noisettes are ready, sprinkle a little Worcestershire sauce over them and place in a dish to keep hot. Pour the heated stock in the grilling pan and add the tomato purée, Bovril, the Madeira and a knob of butter. Transfer the sauce into a pan and boil until thick and glacé. Strain the sauce over the noisettes and then dish up the petits pois on a large serving dish. Arrange the mushrooms and petits pois on one side with the watercress in between.

Serve with mint jelly.

♕ IRISH STEW

To serve 6–8:

2 lbs/1 kg best end of neck of lamb	*4 onions, sliced*
seasoning to taste	*1 lb/500 g potatoes*
	chopped fresh parsley, to garnish

Have the neck chopped in double cutlets and see that the top skin has been removed. Trim away any fat. Put the cutlets in a saucepan of water, bring to the boil for five minutes. Drain off the water, clean out the saucepan and add fresh water to cover. Add salt and pepper to taste, bring to the boil and simmer for half an hour. Add the sliced onions and potatoes and simmer for a further hour until the potatoes are tender and broken. The water should just cover the meat when it is pressed down. Allow to stand and cool, and skim off all fat. Bring to the boil before serving, dish up the cutlets and sieve the potatoes and onions to a thick sauce. Pour over the cutlets and serve some of the juice separately. Garnish with chopped parsley.

GLAZED SADDLE OF VEAL 👑

Pre-heat oven to 220°C/425°F or gas mark 7
To serve 10–12:

1 saddle of veal (about 5 lbs/
   2.5 kg
salt and pepper
oil
1 stick of celery
1 carrot

2 onions
1 oz/30 g butter
pinch of dry thyme leaves
1 tablespoon of fresh chopped
   parsley

For the garnish:
24 small onions
1½ oz/45 g butter
1 teaspoon of sugar

2 carrots, peeled and cut into
   matchsticks
1 lb/500g small French peas
sprig of mint leaves

For the sauce:
kidneys from the veal
1 oz/30 g butter
1 oz/30 g plain flour
½ pint/30 cl stock

pepper, salt and sugar, to taste
½ pint/30 cl double cream
1 glass of port

A saddle of veal is two loins joined together. Get your butcher to chine it, then remove small pieces of bone and any tough skin. Remove the kidneys too, but reserve these for the sauce.

Rub pepper and salt into the veal and brush the outside with a little oil. Roll up the saddle and tie into shape with string. Cut the cooking vegetables into coarse strips and put into a roasting tin with some butter and the herbs. Cover the saddle with grease-proof paper and place in the oven, pre-heated to 220°C/425°F or gas mark 7, and roast for half an hour. Baste and reduce heat to 190°C/375°F or gas mark 5. Continue cooking at the rate of fifteen minutes to the pound, basting frequently.

While the meat is cooking, prepare the garnishing vegetables. Boil the onions in a little salted water with 1 oz/30 g of the butter and half of the sugar. Simmer until the water evaporates and the onions are tender and glazed. Cook the carrots, cut into match-sticks, in the same way with ½ oz/15 g of the butter but without the seasoning. Cook the peas with mint and half a teaspoon of sugar, and glaze with melted butter.

When the meat is ready, place on a hot dish and glaze with the gravy juices.

To make the sauce, cut up the kidneys in thin slices and fry in butter. Add the flour and stir until brown. Pour in the heated stock and boil for ten minutes. Season with pepper, salt and a pinch of sugar. Remove from heat and stir in the cream and port. Place the garnishing vegetables around the veal and serve the sauce separately.

♛ STUFFED LOIN OF VEAL

Pre-heat oven to 220°C/425°F or gas mark 7
To serve 6–8:

1 loin of veal (about 4 lbs/2 kg)
½ lb/250 g minced pork or pork sausage meat
4 ozs/180 g breadcrumbs
1 egg
2 ozs/60 g finely-chopped fresh parsley
1 onion, chopped and fried
½ pint/30 cl single cream
¼ teaspoon of ground white pepper
salt and sugar to taste
bed of roasting vegetables
½ pint/30 cl stock

Ask your butcher to chine the meat and remove small pieces of bone and tough skin. Then make a forcemeat by mixing together the minced pork or sausage meat, breadcrumbs, egg, parsley, chopped onion, cream and seasoning. Lay the loin out flat and spread the stuffing inside. Roll up, starting from the end where the loin bones are thinnest. Tie both ends with string and brush with oil. Cover a roasting tin with a bed of coarsely-cut vegetables and place the stuffed veal on top. Roast in the oven pre-heated to 220°C/425°F or gas mark 7 for fifteen minutes. Reduce heat to 190°C/375°F or gas mark 5 and add a little of the stock. Continue cooking for a further fifteen minutes to the pound adding the remainng stock a little at a time and basting frequently.

When ready, remove string and dish up. Remove the vegetables and strain off the gravy from the pan. Serve the gravy separately with fried mushrooms.

GRATINÉ OF VEAL 👑

Pre-heat oven to 180°C/350°F or gas mark 4
To serve 8–10:

4–5 lbs/2–2.5 kg breast of veal	*3 ozs/90 g butter*
cut into 8 oz/250 g portions	*2 tablespoons of oil*
2 ozs/60 g plain flour	*bed of roasting vegetables*
4 eggs	*salt and pepper*
7 ozs/200 g breadcrumbs	

Dip the veal in the flour, beaten eggs and then the breadcrumbs. Melt the butter and oil in a roasting tin and cover with a bed of mixed vegetables. Place the veal on top, season, cover with foil and roast in the oven at 180°C/350°F or gas mark 4 for one hour and thirty minutes, basting frequently. Remove foil half an hour before cooking time ends to crisp the veal. Dish up the meat, remove the vegetables, strain off the gravy and serve separately.

BRAISED SHOULDER OF VEAL 👑

To serve 6:

4 lbs/2 kg shoulder of veal	*salt and pepper*
2 ozs/60 g butter	*2 sprigs of parsley, chopped*
1 tablespoon of oil	*1 sprig of thyme, chopped*
1 tablespoon of plain flour	*3 onions, sliced*
3 tablespoons of tomato purée	*½ pint/30 cl veal stock or water*
1 teaspoon of Worcestershire	
sauce	

Cut veal into 6 ozs/175 g portions. Melt the butter and oil in a saucepan. Sprinkle flour and seasoning over the meat and brown on both sides. Add the herbs, onions, tomato purée and Worcestershire sauce and mix well. Add the hot stock or water and stir until well mixed. Cover the pan and simmer for two hours. Dish up and serve the veal in its own sauce.

♛ BOILED SHOULDER OF VEAL WITH PRAWN SAUCE

To serve 6:

1 shoulder of veal	½ green pepper, sliced
salt	1 sprig of parsley, chopped
12 white peppercorns	2 onions, sliced

For the sauce:

1 small tin of asparagus tips	1 tablespoon of finely-
¾ pint/40 cl veal stock	chopped fresh parsley
2 tablespoons of plain flour	½ lb/250 g peeled prawns
salt and pepper	1 oz/30 g butter
	¼ pint/15 cl double cream

Ask the butcher to remove the skin from the shoulder and to crack, but not remove, the bones. Place in a saucepan half-filled with water. Bring to the boil and skim. Add salt, peppercorns, sliced pepper, parsley and onions. Cover and simmer until tender.

To make the sauce, strain half the amount of juice from the asparagus tin into the veal stock. Mix the other half with the flour and stir until smooth. Add to the stock and whisk. Season with salt and pepper and add the parsley. Simmer for ten minutes. Add the prawns to the sauce, remove from heat and stir in cold butter and cream.

When the meat is cooked, remove the bones and cut meat in slices. Spread over some of the sauce and garnish with the asparagus tips. Serve the remaining sauce separately.

♛ SAUTÉ OF VEAL WITH ARTICHOKE HEARTS

To serve 8:

8 fillets of veal, one-inch thick	8 artichoke hearts
salt and pepper	½ pint/30 cl green tartare sauce
1 oz/30 g plain flour	(for recipe see page 205)
3 ozs/90 g butter	

Flatten the fillets and then toss them in the seasoned flour. Melt the butter in a pan but do not allow to brown. Blanch the fillets on both sides in the butter, then cook right through. Dish up and garnish with an artichoke heart filled with green tartare sauce.

ROULADE DE VEAU 👑

To serve 4–6:

2 ozs/60 g finely-chopped
   parsley
4 ozs/125 g butter
salt and pepper

2 lbs/1 kg leg of veal cut into
   one-inch thick slices
$\frac{1}{4}$ pint/15 cl stock
$\frac{1}{4}$ pint/15 cl double cream
pinch of sugar

Mix the parsley, 2 oz/60 g of the butter, pepper and salt together. Flatten the fillets and spread with the parsley butter. Roll up the meat and fasten with string. Fry in remaining butter until light brown, add the stock, cover and simmer for about three-quarters of an hour or until tender. Dish up the meat and remove the string. Add the cream to the gravy in the saucepan and bring to the boil. Season and add a pinch of sugar. Strain over the roulades.

Serve with new potatoes and a crisp salad.

CÔTELETTES DE VEAU 👑

To serve 4:

4 cutlets of veal, one-inch thick
salt and pepper
1 oz/30 g plain flour
2 ozs/60 g butter
$\frac{1}{2}$ lb/250 g mushrooms, sliced

$\frac{1}{2}$ pint/30 cl chicken or veal
   stock
1 tablespoon of redcurrant
   jelly
$\frac{1}{4}$ pint/15 cl double cream

Season the cutlets with salt and pepper and dip in the flour. Fry in the butter for fifteen minutes until golden-brown. Remove and toss the sliced mushrooms in the butter to brown. Return the cutlets to the pan, add the stock and whisk to a smooth consistency. Add the redcurrant jelly and the cream. Simmer for five minutes. Strain the sauce over the cutlets.

👑 FRICANDEAU OF VEAL

To serve 4–6:

1 stick of celery	*salt and pepper to taste*
1 onion	*2 ozs/60 g bacon, cut in strips*
2 carrots	*2 ozs/60 g butter*
2 lbs/1 kg veal slices from the	*1 pint/60 cl veal stock*
leg	*1 sprig of parsley*

Clean and cut the celery lengthways. Peel and cut the onion in quarters. Slice the carrots. Pound and flatten the meat and season with salt and pepper. Roll up the slices of veal with a strip of bacon inside and tie with string. Lightly brown the veal in butter in a frying pan. Put the cut vegetables in a casserole dish and place the veal on top. Whisk out the frying pan with half of the stock and strain over the veal. Cover and braise for half an hour. Then turn the veal, add more stock, cover and braise until tender.
    Serve with plain boiled rice, garnished with parsley.

👑 BRAISED VEAL IN THE SWEDISH MANNER

To serve 6:

2 lbs/1 kg leg of veal	*1 large onion, sliced*
2 ozs/60 g butter	*2 sprigs of parsley*
½ pint/30 cl veal stock	*1 clove of garlic*
1 carrot, sliced	*salt and pepper*

For the sauce:	
1 tablespoon of plain flour	*1 tablespoon of redcurrant*
16 fl ozs/45 cl milk	*jelly*
	2 tablespoons of double cream

Tie up the boned veal with string and braise in butter until brown. Add the veal stock, sliced carrot, onion, parsley and the clove of garlic. Season well with salt and pepper. Cover the pan and cook slowly for one and a half hours. When cooked remove meat and untie the string. Remove the vegetables and reduce the gravy by boiling for ten minutes. Glaze the meat with a little of the gravy and keep hot.

To make the sauce, blend the flour with the milk and add to the boiling veal gravy, stirring well. When thickened, strain the gravy into a small saucepan and add the redcurrant jelly. When well absorbed, stir in the cream. Serve separately.

I recommend an accompaniment of lettuce and cucumber salad with a vinegar dressing and small boiled potatoes braised in butter.

VEAL CUTLETS FARCIS 👑

To serve 6:

2 lbs/1 kg of veal from the leg	½ teaspoon of sugar
4 ozs/125 g fresh breadcrumbs	pinch of nutmeg
4 fl ozs/10 cl warm milk	2 ozs/60 g butter
2 eggs	stock, made with the veal bone
salt and pepper	4 fl ozs/10 cl white wine

Cut the meat from the leg and use the bone for making stock. Put the meat twice through the mincer. Mix the breadcrumbs with the milk and work the mixture into the meat. Add the beaten eggs, salt and pepper, sugar and nutmeg. Mix well and mould into cutlets. Fry in butter on both sides for ten minutes. Add more butter to the frying pan if necessary, then pour in a dash of stock and the wine. Boil rapidly to reduce the quantity and pour some onto the cutlets. Serve the rest separately.

Dish up with plain boiled rice and button mushrooms sautéed in butter. Instead of a cooked vegetable, try a cucumber salad.

♛ SCHNITZEL DE VEAU AU DIPLOMAT

Pre-heat oven to 180 °C/350 °F or gas mark 4
To serve 6:

6 cutlets of veal, free from skin
    and bones, about one-inch
    thick
salt and pepper
1 oz/30 g plain flour
2 eggs
4 ozs/125 g fresh breadcrumbs

1 tablespoon of oil
3½ ozs/100 g butter
½ pint/30 cl veal or chicken
    stock
¼ pint/15 cl white wine
¼ pint/15 cl double cream
sugar
2 anchovy fillets

To decorate:
6 anchovy fillets
6 slices lemon

chopped capers
watercress

Flatten the cutlets and score lightly with a knife on both sides. Sprinkle with salt and pepper, dip in flour and coat with egg and breadcrumbs. Fry over a gentle heat in oil and 3 ozs/90 g of the butter until light brown on both sides. Add the heated stock mixed with half the wine and place in the oven pre-heated to 180 °C/350 °F or gas mark 4 and cook for fifteen to twenty minutes. Dish up the schnitzels and add the rest of the wine, the cream, sugar and two anchovy fillets to the sauce. Stir over a low heat and mix well. Add a little more stock if necessary.

Strain the sauce, which should be fairly thick, into a pan. Add the rest of the butter, bring to the boil and pour over the schnitzels. Arrange the anchovy fillets in a ring in the centre of the lemon slices and fill with chopped capers. Then place on each schnitzel.

Garnish with a bunch of watercress.

FRIKADELLER 👑

To serve 4–6:

½ lb/250 g raw pork	2 pints/1.25 litres veal or
½ lb/250 g raw chicken meat	chicken stock
3 tablespoons of breadcrumbs	1 tablespoon of plain flour
½ pint/30 cl single cream	1 egg yolk
2 eggs	juice of ½ lemon
1 teaspoon of salt	1 teaspoon of caster sugar
½ teaspoon of pepper	

I do not believe in nursery meals being dull, but often children develop a craze for a particular dish and you have to keep repeating it until you can interest them in something else. When Prince Charles was a little boy it was meat balls made from chicken or pork. At that time he loved using the house telephone, much to the confusion of the office staff, and he would frequently call me in the kitchen and ask for meat balls. These meat balls – dignified under the Swedish name of Frikadeller – are a classic dish and can be used in a variety of ways. Floated on a dish of clear consommé, for instance, they make a smart first course for a dinner party.

Put the meat through the mincer three times. Soften the bread-crumbs with 4 fl oz/10 cl of the cream and add to the meat in a bowl. Add as much cream again and two eggs, stirring all the time. Season with salt and pepper and roll into small balls. Heat the stock to boiling point and drop in the frikadellers. Boil in batches for fifteen minutes and remove with a straining spoon. Keep hot.

Boil down the stock to about half a pint (30 cl). Mix the flour with some water to form a thin paste. Thicken the stock with the flour mixture, reduce the heat and add the rest of the cream, the egg yolk, lemon juice and sugar. Pour over the frikadellers.

♛ SPICED PORK WITH STUFFED CUCUMBER

Pre-heat oven to 220°C/425°F or gas mark 7
To serve 8:

4 lb/2 kg leg of pork	*1 cucumber*
salt and pepper	*1 lb/500 g cooked spinach*
4 tablespoons of brown sugar	*1 glass of Madeira wine*
8 cloves	*1 teaspoon of mustard*
¾ pint/40 cl stock, made from	*¼ teaspoon of cinnamon*
* pork bones*	*2 tablespoons of tomato purée*

Rinse the pork in scalding water and score the rind with a sharp knife, then dry thoroughly. Rub salt, pepper and half the sugar into the meat and let it stand for one hour. Insert the cloves between the scored rind and roast the meat for one hour and twenty minutes in the oven, pre-heated to 220°C/425°F or gas mark 7. After the first fifteen minutes add the hot stock and baste. Baste every fifteen minutes.

Peel and cut the cucumber into two-inch long pieces. Boil in salted water for ten minutes, then dry on a cloth. Remove the seeds and stuff with cooked spinach.

When the meat is cooked, remove the rind and cloves, skim the fat from the gravy and place the pork on a dish. Add the wine to the gravy, then the mixed mustard, cinnamon, two tablespoons of sugar and the tomato purée. Boil the gravy, reduce to a glaze and strain over the pork.

Serve the meat with the stuffed cucumber and creamed potatoes.

♛ PORK CUTLETS IN PICKLED CUCUMBER SAUCE

Pre-heat oven to 180°C/350°F or gas mark 4
To serve 6:

6 pork cutlets	*¼ pint/15 cl stock*
salt and pepper	*1 tablespoon of tomato purée*
2 ozs/60 g butter	*3 tablespoons of pickled*
6 tablespoons of breadcrumbs	* cucumbers*

Pound the cutlets and season with salt and pepper. Dip in melted butter, then cover with breadcrumbs. Dip in butter again and place under the grill to brown for a few minutes. Put in the oven pre-heated to 180°C/350°F or gas mark 4 for about twenty minutes. Then place on a serving dish. Add the stock and tomato purée to the juice from the pork cutlets. Cut up the pickled cucumber, add to the sauce and bring to the boil. Pour over the cutlets.

STUFFED SPARERIBS OF PORK

Pre-heat oven to 180°C/350°F or gas mark 4
To serve 4:

4 lbs/2 kg sparerib of pork
1 teaspoon of mustard
1 lb/500 g apples, peeled and
 cored
½ lb/250 g dried prunes, soaked

3 or 4 cloves
½ pint/30 cl stock
1 tablespoon of plain flour
salt and pepper

Ask the butcher to break the sparerib bones in two places. Spread mustard over the pork on the side nearest the bone. Fill with the peeled and cored apples and the soaked prunes. Insert cloves and roll up and tie with string. Put in a tin and braise in the oven pre-heated to 180°C/350°F or gas mark 4, adding the stock a little at a time and basting frequently. When cooked, remove string and take out the cloves, prunes and apples. Serve the prunes and apples as a garnish.

Add the flour to the gravy in the pan, mix well and season to taste. Stir and boil for six minutes. Strain and serve with the pork.

Serve with apple purée and redcurrant jelly.

👑 BRAISED FILET MIGNON OF PORK

To serve 8:

8 fillets of pork	$\frac{1}{4}$ pint/15 cl milk
salt and pepper	$\frac{1}{4}$ pint/15 cl single cream
2 ozs/60 g butter	pinch of sugar
1 tablespoon of tomato purée	

Flatten the fillets and sprinkle with salt and pepper. Fry in butter until brown. Add the tomato purée, milk, cream and sugar and braise for half an hour.

Dish up and strain the sauce over the fillets.

Serve with creamed potatoes and spinach.

👑 MARINADE OF PORK LUCULLUS

Pre-heat oven to 220 °C/425 °F or gas mark 7
To serve 6:

$3\frac{1}{2}$ lbs/1.6 kg loin of pork	1 tablespoon of plain flour
1 teaspoon of salt	$\frac{1}{2}$ pint/30 cl good stock
$\frac{1}{2}$ teaspoon of white pepper	1 tablespoon of redcurrant
$\frac{1}{2}$ pint/30 cl dry white wine	jelly
2 ozs/60 g butter	$\frac{1}{4}$ pint/15 cl double cream

Get the butcher to bone the loin and cut away the rind and surplus fat. Rub in salt and pepper. Place in a deep dish and pour over the wine. Marinade the fillet for ten to twelve hours, turning occasionally. Put the butter in a roasting tin to brown and turn the meat in the butter. Place in the oven pre-heated to 220 °C/425 °F or gas mark 7 for $1\frac{3}{4}$ hours, basting frequently with the marinade. When cooked, remove and keep warm. Add the flour to the gravy in the roasting tin and pour in the stock. Stir and boil until smooth.

Strain into a small saucepan and add the redcurrant jelly. Stir until it dissolves, then stir in the cream. Season to taste.

Serve with small round potatoes fried in butter and Brussels sprouts.

ESCALOPES OF PORK WITH CREAM SAUCE 👑

Pre-heat oven to 180°C/350°F or gas mark 4
To serve 3–4:

1½ lbs/750 g fillet of pork
2 tablespoons of plain flour
salt and pepper to taste
¼ lb/125 g butter

½ pint/30 cl good stock
1 tablespoon of white wine
½ lb/250 g dried prunes, soaked
pinch of sugar
¼ pint/15 cl double cream

Cut the fillet into escalopes an inch thick. Dip in flour and season with salt and pepper. Fry in butter until light brown. Place in a casserole dish. Add the stock to the frying pan and stir until smooth. Strain over the escalopes, add the wine, the drained prunes and a pinch of sugar. Cover with the lid and braise in the oven for thirty minutes until tender. When cooked, dish up the escalopes in a circle on a hot dish. Place the prunes in the centre of the dish.

Add the cream to the sauce, bring to the boil and pour over the escalopes. Serve with redcurrant jelly, green peas, spinach and fried potatoes.

BRAISED CUTLETS OF PORK 👑

Pre-heat oven to 180°C/350°F or gas mark 4
To serve 4–6:

4 or 6 cutlets of pork, cut ½-
  inch thick
salt and pepper
2 ozs/60 g butter
2 carrots, cut in slices
  lengthways
½ onion, cut in thick slices

2 sprigs of parsley
¼ pint/15 cl stock
1 tablespoon of tomato purée
½ glass of wine
¼ pint/15 cl double cream
pinch of sugar

Trim the cutlets and remove unwanted fat. Season with salt and pepper and fry in butter for five minutes until light brown. Place in a roasting tin on the carrots and onion with the parsley.

Add the stock to the frying pan and stir in with the gravy. Add the tomato purée and the wine, stir and bring to the boil. Strain the gravy over the cutlets and place in the oven pre-heated to 180°C/350°F or gas mark 4. Do not cover. Cook for thirty minutes and baste once or twice. When the cutlets are tender, dish up and strain the gravy. Stir the cream into the gravy, add a pinch of sugar and pour over the cutlets.

Serve with apple sauce, creamed potatoes and baked tomatoes.

♔ SCHNITZEL OF PORK À LA SCALA

To serve 4:

> *1 lb/500 g loin of pork fillet,*
> *cut ½-inch thick*
> *salt and pepper*
> *2 tablespoons of plain flour*
> *1 egg*
>
> *6 tablespoons of breadcrumbs*
> *1 tablespoon of lard*
> *a little stock*
> *redcurrant jelly and slice of*
> *orange, to garnish*

Pepper and salt the pork. Dip in flour, beaten egg and then coat in breadcrumbs, and fry slowly in the lard for about half an hour until golden-brown. Remove and place in the centre of a serving dish. Whisk out the pan with a little stock. Strain and pour over the pork. Garnish with a slice of orange with redcurrant jelly in the centre.

If you like, pipe a border of sweet potato purée (for recipe see page 131) around the dish. Tomato sauce (for recipe see page 208) makes an excellent accompaniment to this dish. Serve it in a sauce boat.

GLAZED BACON WITH ORANGE SAUCE 👑

Pre-heat oven to 220°C/425°F or gas mark 7
To serve 6:

3 lbs/1.5 kg smoked Danish back bacon, boned and rolled
10 white peppercorns
3 cloves
1 teaspoon of mustard powder

1 teaspoon of cinnamon
1 tablespoon of caster sugar
2 tablespoons of grated orange rind
orange sauce (for recipe see page 209)

For decoration:
3 bananas
½ oz/15g butter

1 tablespoon of sherry

Soak the bacon overnight. Then put in a large saucepan, cover with water and bring to the boil. Skim, add the peppercorns and cloves, cover with a lid, reduce heat and simmer for 1½ hours. Remove from the heat and allow to cool in the stock. When cold, remove the skin.

Spread mustard powder over the fat. Mix together the cinnamon and caster sugar and the grated orange rind. Sprinkle over the bacon pressing well into the fat. Place in the oven which has been pre-heated to 220°C/425°F or gas mark 7, until the fat turns a glazed golden-brown.

Cut each banana in half lengthwise, then across. Fry in butter and pour sherry over them. Cut the pork into thin slices and place together again on a dish. Arrange the banana on top.

Make the orange sauce from the recipe on page 209 and serve separately.

👑 BAKED PRAGUE HAM

Pre-heat oven to 220 °C/425 °F or gas mark 7
To serve 10–12:

4–5 lbs/2–2.5 kg Prague ham
2 lbs/1 kg shortcrust pastry
  (for recipe see page 215)
1 egg yolk diluted in water
1 tin of sauerkraut
butter
1 onion, chopped
½ pint/30 cl consommé

3 fl ozs/8 cl vinegar
1 tablespoon of syrup
1 lb peas, cooked and drained
12 baby beetroots (boiled)
¾ pint/40 cl brown sauce
1 glass of sherry
1 tablespoon of tomato purée
salt and pepper to taste

This is the most delicious recipe. For a special occasion Prague ham is well worth tracking down, for it is sweet and succulent beyond belief.

Cover ham in water and bring to the boil. Skim, then simmer for fifteen minutes to the pound after boiling. Peel off the rind and drain in a cloth. Allow to cool. Roll out the pastry and when the ham is cold, place it in the centre of the pastry and cover completely. Decorate with cut-out pieces and brush over with egg yolk diluted in water. Place the ham in the oven which has been pre-heated to 220 °C/425 °F or gas mark 7, and bake until golden-brown.

Braise the sauerkraut for one hour in a little butter with the chopped onion and add the consommé, vinegar and syrup.

Dish up the ham and surround with the sauerkraut, peas and beetroots. Heat the brown sauce, add sherry and tomato purée, season, dilute with a little stock or water if the sauce is too thick, and serve separately.

FARCE DE JAMBON 👑

Pre-heat oven to 180°C/350°F or gas mark 4
To serve 6:

¾ oz/20 g butter
1 truffle, peeled and cut into
    thin slices
5 stuffed olives
1¾ lbs/850 g raw minced pork
4 ozs/125 g minced smoked
    ham
½ lb/250 g bread panade (for
    recipe see page 213)

½ lb/250 g puréed mushrooms
1 egg yolk
3 fl ozs/8 cl Madeira wine
½ pint/30 cl double cream
½ pint/30 cl good meat stock
salt and pepper
pinch of sugar
6 slices of smoked bacon

For the stuffed tomatoes:
5 firm tomatoes

8 ozs/250 g peas, cooked and
    sieved

Grease a round soufflé dish with butter and decorate the bottom with the sliced truffle and olives. Make a forcemeat of the finely-minced pork and ham and the bread panade. Stir in all the other ingredients except the bacon.

Fill the dish with the forcemeat and top with the bacon slices. Place the dish in a tin of water and poach in the oven which has been pre-heated to 180°C/350°F or gas mark 4, for one and a half hours. Turn out when cooked.

Garnish with stuffed tomatoes, made by cutting five firm tomatoes in half, scooping out the seeds and filling with purée of green peas.

♔ GRILLED GAMMON WITH SWEET HORSERADISH SAUCE

To serve 4:

4 gammon rashers, cut ½-inch thick	½ lb/250 g fresh or frozen spinach
2 lbs/1 kg potatoes	2 cooking apples
2 tablespoons of butter	¼ pint/15 cl water
3 tablespoons of single cream	1 tablespoon of sugar
salt and pepper	1 tablespoon of horseradish sauce (bottled)
1 egg yolk	
4 tomatoes	

Grill the gammon rashers for five minutes on each side. Boil potoatoes, drain and mix in a tablespoon of the butter, the cream, seasoning and egg yolk. Beat thoroughly and place in peaks on a large dish with the grilled gammon.

Peel and de-seed the tomatoes, season and put a dot of butter inside each one. Put on the dish and keep warm. Cook the spinach, drain, and add the rest of the butter. Mix well, season and fill the tomatoes with the spinach.

To make the sauce, peel and core the apples, cook in ¼ pint/ 15 cl of water until soft, and sieve. Add sugar and mix with the horseradish sauce. Serve separately.

♔ DANISH GAMMON

Pre-heat oven to 220 °C/425 °F or gas mark 7
To serve 8–12:

1 Danish smoked gammon	2 or 3 cloves
1 apple, peeled and cut in four	mustard powder
30 cl of pineapple juice	4 tablespoons of demerara sugar mixed with ½ teaspoon of ground cinnamon
bay leaf	
6 peppercorns	

This is a disarming little dish for a luncheon party. It looks, and is, simple to prepare but there will be pleasant surprises in store.

Soak gammon overnight and scrub skin thoroughly. Cover with water in a large pan, bring to the boil and skim. Add the apple, pineapple juice, bay leaf, peppercorns and cloves, and simmer for thirty-five minutes to the pound. Allow to cool in its own juice overnight. Skin carefully and smear the fat first with mustard powder and then with demerara sugar mixed with cinnamon. Rub well into the fat and then roast in the oven at 220°C/425°F or gas mark 7, for ten to fifteen minutes, or until brown.

BRAISED VENISON ♔

Pre-heat oven to 160°C/325°F or gas mark 3
To serve 8–10:

¾ lb/350 g fat larding bacon	salt, pepper and garlic salt
4 lbs/2 kg fillet of venison	2 tablespoons of plain flour
1 oz/30 g butter	2 tablespoons of redcurrant
1 carrot	jelly
1 onion	1 wine glass of burgundy
1 pint/60 cl stock or water	¼ pint/15 cl double cream

Wrap the larding bacon round the fillet of venison. Melt the butter in a saucepan and brown the meat. Cut up the carrot and onion and put in the pan with the stock or water. Add the salt, pepper and garlic salt and braise in the oven set at 160°C/325°F or gas mark 3 for two hours. Remove the meat and vegetables from the pan and skim off the fat. Mix the flour with a little water and stir into the gravy. Let it boil on top of the cooker for a few minutes to reduce the gravy. Strain into another saucepan and add the redcurrant jelly and more stock if necessary. Add the wine and simmer for three minutes. Remove from heat. Dish up the venison and spoon a little of the sauce over it. Stir in the cream with the rest of the sauce and serve separately.

Only the plainest of vegetables, such as small boiled potatoes, peas or beans, are necessary with this dish.

♛ TURKEY LIVER LUNCH

Pre-heat oven to 180°C/350°F or gas mark 4
To serve 2:

2 large turkey livers	*salt and pepper*
1 large onion	*1 tablespoon of plain flour*
1 lb/500 g potatoes	*6 rashers of streaky bacon*
2 ozs/60 g butter	

Turkey livers can be bought all year round, but in this country they seem to be an unappreciated delicacy. In Sweden, we consider them to have delicate and exceptional flavour and they are always well received.

Clean and cut the turkey livers into slices, rinse and dry well. Chop the onion and cut potatoes into slices. Use 1 oz/30 g of the butter to grease an ovenproof dish and line with the sliced potatoes. Sprinkle the onion on top and season.

Melt the rest of the butter and dip the sliced liver first in butter, then in flour. Place liver on top of the potatoes, cut the bacon in strips and place over the liver. Bake in the oven which has been pre-heated to 180°C/350°F or gas mark 4, for half an hour.

♛ KIDNEYS WITH BRANDY

To serve 2:

4 lambs' kidneys	*1 tablespoon of tomato sauce*
butter	*salt and pepper*
2 tablespoons of brandy	*¼ pint/15 cl creamy milk*
1 teaspoon of plain flour	

Cut the kidneys in half and fry them in a little butter. Put them in a saucepan and pour in the brandy. Then set the brandy alight. Add the flour, tomato sauce and seasoning. Mix well and add the milk. Simmer for half an hour.

Serve with boiled rice or creamed potatoes.

BRAISED OXTAIL 👑

To serve 4:

1 oxtail	*2 onions, sliced*
2 tablespoons of plain flour	*1 bay leaf*
salt and pepper	*sprig of thyme*
2 carrots, sliced	*sprig of parsley*
1 celery bunch, sliced	*1 glass of sherry*

Trim and cut the oxtail at the joint sections into pieces about two inches long. Remove excess fat and place in a saucepan of boiling water and parboil for ten or fifteen minutes. Strain off the water and wipe each piece dry with a cloth. Sprinkle over flour, salt and pepper and braise in an iron saucepan for a few minutes.

Add the cut up vegetables and braise with the meat for another five or ten minutes, stirring all the time. Cover the meat with warm water, stir and bring to the boil. Remove the scum and add the bay leaf, thyme and parsley. Cover the pan and braise for three or four hours on a low heat. When cooked put the oxtail in a casserole dish, then add a glass of sherry to the gravy remaining in the pan, bring to the boil and strain over the oxtail.

SAUTÉ OF LIVER WITH MUSHROOMS 👑

To serve 2:

6–8 ozs/175–250 g calves' or lambs' liver	*1 oz/30 g plain flour*
	¼ pint/15 cl stock or water
1 large onion	*salt and pepper*
2 ozs/60 g butter	*1 tablespoon of Madeira wine*
¾ lb/350 g mushrooms, sliced	*¼ pint/15 cl double cream*

Cut the liver into strips and finely chop the onion. Put the butter in a saucepan on a medium heat and brown the liver. Add the onion and lower the heat. Add the sliced mushrooms and stir. Sprinkle the flour over the mixture and stir the ingredients together. Add the heated stock or water a little at a time and season. Add the wine, stir well and bring to the boil. Lower the heat and simmer for fifteen minutes. Stir in the cream and simmer for a further ten minutes. Serve with rice.

♛ LIVER IN REDCURRANT SAUCE

To serve 4:

1 lb/500 g calves' liver (leave whole)
equal mix of milk and water
½ lb/250 g bacon rashers
2 ozs/60 g butter
salt and pepper

¾ pint/40 cl hot milk
1 tablespoon of redcurrant jelly
1 tablespoon of plain flour
gravy browning (optional)

This is a dish that everyone will enjoy. Simple ingredients, easy to prepare in advance and served with a rich and delicious sauce.

Soak the piece of liver in equal parts of milk and water for half an hour. Drain and dry in a cloth. Tie the bacon rashers round the liver and braise in 1½ ozs/45 g of butter in an iron saucepan over a gentle heat. When brown, add salt and pepper. Put ¼ pint/ 15 cl of the hot milk into the pan, cover and braise for an hour, turning the liver over at intervals.

Add the rest of the milk a little at a time. When the liver is cooked, take out of the saucepan, untie bacon and keep hot. Add the redcurrant jelly to the gravy with one tablespoon of flour, and mix well over a low heat. Add a little gravy browning if necessary. The sauce should be a creamy, light brown colour. Add a knob of butter and stir.

Cut the liver into thin slices and place on a hot serving dish. Strain some of the sauce over the liver and serve the rest separately. Serve with rice and spring greens and redcurrant jelly.

TONGUE WITH CUMBERLAND SAUCE ROYAL 👑

To serve 6–10:

*1 large ox tongue, smoked or
    pickled in brine
1 apple, peeled and sliced
½ pint/30 cl red wine
1 teaspoon of Bovril*

*1 orange, peeled and sliced
2 or 3 cloves
10 peppercorns
chopped aspic, shredded
    lettuce and parsley, to
    garnish*

For the Cumberland sauce royal:
*3 tablespoons of redcurrant
    jelly
juice of ½ lemon
½ tablespoon of mustard
    powder*

*1 tablespoon of thick-cut
    marmalade
1 wine glass of sherry*

Order the ox tongue in good time from the butcher so that he can soak it in brine for at least three weeks. The worst disaster that can befall a tongue is that it should be grey, tasteless and insufficiently salted. If you can find a smoked tongue, this is the best of all.

Place tongue in a large saucepan without tying up, and cover with water. Bring to the boil and skim. Add the cut-up apple and orange, cloves and peppercorns, bring to the boil, reduce heat and simmer for four hours or until tongue is tender.

When cooked, carefully remove skin and the small bones in the root of the tongue, and trim. Strain off stock, reserving ¾ pint/ 40 cl. Replace tongue in the pan and pour over the stock and red wine. Bring to the boil and allow to simmer, turning the tongue so that it cooks twenty mintues each side.

Allow to cool in its juice, then dish up. Arrange the tongue on a plate so that it is slightly arched in the middle. When cold, slice the tongue almost in half, lengthways. Then cut in thin vertical slices so that it is ready for serving. Heat sauce made from stock and red wine and add the Bovril, boil down and reduce to a demi-glaze. Cool slightly and pour over the tongue. Sprinkle some chopped aspic on either side of the glazed tongue. Decorate the dish with a little parsley and lettuce.

To make the sauce, mix all the ingredients together roughly. Serve the Cumberland sauce separately – if you like, in a hollowed-out orange.

The Bird

UNLESS YOU ARE PREPARED TO REAR AND KILL YOUR OWN FARMYARD roosters, or pay a premium for organic or free range birds from an assured supplier, you must accept battery chickens which are tender and cheap but lack flavour. This means, therefore, a change of approach in cooking methods. What has disappeared from the chicken must be put back by the cook. You cannot hope just to pop it in the oven and have something super-tasty at the end.

This is how I treat a chicken. First, I flavour it from inside. Always season *inside* the chicken; salt and pepper on the outside makes very little difference. A pat of parsley butter, a squeeze of lemon or some good stuffing means that the delicate juices are used to the best advantage and the bird absorbs the flavour.

Secondly, there is only one way to get the professional look with a roasted chicken, and that is to rub it with oil before it goes in the oven. This means that the finished bird will have that glorious, all-over sheen instead of looking like a patchy brown and white cocker-spaniel. Furthermore, a good rub with oil seals the skin so that the chicken is cooked from inside. Never insult a bird by roasting it in a pan swimming with animal fats. Instead, massage a little vegetable oil all over the skin before cooking, then you won't have to baste so often either.

Some of my recipes ask you to bone the birds. You may regard this as rather finicky but the heap of bones left behind on the plate is never a pleasant sight. Chicken bones have their beauty of course, but only in the stockpot, which is where they belong.

Most professional cooks do some boning. I never once sent a chicken to the table at Clarence House without removing the bones. When I first worked for the late Lord Rothermere I was told that he refused to eat chickens altogether because he hated the bones. I agreed with him because by the time you have dissected a chicken on your plate, the meat has grown cold.

Boning should be done in the kitchen, and is really quite a

simple operation. It is not necessary to hack the bird to pieces. After the chicken is cooked, grasp the bones with your fingers, twist sharply and pull out; they will come away quite easily. This additional attention can lend extra pleasure and delight to good food.

👑 GLAZED CHICKEN RISOTTO

Pre-heat oven to 220 °C/425 °F or gas mark 7
To serve 6:

3 spring chickens weighing about 1¾ lb/750 g each	3 rashers of smoked bacon
	3 cloves of garlic
salt and pepper	sunflower oil

For the risotto:

8 ozs/250 g rice	½ lb/250 g mushrooms, sliced
livers from the 3 chickens	salt and pepper
1 oz/30 g butter	pinch of sugar
4 slices of bacon, chopped	

This is a perfect example of how to cook chicken so that it has that appetizing, glazed appearance.

Clean chickens and dry thoroughly. Season the inside of each with salt and pepper, and insert in each a piece of rolled-up bacon and a clove of garlic. Rub the skins all over with a little oil. Put the chickens in a large pan and roast in the oven which has been pre-heated to 220 °C/425 °F or gas mark 7, until brown on top. Reduce heat, and turn the chickens on their side so that they brown evenly.

Meanwhile boil the rice for twenty minutes. Drain and keep warm. Braise the chicken livers in a little butter, add the cut-up bacon and sliced mushrooms. Cut the chickens' livers into small pieces and mix all together with the rice. Season and add a little sugar.

When the chickens are ready, remove from the oven and allow to cool so that you can handle them. Cut cleanly in half and pull out all possible bones without disfiguring the shape. Remove the garlic and stick the chicken halves together with their own juices. Save the rest of the juice from the pan.

Arrange the risotto on a dish and place the chickens on top. Heat the juice left in the roasting pan and glaze the birds with it.

CHICKEN WITH ITALIAN RISOTTO 👑

To serve 6:

1 boiling fowl (about 4–5 lbs/2–2.5 kg)
½ lemon
salt
1 carrot
1 onion
½ celery stick
bouquet garni

½ teaspoon of ground pepper
½ lb/250 g mushrooms
1 oz/30 g butter
2 tablespoons of breadcrumbs
2 teaspoons of cornflour
¾ pint/40 cl chicken stock

For the Italian risotto:
1 onion
1 dessertspoon of olive oil
2 ozs/60 g butter
8 ozs/250 g rice
1¼ pints/¾ litre chicken stock
pinch of saffron

½ glass of wine or brandy
1 tablespoon of tomato purée
dash of cayenne pepper
4 ozs/125 g grated Parmesan cheese
seasoning

When combining chicken meat with other ingredients, it is nearly always preferable to use a boiling fowl. The way it is cooked means that the flesh is more moist and less liable to shrink. Quite a lot of care should be taken in buying the right sort of chicken for boiling for, although it is older than a roaster, it is not – or should not be – old. A chicken is fully grown at four months; by six months it should have put on quite a bit of weight. After its first birthday it begins toughening up, and soon becomes fit only for soup.

This is a useful recipe, using a previously-boiled bird. It is good for feeding large numbers and will stretch to that odd extra guest. It is very tasty, and grand enough for a smallish evening party. You can keep it waiting a bit, too.

Rub the chicken with lemon and salt. Cover with water in a large pan and add more salt. Bring to the boil over a medium heat and skim. Add vegetables, bouquet garni and pepper, and bring to the boil again. Reduce heat and simmer for an hour and a half or until the chicken is tender.

To make the risotto, chop onion and fry in the oil and half the amount of butter until light brown. Add rice, stir and cook until it becomes transparent; add the stock from the chicken and cook for twenty-five minutes. Dissolve the saffron in the wine and add it to the rice with the tomato purée. Season well, add the rest of the butter and lastly some of the Parmesan cheese. Let the risotto stand for a few minutes.

When the chicken is cooked, remove it and strain the stock. Remove bones and skin from the chicken and cut the meat in small pieces. Peel and slice the mushrooms and braise in butter. Add the chicken and breadcrumbs. Dissolve the cornflour in chicken stock, season and pour over. Simmer over a low heat for a few minutes.

Dish up, making a well in the middle of the rice into which you pour the chicken mixture. Sprinkle more cheese over the top.

♛ FRIKADELLER WITH MUSHROOM SAUCE

To serve 6:

½ lb/250 g raw chicken meat	2 eggs
2 ozs/60 g butter	salt and pepper
¼ pint/15 cl double cream	pinch of nutmeg
3 ozs/90 g bread panade (for recipe see page 213)	½ teaspoon of sugar
	1 pint/60 cl chicken stock

For the mushroom sauce:

½ lb/250 g mushrooms	salt and pepper
½ pint/30 cl creamy milk	½ teaspoon of sugar
1 tablespoon of plain flour	1 oz/30 g butter
a little chicken stock	

To any Swedish ex-patriate, the word 'frikadeller' conjures up a hundred dreams. Of all the classic ingredients, the frikadeller mixture is perhaps the most versatile. Moulded into small balls and served with a creamy sauce, it is delicious. Used as a stuffing or steamed in the oven as a chicken cream, the mixture takes on another delectable form. I am proud to have introduced one of Sweden's best advertisements to the British Royal Family.

Cut breast from uncooked chicken and mince finely. Put minced chicken into a basin with the softened butter, cream and bread panade and mix very thoroughly. Add the eggs one at a time with seasoning, nutmeg and sugar, stirring for about one minute each time. Mould the mixture into about 30 small round balls and poach in boiling chicken stock for ten to fifteen minutes.

To make the sauce, clean and cut the mushrooms and boil in the milk for five to ten minutes. Mix flour with stock until smooth, then add the milk. Bring to the boil, add seasoning and sugar and simmer for ten minutes on a low heat. Remove from heat and add the cold butter in small lumps. Pour over the frikadellers.

FRIKADELLER WITH LOBSTER SAUCE

To serve 5:

½ lb/250 g raw chicken meat
2 ozs/60 g softened butter
3 ozs/90 g bread panade (for recipe see page 213)
¼ pint/15 cl double cream
pinch of nutmeg

½ teaspoon of sugar
2 eggs
salt and pepper
1 pint/60 cl chicken stock
½ pint/125 g frozen peeled prawns

For the lobster sauce:
1 small tin of lobsters
1 tin of lobster soup
¼ pint/15 cl double cream
½ glass of port wine
1 tablespoon of tomato purée

salt and pinch of sugar
cayenne pepper
1 oz/30 g butter
1 oz/30 g Gruyère cheese

Cut the meat from the uncooked chicken and mince very finely. Put minced chicken into a bowl with softened butter and bread panade and mix well. Add the cream, nutmeg, sugar and the eggs, one at a time. Season and stir hard. Shape the mixture into ten portions with a tablespoon so that each is about the size of a poached egg. Poach in chicken stock for about fifteen minutes.

Heat the prawns in their own juice. To make the lobster sauce, sieve the tinned lobster, add the lobster soup and heat slowly. Stir in the cream, wine, tomato purée and seasonings. Bring to the boil, stir well and add butter in small pieces. Remove from heat and add the cheese. The sauce should not be thick and if necessary can be diluted with milk to taste.

Arrange the prawns in the centre of a serving dish and pour over the lobster sauce. Surround with the frikadellers. Serve with rice mixed with chopped-up cooked gammon and garnished with parsley and black olives.

♛ CHICKEN CHAUD-FROID

To serve 6 as a first course:

1 previously boiled chicken   *1 green pepper, sliced thinly*
¼ pint/15 cl supréme sauce (for   *1 red pepper, sliced thinly*
   recipe see page 202)   *1 pint/60 cl aspic*
1 truffle, peeled and sliced

To garnish:
lettuce   *green pickled tomatoes*
black olives   *tinned peppers*

This is what I call one of my Proud Hostess dishes. The chaud-froid sauce, made with supréme sauce and coated with aspic, is not hard to achieve but requires attention to detail and good judgement. The result is satisfyingly grand.

Remove the skin of the boiled chicken, cut out the breasts and divide them into six portions. Cook the supréme sauce so that it is thick, but still liquid.

With two forks dip the chicken portions into the supréme sauce so that they are well coated. Place on a wire tray and decorate artistically with sliced truffle and thin strips of red and green pepper, making flower shapes or whatever takes your fancy. Have the aspic jelly cooled just at setting point and carefully coat the decorated chicken portions. Put in the refrigerator.

Line a silver dish with the rest of the aspic, leaving a little in the bottom of the jug to set. When everything is firmly set, decorate the dish with lettuce leaves, olives and pickled tomatoes. Place the chicken portions on the dish and arrange the tinned peppers cut in halves. Finish by sprinkling here and there a little chopped aspic from the jug.

Serve with Salade Charlotte (for recipe see page 144).

CHICKEN SAUTÉ ♔

To serve 6:

1 chicken	½ lb mushrooms, peeled and
1 oz/30 g butter	sliced
5 small onions	1 tablespoon of plain flour
¼ lb/125 g bacon, cut into strips	salt and pepper
liver from the chicken, sliced	½ pint/30 cl stock

Joint the chicken and place in a saucepan with the butter to braise until light brown. Add the onions, bacon, the sliced liver of the chicken and the mushrooms. Sprinkle with flour and season. Stir over a high heat, add the stock and mix well. Cover the pan with the lid and simmer gently for one hour.

Serve hot with seasonal vegetables and boiled rice.

CÔTELETTES DE POULET SAUTÉES ♔

Pre-heat oven to 180°C/350°F or gas mark 4
To serve 4:

1 large chicken	1 tablespoon of mushroom
3 ozs/75 g butter	purée
1 tablespoon of chopped fresh	1 tablespoon of Madeira wine
parsley	or sherry
juice of ½ lemon	3 fl ozs/8 cl single cream
salt and pepper	1 truffle, peeled and sliced
2 tablespoons of plain flour	sprig of parsley or watercress
¼ pint/15 cl chicken or veal	to garnish
stock	

Cut the breast from the chicken and save the rest of the bird for making stock. Cut breasts into two pieces and then pound to flatten. Make into four cutlets, and insert a slit in each.

Cream 1 oz/30 g of butter with the parsley, lemon juice and seasoning and stuff each breast with the mixture. Dip the cutlets into flour and fry in 1 oz/30 g of butter over a gentle heat until golden-brown, basting all the time. Put in the oven pre-heated to 180°C/350°F or gas mark 4, and cook for ten to fifteen minutes.

Pour the stock into the pan in which the cutlets have been sautéed and heat. Add the mushroom purée, wine and seasoning. Boil quickly over a high heat. Reduce heat and stir in the remaining butter and cream. Strain and pour over the cutlets. Place a slice of truffle on top of each cutlet and garnish with watercress or parsley.

Serve with fried potatoes and a salad of French beans and one red chilli cut in strips on a bed of lettuce. Sprinkle with French dressing.

♛ BRAISED CHICKEN À LA GOURMAND

To serve 4:

1 chicken	½ orange, cut into four pieces
2 sprigs of parsley	with rind
2½ ozs/75 g butter	1 glass of white wine
salt and pepper	1 teaspoon of redcurrant jelly
1 tablespoon of oil	½ pint/30 cl double cream
½ pint/30 cl good chicken stock	1 egg yolk
2 sticks of celery	

Rinse and dry but do not truss chicken. Chop parsley and mix with 1 oz/30 g of butter. Season the inside of the chicken and place the parsley butter inside. Melt the rest of the butter and the oil in a saucepan and braise the chicken light brown all over. Lower the heat, cover the saucepan and cook gently for fifteen minutes. Add a little chicken stock, the celery and orange. Cover and braise for a further fifteen minutes, turning the chicken on its side. Add more stock and the wine at intervals of ten minutes. Turn the chicken once more and cook for about one hour.

Remove the chicken and simmer the sauce down to a glaze.

Then add the remainder of the liquid and mix in the redcurrant jelly. Strain this sauce into another pan. Add the cream, whisk well and heat the sauce gently, but do not bring it near boiling point. Add the beaten egg yolk. Remove from heat and keep hot, then stir in a knob of butter. Cut chicken into portions and serve with the sauce.

An excellent accompaniment is pimento rice, which is made by mixing in a sliced red or green pepper with a dish of boiled rice.

CHICKEN SAUTÉ PROVENÇALE

To serve 6:

1 chicken (3 lbs/1.5 kg in weight)	$\frac{1}{4}$ pint/15 cl white wine
2$\frac{1}{2}$ ozs/75 g butter	1 tablespoon of tomato purée
1 tablespoon of olive oil	pinch of sugar
plain flour	$\frac{1}{4}$ pint/15 cl double cream
salt and pepper	8 stuffed olives, to garnish
$\frac{1}{2}$ pint/30 cl chicken stock	

Remove the legs from the chicken, cut away the breast and remove skin. Cut the legs in two at the joint and cut each breast, diagonally, in two. Melt 2 ozs/60 g of butter and the oil in a frying pan. Dip the chicken pieces in flour and fry over a gentle heat for twenty-five to thirty minutes. Add salt and pepper. Allow a longer cooking time for the legs. When cooked, dish up the chicken on a serving dish.

Add the stock to the frying pan, then the wine, tomato purée and a pinch of sugar. Reduce to half the quantity by boiling rapidly. Lower the heat and add the cream and the rest of the butter.

Strain the sauce over the chicken and garnish with the olives.

♛ POUSSINS WITH POMMES AU GRATIN

Pre-heat oven to 220 °C/425 °F or gas mark 7
To serve 4:

4 tablespoons of sunflower oil	2 lbs/1 kg potatoes
1 teaspoon of tomato sauce	2 ozs/60 g butter
1 teaspoon of Bovril	$\frac{1}{4}$ lb/125 g grated Parmesan
salt and pepper	cheese
2 large poussins	bread sauce (for recipe see
	page 207)

Mix the oil, tomato sauce, Bovril and seasoning together in a bowl. Cut the poussins in half and brush with the oil mixture.

Peel and slice the potatoes and place them in a buttered oven-proof dish. Sprinkle with pepper and salt and dot knobs of butter on top. Place the cut poussins on a grilling rack and roast in the oven at 220 °C/425 °F or gas mark 7 for about thirty minutes along with the potatoes. Brush the birds with the oil mixture once or twice during cooking. When cooked, remove and keep hot. Sprinkle cheese on top of the potatoes and let them cook for another ten minutes. Place poussins on top of the potatoes and serve with bread sauce.

♛ POUSSINS ROYAL

Pre-heat oven to 220 °C/425 °F or gas mark 7
To serve 4:

4 poussins	$\frac{1}{4}$ lb/125 g bread panade (for
salt and pepper	recipe see page 213)
sunflower oil	$\frac{1}{2}$ pint/30 cl single cream
2 tablespoons of chopped fresh	4 egg yolks
parsley	1 tinned truffle, peeled and
2 ozs/60 g butter	finely-chopped, plus the
$\frac{1}{2}$ lb/250 g minced veal	juice from the tin
$\frac{1}{4}$ lb/125 g smoked ham	$\frac{1}{2}$ pint/30 cl stock

Whenever I think of that great and lovable Prime Minister, the late Sir Winston Churchill, I am reminded of turtle soup. Not that I ever cooked any for him, but he consumed vast quantities of it and always took it with him when staying away from home. I remember seeing this turtle soup in the refrigerator at Balmoral Castle and being told that he liked to have it in a thermos in his room at night. The trouble was that poor Sir Winston suffered greatly from his teeth at the time and, being unable to tackle ordinary meals, kept his strength up with turtle soup. Unfortunately, therefore, I cannot say with confidence that Sir Winston ever actually *enjoyed* a meal of mine, but here is a dish, part of which at least, might have helped to fortify the turtle soup.

Season the poussins inside and out with salt and pepper. Brush all over with oil and place some parsley inside each one. Place in the oven, which has been pre-heated to 220°C/425°F or gas mark 7, with the butter and cook for forty minutes, basting occasionally.

In the meantime, mince the veal and ham together and mix with the bread panade. Add seasoning to taste. Whisk the cream and egg yolks together and stir very thoroughly. Add the chopped truffle and the juice from the tin. Mix well together to make a forcemeat.

When the poussins are half-cooked, remove from the oven and allow to cool a little. Then cut in half and remove the bones gently. Stuff the poussins with the forcemeat, stick the halves back together, cover with greaseproof paper and return to the oven at a temperature of 180°C/350°F or gas mark 4, for twenty minutes. Then place on a serving dish and decorate with asparagus tips and mushrooms braised in butter.

To make a gravy, skim fat from the juices in the pan, add the stock, bring to the boil, strain and serve separately.

Serve with French beans and new potatoes.

♛ BRAISED PHEASANT WITH CELERY

Pre-heat oven to 180 °C/350 °F or gas mark 4
To serve 4:

1 brace of pheasants	*2 pints/1.2 litres good veal or*
salt and pepper	*beef stock*
½ lb/250 g fat bacon rashers	*2 ozs/60 g plain flour*
4 celery hearts	*1 glass of white wine*
sprigs of parsley	*¼ pint/15 cl double cream*
butter	*pinch of sugar*

Anyone who has ever worked for the British Royal Family would know all about game. From the beginning to the end of the shooting season, all the Royal Households would be flooded with the plentiful produce of the estates. It was my job at Clarence House to think of fresh ways of dealing with this rich stream of pheasant, grouse, partridge etc, and I can remember that I was quite pleased when the shooting season was over. Now that I have to buy my game like anyone else, I think longingly of those vanloads of royally-shot birds.

For this recipe, sprinkle the inside of the pheasants with salt and pepper and tie the bacon round the birds. Put them in a saucepan with two celery hearts, chopped parsley and a knob of butter, and brown over a medium heat. Then add ½ pint/30 cl of heated stock, cover the pan and braise for ten minutes over a high heat. Add the rest of the stock and bring to the boil. Put in a covered dish and cook in the oven at 180 °C/350 °F or gas mark 4 for about thirty minutes. When cooked, remove the birds and reduce the stock to about half the amount over a high heat. Strain the stock and keep hot.

To make the sauce, first cut the two remaining celery hearts and boil in salted water until tender. Drain and braise in butter on a low heat until golden-brown. Cover and keep hot.

Then melt 1 oz/30 g of butter in a saucepan, add the flour, mix well with a whisk and add the stock, gradually bringing to the boil. Lower heat and simmer for five or six minutes. Add the wine and cream, season with salt and pepper and a pinch of sugar. The sauce should be a creamy golden colour. Lastly, stir in a knob of butter.

Cut the breasts from the pheasants and divide each into two portions. Place the braised celery on a serving dish and put the breasts of pheasant on top of the celery. Coat the pheasants with some of the sauce and serve the rest separately.

Serve with redcurrant jelly, plain boiled potatoes in a napkin and a chicory salad with French dressing.

ROULADE OF PHEASANT WITH SMOKED HAM ♛

Pre-heat oven to 220°C/425°F or gas mark 7
To serve 6:

1 pheasant	½ lb/250 g pork sausage meat
liver from the pheasant	1 lb/500 g raw smoked ham,
¼ pint/15 cl double cream	sliced
salt, pepper and sugar to taste	butter

For the sauce:
¾ pint/40 cl stock made from the pheasant bones	1 tablespoon of tomato purée
	knob of butter
	6 pastry bouchée cases

Skin the pheasant, remove the meat and put through the mincer twice. Mix with the sausage meat. Lightly fry the pheasant liver in butter and mix with the forcemeat. Stir in the cream. Season with salt, pepper and a little sugar.

Remove the rind from the ham and put a tablespoon of creamed pheasant on each slice, and fold into a roll. Put the filled ham in a roasting tin and spread with a little melted butter. Bake in the oven at 220°C/425°F or gas mark 7 for fifteen to twenty minutes.

To make the sauce, reduce the stock to half by rapid boiling. Add the tomato purée and knob of butter and boil for two minutes over a high heat. Glaze the roulades with the sauce and serve on a hot dish with bouchées filled with creamed spinach (for recipe see page 140) and braised celerey (for recipe see page 125).

♛ PHEASANT PIE

Pre-heat oven to 220 °C/425 °F or gas mark 7
To serve 6:

For the pastry:
1 lb/500 g plain flour   2 egg yolks
2 ozs/60 g lard   salt and pepper
6 ozs/175 g butter   water to mix

For the filling:
2 pheasants   1¼ pints/¾ litre good stock
¼ lb/125 g fat bacon rashers   salt and pepper
butter   ½ red pepper

For the sauce:
1 oz/30 g butter   ¼ pint/15 cl double cream
1 tablespoon of plain flour   salt, pepper and a pinch of
stock   sugar

First, make the pastry according to the short pastry recipe on page 215.

Tie the bacon round the birds and braise in butter until light brown. Add ¼ pint/15 cl of stock, season with salt and pepper, cover the saucepan and braise for twenty minutes. Add 1 pint/60 cl more of stock, turn the birds, cover and cook over a gentle heat until they are tender. Remove the birds, cut in half length-ways, remove the bones and put them back in the pan with the gravy. Simmer for half an hour. Cut the birds into small portions.

Blanch the pepper in boiling water, remove the seeds, cut into strips and mix with the pheasant. Line a pie form with pastry, fill it with the meat and cover with the stock. Put on the pastry lid, decorated with some appropriate pastry cut-outs, brush with beaten egg, and place in the oven at 220 °C/425 °F or gas mark 7 for fifteen minutes. Turn down the heat, cover the pie crust and cook for a further thirty minutes. Serve hot or cold.

If serving hot, make the following sauce. Strain the remaining gravy and skim off the fat. Put the butter in a pan, add flour and mix well over the heat until brown. Add some gravy and stir until smooth. Add more gravy and simmer for five minutes. Then add the cream and season with salt, pepper and a pinch of sugar. The sauce should be golden-brown and quite thick.

PARTRIDGES EN CASSEROLE 👑

To serve 4:

$\frac{1}{4}$ lb/125 g minced pork and
    chicken, mixed
2 partridges
$\frac{1}{4}$ lb/125 g fat bacon rashers
$\frac{1}{4}$ pint/15 cl chicken stock
1 onion

1 carrot
salt and pepper
$\frac{1}{2}$ lb/250 g mushrooms
$\frac{1}{2}$ red or green pepper
butter

Mix the minced pork and chicken together to make a forcemeat. Cut the mushrooms in half and the pepper in strips. Stuff the partridges with the forcemeat and tie the bacon fat round them. Braise in an ovenproof dish on a gentle heat and add a little stock at intervals. Add the onion, carrot and seasoning. Cover and cook for an hour. Meanwhile, braise the mushrooms in a little butter with the pepper.

When the partridges are cooked, remove them and strain the stock. Remove the bacon and cut the partridges in half. Put them in a clean casserole dish with the pepper and mushrooms and pour the sauce over. Simmer for ten or fifteen minutes.

STUFFED PARTRIDGE 👑

Pre-heat oven to 220°C/425°F or gas mark 7
To serve 4:

2 partridges
salt and pepper
1 lb/500 g minced chicken
1 tablespoon of oil
1 tablespoon of melted butter

1 lb/500 g button mushrooms
$\frac{1}{2}$ lb/250 g sliced bacon
good stock
1 glass of Madeira wine

Cut the partridges in half and remove the backbones. Season well and fill each half with the minced chicken. Stick the partridges together again, place in a roasting tin and coat them with a mixture of oil and melted butter. Roast in the oven at 220 °C/425 °F or gas mark 7 for twenty-five minutes, basting frequently.

Remove from the oven, divide the halves and keep hot. Serve with quickly-braised mushrooms and rolls of grilled bacon. Make the rest of the chicken into balls, fry them and add to the dish.

Swirl out the pan with some stock, add the Madeira wine and a knob of butter. Heat, reduce the gravy by boiling and strain over the partridges.

☸ WILD DUCK

Pre-heat oven to 220 °C/425 °F or gas mark 7
To serve 4:

2 small wild duck	salt and pepper
½ lb/250 g mushrooms	¼ pint/15 cl stock
1 onion	1 tablespoon of double cream
butter	1 glass of port wine
1 tablespoon of plain flour	brown breadcrumbs

Roast the wild duck in the oven at 220 °C/425 °F or gas mark 7 for about twenty-five to thirty minutes. When cooked, remove the breasts, cut in slices lengthways and replace on the breast bones. Remove the legs and cut in two at the joints, then replace. Spoon over some of the gravy from the roasting tin. Skim the fat off the rest of the gravy and keep hot.

Chop up the mushrooms and onion and braise in a little butter for one or two minutes. Add the flour and seasoning and stir over a high heat, pour in the stock and cook until thickened. Then add the cream and the wine and simmer for five minutes. Pour the thick mixture over the breasts of the duck.

Mix the breadcrumbs with a knob of butter and put on top of the ducks. Put in the oven at 150 °C/300 °F or gas mark 2 for fifteen minutes.

Serve with redcurrant jelly and a sharp salad.

ROAST GROUSE 👑

Pre-heat oven to 230 °C/450 °F or gas mark 8
To serve 2:

> 2 young grouse, well hung   ¾ pint/40 cl beef stock
> fat bacon rashers   brown breadcrumbs

Grouse have their own distinctive flavour and are best cooked plainly.

Tie the birds with bacon fat and roast for fifteen to twenty minutes in the oven at 230 °C/450 °F or gas mark 8, basting every five minutes. When cooked, cut the grouse in half lengthways and remove the backbones. Keep warm. Boil the bones in the beef stock.

Add a little stock to the roasting pan and stir. Strain into the beef stock. Reduce the stock to half the amount by boiling, and strain. Serve with the grouse. Serve the birds on a bed of fried brown breadcrumbs.

Garnish with straw potatoes and watercress. Serve with bread sauce, French beans and a crisp green salad.

GALANTINE OF GAME 👑

Pre-heat oven to 180 °C/350 °F or gas mark 4
To serve 6–8 as a first course:

> 1 cooked grouse   1 carrot
> 1 cooked pheasant   parsley
> ½ lb/250 g mixed minced pork   salt and pepper
>   and veal   ½ oz/15 g gelatine
> 1 onion   ¼ pint/15 cl red wine

For a party, nothing looks nobler than a beautiful home-made galantine of game.

Cut some fillets from the grouse and pheasant and put to one side. Mince the rest of the game and add to the pork and veal forcemeat and season well. Put the game carcasses in a saucepan with the vegetables, parsley and some seasoning. Cover with water, bring to the boil and simmer for two hours. Strain, and reduce liquid to about 1 pint/60 cl.

Line a terrine dish first with a layer of the game fillets, then with the forcemeat and season between each layer. Leave room in the dish for the liquid to be added later. Place the dish in a tin of hot water and bake in the oven at 180°C/350°F or gas mark 4 for an hour.

Heat the strained stock, dissolve the gelatine in it and add the wine. Allow to cool a little and pour the aspic mixture over the meat in the tin.

When set, turn out on a dish and garnish with any remaining aspic, chopped, and with lettuce and thinly-sliced sweet red pepper.

👑 TERRINE OF GAME

To serve 6–8:

1 pheasant	$\frac{1}{2}$ teaspoon of salt
2 partridges	$\frac{3}{4}$ lb/350 g shin of veal
2 ozs/60 g butter	3 tablespoons of powdered
3 pints/1.75 litres good stock	aspic
3 cloves	$\frac{1}{4}$ pint/15 cl white wine
8 white peppercorns	2 hard-boiled eggs

Braise the pheasant and partridges in the butter, add stock, cloves, peppercorns and seasoning. Cut the veal into large pieces, wash in hot water and put in the saucepan with the birds. Bring slowly to the boil and skim. Simmer for one and three-quarter hours with the lid on. Remove the birds and meat, and cut the flesh into pieces. Replace the bones in the stock, simmer and reduce to 2 pints/1.25 litres. Remove and cool. Strain the stock and skim off as much fat as possible.

Stir in the aspic powder and dissolve. Add the wine and leave to cool.

Arrange the cut meat in a terrine dish with slices of hard-boiled egg. Then pour over the aspic, cool but not yet set, and leave in a cold place to set.

TURKEY WITH WALNUT STUFFING 👑

Pre-heat oven to 220°C/425°F or gas mark 7
To serve 15:

<table>
<tr><td>½ lb/250 g ground walnuts</td><td>salt and pepper</td></tr>
<tr><td>butter</td><td>2 lbs/900 g sausage meat</td></tr>
<tr><td>¼ lb/125 g breadcrumbs</td><td>1 turkey (about 15 lbs/7 kg)</td></tr>
<tr><td>2 tablespoons of double cream</td><td>vegetable oil</td></tr>
</table>

Mix together the walnuts, a knob of butter, breadcrumbs and cream, and season. Stuff the rear end of the turkey with the sausage meat and the neck end with the walnut stuffing.

Rub oil all over the skin of the bird. Place in the oven pre-heated to 220°C/425°F or gas mark 7 and roast for fifteen minutes, then baste. When the turkey has turned a light brown colour, reduce the heat, turn on its side and cook for ten to fifteen minutes per pound. Baste and turn the turkey every fifteen minutes.

When cooked, strain the juice and skim off the fat. Garnish with chipolata sausages. Serve with cranberry sauce and bread sauce.

TURKEY AND HAM PIE 👑

Pre-heat oven to 220°C/425°F or gas mark 7
To serve 4:

<table>
<tr><td>1½ lbs/750 g leftover turkey
and ham</td><td>1 pint/60 cl chaud-froid sauce
(for recipe see page 210),</td></tr>
<tr><td>8 ozs/250 g short pastry
(for recipe see page 214)</td><td>made from chicken or veal
stock</td></tr>
<tr><td></td><td>4 hard-boiled eggs</td></tr>
</table>

Cut leftover turkey and ham into pieces – chicken too if you have any. Line an 8 inch/20 cm pie tin with short pastry, cover the bottom with sauce, then with the mixed meat. Place the hard-boiled eggs on top and fill up with the rest of the meat. Finish by pouring over the rest of the sauce, then cover with pastry. Decorate with pastry cut-outs, brush with beaten egg and bake in the oven pre-heated to 220°C/425°F or gas mark 7. Reduce the heat after the first fifteen minutes and bake for a further half-hour. Serve hot or cold.

♔ ROAST DUCK SCANDINAVIAN STYLE

Pre-heat oven to 220 °C/425 °F or gas mark 7
To serve 4:

$\frac{1}{2}$ lb/250 g chicken
$\frac{1}{2}$ lb/250 g smoked gammon
6 ozs/175 g bread panade (for
   recipe see page 213)
1 onion

butter
$\frac{1}{2}$ pint/30 cl creamy milk
salt, pepper and sugar to taste
2 young ducks

For the sauce:
1 tablespoon of fat from duck
   gravy
1 tablespoon of plain flour
$\frac{1}{2}$ pint/30 cl chicken stock
gravy from the duck
raw livers from the ducks
   (sieved)

1 glass of Madeira wine
$\frac{1}{2}$ lb/250 g prunes, cooked,
   stoned and chopped
salt and sugar to taste

Mince the chicken and gammon twice together and mix with the bread panade. Cut the onion finely and braise in butter, then add to the meat mixture with the milk and seasoning. Mix thoroughly.

Split the ducks open and remove the breast bones. Sprinkle salt and pepper inside and stuff with the forcemeat. Tie the ducks up in their natural shape and cover with foil. Place in the oven pre-heated to 220 °C/425 °F or gas mark 7, to cook for one hour and fifteen minutes. After an hour, remove the foil, baste the ducks with their own gravy and let them brown for the remaining fifteen minutes. Place on a serving dish to keep hot.

To make the sauce, remove fat from the gravy and put 1 tablespoon of the fat into a saucepan. Add the flour to the duck fat, pour in the stock, stir well, add the duck gravy and the livers. Cook for five minutes. Add the wine and the prunes and season with salt and sugar. Simmer for ten minutes.

Dish up the ducks on a serving dish and serve with green peas mixed with red peppers cut in strips and creamed potatoes. Serve the sauce separately.

ROAST DUCKLING ♔

Pre-heat oven to 220 °C/425 °F or gas mark 7
To serve 4–6:

2 ducklings	*3 dessert apples, sliced*
liver from the ducklings	*½ lb/250 g dried prunes, soaked*
salt and pepper	

For the sauce:
2 tablespoons of plain flour	*1 glass of sherry*
juice from the roasted	*1 tablespoon of redcurrant*
* ducklings*	* jelly*
½ pint/30 cl beef stock	*salt and pepper to taste*

Rub the breasts of the ducklings with the liver, sprinkle inside and out with salt and pepper and stuff with the cut-up apples and the prunes.

Roast in the oven which has been pre-heated to 220 °C/425 °F or gas mark 7, basting every fifteen minutes. After the first fifteen minutes, lower the heat and continue roasting for one hour and fifteen minutes. When ready, the skin should be crisp and light brown. Remove from the oven and keep hot.

To make the sauce, add flour to the juice from the ducklings and stir well. Add the heated stock, stir until smooth and add the wine, redcurrant jelly and seasoning. If the sauce is thick, add a little more stock and some juice from the prunes. Taste, adjust seasoning and strain. Serve separately with the ducklings.

♛ ROAST DUCK SUÉDOISE

Pre-heat oven to 220 °C/425 °F or gas mark 7
To serve 2–4:

1 lb/500 g dried prunes   *1 duck*
2 dessert apples   *salt and pepper*
2 cloves

For the sauce:
skimmed gravy from the   *½ glass of prune juice*
   cooking juices   *1 glass of claret*
1 tablespoon of plain flour   *1 dessertspoon of orange*
½ pint/30 cl stock (preferably   *marmalade*
   beef)

Soak the prunes overnight in cold water and remove the stones. Core and quarter the apples and insert the cloves. Season the duck generously with salt and pepper, inside and out. Rub the breast with the liver from the bird.

Stuff the duck with the apples and half the prunes. Cover the breast with buttered greaseproof paper and roast in the oven, which has been pre-heated to 220 °C/425 °F or gas mark 7, for an hour and twenty minutes. Lower the heat after the first half hour and baste occasionally. Remove the paper fifteen minutes before the cooking time is up, and let the duck brown without basting.

While the duck is cooking, simmer the remaining prunes in water until soft. When cooked, add a pinch of salt and keep warm on a low heat.

When the duck is cooked, remove from the oven, place on a dish and keep warm. Skim the fat from the gravy in the pan. To make the sauce, add flour to the skimmed gravy, and stir until smooth. Add the stock and simmer for ten minutes. Add the prune juice, half the glass of claret and the marmalade. Check seasoning, strain and keep hot.

To garnish, pour a tablespoon of the fat from the duck on to the strained prunes, add the rest of the claret and simmer for a few minutes so that the prunes become glazed. Arrange them round the duck.

Serve with red cabbage and new potatoes.

ROAST GOOSE 👑

Pre-heat oven to 220°C/425°F or gas mark 7
To serve 10:

1 goose	*1 cup breadcrumbs*
2 onions	*salt and pepper*
sage	
1 oz/30 g butter	

Chop the onions and the sage leaves and sauté the onion and sage in butter. Add the breadcrumbs and the salt and plenty of pepper and stuff the goose with this. Prick the goose all over with a fork.

Goose is so fat that I shouldn't lard it and I shouldn't even cook it in fat – just put enough water in the baking tin to prevent the goose sticking. Heat.

Put the goose in the oven. Turn down the heat after twenty minutes to 190°C/375°F or gas mark 5. Baste the bird with its fat every half hour. A nice plump young goose of about 7 lbs should take about 1½ hours. Season with salt and milled pepper towards the end of the cooking.

The conventional English sauce with goose is apple sauce – a couple of cooking apples, peeled, cored, sliced and cooked in as little water as possible to a mush, with a very little sugar added.

♔ ROAST GOOSE WITH FRUIT STUFFING

Pre-heat oven to 220°C/425°F or gas mark 7
To serve 10:

1 goose, about 8 lbs/4 kg	*1 orange*
½ lemon	*1 lb/500 g dried prunes, stoned*
salt and pepper	*1 small pineapple*
2 dessert apples	*1 tablespoon of port*
2 or 3 cloves	

For the sauce:

juice from the roasting pan, skimmed of all fat	*1 tablespoon of redcurrant jelly*
1 teaspoon of cornflour	*salt and pepper*
1 glass of red wine	*giblets from the goose, minced*
1 tablespoon of orange marmalade	

Soak the prunes in warm water until swollen, then remove the stones.

Rub the goose inside and out with the lemon. Season inside with salt and pepper. Cut the apples in quarters and stick with cloves. Quarter the orange, leaving the skin but removing the pips.

Stuff the goose with the orange and apples and half the stoned prunes. Close the opening with a skewer. Roast in the oven which has been pre-heated to 220°C/425°F or gas mark 7, for twenty minutes. Lower the heat to 190°C/375°F or gas mark 5 and cook for one and three-quarter to two hours, basting every twenty minutes.

When cooked, serve on a dish garnished with pineapple slices and the rest of the prunes which have been previously cooked in water with a tablespoon of port wine and reduced to a glaze. Cut the breast of the goose in slices from the top and replace into its natural shape.

To make the sauce, thicken the juice from the roasting pan with the cornflour and add the wine, marmalade and redcurrant jelly. Season and simmer. Then add the minced giblets to the gravy. Simmer for five minutes, sieve and serve with the meat.

Vegetables and Salads

UNTIL I CAME TO ENGLAND I HAD NEVER BOUGHT A VEGETABLE – I always picked them. I worked in the huge, beautiful and still rather feudal castles in Sweden which were entirely self-supporting. From the beginning I was a keen cook-gardener, using everything that came out of the earth when it was young and fresh and preserving nature's surplus for when it was out of season. Nowadays people have little time for the simple satisfactions of bottling peaches, pears and tiny beetroots or the pleasure of picking young vegetables in season.

Although at Clarence House I was lucky enough to have a choice of fresh vegetables from the royal estates at Windsor, the 1950s were a time when shopping was difficult and the busy housewife fell back on tinned produce. My standbys were tinned artichoke hearts, asparagus tips and red peppers; luxuries which were often hard to find or out of season. Accordingly, I have included some 'easy way out' dishes which can be quickly assembled.

I grow only a few of my own vegetables now. I appreciate what can be bought in convenient cans and packets, and make full use of them, while at the same time being rather choosy about brands. But something is wrong when we ignore fresh spring cabbage – as tender as asparagus if properly treated – in favour of frozen peas, wrapped up in green packets which describe the exact moment that the pod went pop! And have we forgotten the beauty of the Jerusalem artichoke which proves its goodness by the jellied stock it leaves in the pan? There is nothing more delicious than French beans in season; make a great fuss of them and serve as a special dish for a lunch or dinner party.

Everyone has their own way of cooking and serving vegetables, of course, and people do not usually compare recipes on how to cook, say, Brussels sprouts. However, I feel such things are important for it is surprising how often vegetables are overcooked: time runs away when cooking a meal and the poor old vegetables are not rescued until soft and mushy. When this happens, you might as well drink the cooking water, for the vegetables will have lost all their Vitamin C, and will look most unappetising too. Leaving the lid off the pan is another way of wasting the nutrients.

Vegetables properly cooked and appetisingly served and garnished, will go a long way to boosting the morale of any dish – and will do you a lot of good too.

You will see that I have first listed a number of vegetables and given you advice on how they should be prepared and served as accompaniments to main courses. More elaborate recipes for vegetables and salads, some of which form meals in themselves, follow.

♔ BEANS, BROAD

Pod the beans. Boil in salted water for five minutes with the lid on. Drain and remove the skins, put back in the saucepan with a lump of butter, cover and simmer for five to ten minutes. Add half a tablespoon of chopped parsley and a pinch of sugar. Or, if you can find it, sweet savory chopped and mixed with the juice of half a lemon.

♔ BEANS, FRENCH

Top and tail the beans, rinse and tie them into bundles. Place in salted boiling water with a pinch of bicarbonate of soda. Boil until tender, about ten to twelve minutes, but do not overcook. Drain and wash over with cold water, then place on a cloth to drain.

♔ BRUSSELS SPROUTS

Cut off any wayward outer leaves and slice the ends off the stalks. Cross with a knife. Put in cold water for half an hour, so as to get rid of any foreign bodies.

Plunge into *boiling* salted water and whatever anyone tells you, there is nothing wrong with that old cook's trick of adding a pinch of bicarbonate of soda; it makes them remain green instead of going grey. Bring up to the boil again and lower the heat considerably. Let them stand in this simmering, not boiling, water for ten minutes until they sink down and are still nutty. It is all the hectic boiling that makes them mushy. Keep the lid on all the time.

Strain very thoroughly and then return to the empty saucepan adding some butter. Swirl the sprouts in the butter and dish up.

Alternatively, you could prepare sprouts as above, dry in a cloth and then fry gently in butter until golden-brown. They are delicious like this, too.

CABBAGE

Cut cabbage in half and remove the outer leaves. Cut out the stalk and pare off some of the thick veins. Leave in cold water for fifteen minutes. Then put in boiling water; push the leaves down so that the water almost covers. Add a pinch of bicarbonate of soda and cook for ten minutes with the lid on. When cooked, drain very thoroughly, pressing the cabbage gently with a plate to rid it of excess water. Spread some butter inside and roll up.

CARROTS

Top and tail, scrape and cut downwards in fairly thin sticks; then cut the sticks in half. Just cover in plain water and boil quickly so that the water evaporates. When all the water has gone the carrots are cooked. If any excess water is left, drain it off and add half a tablespoon of butter to the carrots in the pan; swirl the carrots around in the steam, add pinches of salt, pepper and sugar and glaze the carrots in the butter. Salt in the cooking water causes carrots to discolour.

♔ CARROTS VICHY IN WINE

Scrape small, new carrots. Boil in a little water until tender, drain off, add a knob of butter, sugar to taste and half a glass of white wine. Cooked in this way, they are a delicious garnish to a main meal.

♔ CARROT TIMBALES

Carrot timbales make a vivid splash of colour and are impressive served with a main course or as a first course surrounded by glazed baby onions.

Pre-heat oven to 200 °C/400 °F or gas mark 6

1 lb/450 g carrots, peeled and cut into medium slices	*6 tablespoons milk*
	salt and freshly ground pepper
1 oz/25 g butter	*pinch of sugar*
3 eggs	*pinch of salt*

Butter four ramekins. Put carrots in a saucepan, cover with water. Bring to the boil, cover and cook for about fifteen minutes or until very tender. Strain and mix to a smooth purée with half an ounce of butter and a pinch of salt. Melt remaining butter in the saucepan used to cook carrots and cook purée over low heat, for about three minutes, stirring often until excess moisture evaporates. Remove from heat. Whisk egg whites with milk in a medium sized bowl. Gradually whisk in carrot purée. Season to taste with salt, pepper and sugar. Fill the ramekins with carrot purée. Smooth over top and place ramekins in a bain-marie. Add boiling water to come halfway up the sides of the ramekins. Bake for thirty-five to forty minutes or until firm to the touch. Remove ramekins when a skewer inserted into the middle comes out dry. Allow to cool for about three minutes then slide a thin bladed knife around the edge of each one, set a small plate on top, invert and gently lift off ramekin.

CAULIFLOWER 👑

Cut off the stalk and divide the cauliflower into sprigs. Choose a few good leaves and dice the tender part of the stalk if desired. Soak in cold water for a few minutes.

Put in the pan enough boiling salted water to cover the cauliflower and cook rapidly for ten minutes or less with the lid off. Unfortunately, cauliflower produces an unpleasant smell which permeates the vegetable if the lid is left on. Drain in a cloth and serve with melted butter.

CELERY, BRAISED 👑

Clean and cut a celery heart in half, boil in salted water until tender. Drain on a cloth, cut each half in two pieces and braise in butter until golden.

GLOBE ARTICHOKES 👑

These look a little like thistles; the short ones are the best. Cut off all the thorny bits at the top of the leaves and level the base. Soak in cold water for one hour to get rid of any bitterness.

Place in about 3 pints/180 cl of boiling salted water in a deep pan with a pinch of bicarbonate of soda to keep from greying. Boil for twenty minutes to half an hour with the lid on. Test for readiness by pulling a leaf – if it comes away easily the artichokes are done. Drain, head down, in a cloth and keep warm. Serve on a napkin with melted or creamed butter, and a little lemon juice served separately.

JERUSALEM ARTICHOKES 👑

These are a bit of a bother to peel, but persevere until the artichokes are clean and white. Put in cold water for a few minutes. Then boil in salted water for ten or fifteen minutes.

Strain and serve with knobs of butter on top. Don't whatever you do throw away the cooking water as it is wonderful for soups. Watch it jellify in the pan.

👑 PURPLE SPROUTING BROCCOLI

Remove any pieces you don't like. Then chop the stalks so that all pieces of the broccoli are the same length. Tie up in bundles and leave in cold water for half an hour.

Boil for about eight minutes in just enough water to cover, adding a small piece of garlic, salt and a pinch of bicarbonate of soda. When cooked, drain carefully and put in a cloth until wanted. Serve with melted butter.

👑 SEA-KALE

Trim and remove the root, rinse well and tie in bundles. Boil in enough salted water to cover with the lid on for ten minutes. Remove, drain and serve with melted butter. If you add crisply-fried pieces of bacon, this can be a course in itself.

👑 SPINACH

Pick over the spinach very carefully, removing coarse veins. Soak in lots of cold water to get rid of all the grit.

Put very, very little water in the saucepan, just enough to cover the bottom of the pan. Add salt and a pinch of bicarbonate of soda to make it cook quicker. Pack the spinach well down in the pan and start cooking at a moderate temperature, increasing the pace for five minutes. Remove the lid during the last few minutes to let surplus moisture evaporate. To serve, roll the leaves up and sprinkle them with melted butter.

Potatoes are the most versatile of all vegetables. It saddens me when I hear people dismiss them by saying they are fattening. *Any* food is fattening is you eat too much of it. I have eaten potatoes all my life and I am not fat. Her Majesty the Queen always eats potatoes and retains a wonderful figure. Try some of the following dishes and you will see just what I mean about potatoes being versatile.

POTATO SOUFFLÉ ♔

To serve 4:

1 egg
½ lb/250 g potatoes, mashed
2 rashers fried bacon, cut up
1 onion, finely-chopped and
    fried with the bacon

salt and pepper
6 medium-sized tomatoes
¼ lb/125 g Gruyère cheese,
    grated

Beat in the egg with the mashed potatoes and add the cut-up fried bacon, the chopped onion and salt and pepper. Cut the tops off the tomatoes and remove the seeds. Fill the tomatoes with the potato mixture. Sprinkle with cheese and place in a hot oven for ten minutes.

Delicious with roast lamb.

SPECIAL DUCHESSE POTATOES ♔

To serve 2–4:

½ lb/250 g potatoes, mashed
1 tablespoon of cold butter
1 egg

¼ lb/125 g chopped and fried
    mushrooms
salt, pepper and sugar
ground almonds

Mix the potatoes, 1 tablespoon of cold butter, egg, mushrooms, seasoning and a pinch of sugar, and shape into small balls. Roll in ground almonds and fry in butter until light brown.

Wonderful with chicken.

HASSELBACK POTATOES ♔

Pre-heat oven to 220°C/425°F or gas mark 7

6 medium sized potatoes
butter for the baking dish
1 oz/30 g melted butter

1 teaspoon salt
1 oz/30 g dried breadcrumbs

Peel potatoes and drop them into a bowl of cold water to prevent discolouration. Place one potato at a time in a large wooden spoon and with a sharp knife, slice down at intervals along the length of the potato. The deep curved bowl of the spoon will prevent the knife from cutting right through. Drop each semi-sliced potato back into the cold water to keep until ready to roast in the oven, first patting them dry with a cloth. Generously butter a baking dish and place the potatoes in it, cut side up. Baste the potatoes with the melted butter, sprinkle with salt and bake for thirty minutes. Then sprinkle each potato with breadcrumbs, baste again with melted butter and continue to roast for another fifteen minutes until fan shaped, scrunchy and brown.

👑 BAKED POTATOES BOHEMIAN

1 potato per person	*salt and pepper*
2 tablespoons of sausage meat	*butter*
per person	*tomato purée*

This is a useful supper dish when faced with a gang of hungry teenagers, or an unexpected guest. Highly popular with the children too.

Bake large potatoes in their jackets, cut a lid and scoop out the inside. Mash the scooped-out potato, mix with sausage meat, and season. Replace the mixture in the jackets and brush the top with melted butter and a little tomato purée mixed together. Bake in the oven for twenty minutes.

👑 POTATO PANCAKES

To serve 2–4:

1 lb/500 g potatoes	*1 egg*
2 or 3 tablespoons of plain	*salt and pepper to taste*
flour	*½ lb/250 g green bacon or pork*
2 tablespoons of milk	

Wash, peel and grate the potatoes into a bowl. In another bowl, mix the flour, milk and egg to a smooth paste. Season, and add to the grated potatoes. Cut the bacon or pork into small pieces and fry gently until golden-brown. Add to the mixture. Using about two tablespoons of the mixture at a time, shape into small pancakes and fry in bacon fat. Allow the mixture to set on top before turning to fry on the other side.

This is delicious served hot and golden with cranberry sauce and watercress salad.

STUFFED POTATO DUMPLINGS

To serve 6:

1 lb/500 g potatoes, mashed (cold and seasoned)	6 ozs/175 g plain flour
2 eggs	1 onion
	$\frac{1}{2}$ lb/250 g bacon

Add the eggs and 4 ozs/125 g of the flour to the cold seasoned potato and mix to a dough. Pat the dough on a floured board and work in the rest of the flour.

Fry the chopped-up onion and bacon gently until brown and remove from pan. Roll the potato dough into a loaf and cut into pieces the size of medium potatoes. Roll out and stuff each one with the bacon and onion mixture. Shape into dumplings. Have ready 3 pints/180 cl of boiling salted water and drop dumplings in a covered pan. When they rise to the surface, they are cooked. Remove with a draining spoon and serve with melted butter.

POTATO MIGNON

To serve 4:

1 lb/500 g potatoes, mashed	pepper, salt and sugar to taste
2 eggs	plain flour
butter	

Mix the potatoes, eggs, butter and seasoning together and roll into cakes one-inch thick. Roll in flour and fry in butter until light brown.

Good served with fried bacon.

 POTATOES MACRÉE

To serve 4:

> 1 lb/500 g potatoes, boiled in   1 onion, sliced
>   their skins   salt and pepper
> 1 oz/30 g butter

Peel the cooked potatoes, cut in slices and fry in butter with the onion. Season and fry gently until brown.

PARSLEY POTATOES

To serve 4:

> 1 lb/500 g potatoes, boiled   1 tablespoon of chopped fresh
> ½ pint/30 cl béchamel sauce (for   parsley
>   recipe see page 201)   salt, pepper and sugar
> knob of butter

Cut potatoes into cubes. Heat the béchamel sauce and add the butter, parsley and seasoning. Mix in with the potatoes.

Good with salt beef.

SCANDINAVIAN POTATO BALLS

To serve 4:

> 1 lb/500 g potatoes, boiled in   2 ozs/60 g butter or bacon fat
>   their skins   salt, pepper and sugar to taste
>   brown breadcrumbs

Peel potatoes and shape into balls. Fry in butter, add salt and pepper and enough breadcrumbs to coat. Stir and turn gently over a low heat. When golden, sprinkle a little sugar on top and serve.

NEW POTATOES 👑

To serve 6–8:

> *2 lbs/1 kg new potatoes*   *mint*
> *salt*   *a knob of butter*

Wash and scrape the potatoes, place in salted, boiling water with a sprig of mint, cover and cook for fifteen minutes. Strain off the water, replace on low heat to dry and add the knob of butter. Keep some fresh mint aside for decoration and serve in a hot dish.

POTATOES SUÉDOISE 👑

To serve 6–8:

> *2 lbs/1 kg potatoes*   *salt, pepper and sugar to taste*
> *¼ lb/125 g butter*

Peel the potatoes and cut in boat-shaped quarters. Melt the butter in a baking tin and add the potatoes, sprinkle with pepper and salt and bake in the oven until they are light brown. When cooked, sprinkle a little sugar on top and serve.

PURÉE OF SWEET POTATOES 👑

To serve 6–8:

> *2 lbs/1 kg sweet potatoes*   *1 tablespoon of double cream*
> *1 tablespoon of butter*   *pinch of cayenne pepper*

Sweet potatoes can be bought at most high-class greengrocers and supermarkets. They have a slightly sweet taste which goes particularly well with pork. Simply cook in the same way as ordinary potatoes. Mash, add butter, cream and pepper and beat very thoroughly.

♔ HARICOTS VERTS À LA CRÈME

To serve 6–8:

> 2 lbs/1 kg French beans
> salted water
> 3 fl oz/8 cl wine vinegar
> 2 egg yolks
>
> $\frac{1}{2}$ pint/30 cl single cream
> juice of $\frac{1}{2}$ lemon
> 1 oz/30 g cold butter
> chopped fresh parsley

Top and tail the beans, tie into bundles and boil in salted water for ten minutes.

Make the sauce by boiling and reducing the vinegar to a third of the quantity. Remove from heat. Whip the egg yolks and cream in another saucepan over a gentle heat until thickened. Remove from heat and add the lemon juice and vinegar in small quantities. Lastly, whisk in the butter (slightly softened, but cold) in small lumps. Keep hot. Pour the sauce over the beans and sprinkle with chopped parsley.

♔ SAVOURY FRENCH BEANS

To serve 6–8:

> 2 lbs/1 kg French beans
> salted water
> $\frac{1}{2}$ oz/15 g melted butter
> 1 clove of garlic, crushed
>
> 2 tablespoons of grated
> Parmesan cheese
> fried bacon, cut in strips

Top and tail the beans and boil in salted water for ten minutes. Drain on a cloth. Fry the beans in butter with the garlic, sprinkle with the grated cheese and fry for two minutes over a low heat.

Serve very hot with strips of fried bacon sprinkled on top.

CHICORY IN CREAM SAUCE 👑

To serve 3:

> 6 whole chicory
> salted water
> 2 egg yolks
> pinch of cayenne pepper

> 2 tablespoons of grated
> Gruyère cheese
> ½ pint/30 cl single cream

Chicory, the small cigar-shaped vegetable, is useful chopped and added raw to winter salads. Cooked, it has a slightly bitter flavour which goes particularly well with cheese. This recipe uses the distinctive nutty flavour of chicory to make an unusual dish. It can be served as a separate vegetable course or with meat.

Remove the outer leaves of the chicory and make a cross with a knife at the root. Rinse and boil in salted water until soft. Drain on a cloth and keep hot.

Whip the egg yolks with the cream and stir over a gentle heat until thickened. Add the cayenne pepper and stir in the cheese. Pour over the chicory.

CHICORY AND HAM AU GRATIN 👑

To serve 4:

> 8 chicory
> ¾ lb/350 g sliced ham
> 1 pint/60 cl creamy béchamel
>   sauce (for recipe see page 201)

> 4 tablespoons of grated
> Parmesan cheese
> 2 hard-boiled eggs
> 2 tablespoons of breadcrumbs

This makes a delicious lunch or supper dish. Remove the outer leaves of the chicory and cross the root with a knife. Boil for ten minutes or until soft. Drain thoroughly and when sufficiently cool to handle wrap a slice of ham securely round each chicory. Put in a deep ovenproof dish to keep hot.

Heat the béchamel sauce and add most of the grated cheese, stir well. Pour the sauce over the chicory and add the hard-boiled eggs cut into quarters. Sprinkle on top the breadcrumbs and the rest of the grated cheese. Put in a hot oven for fifteen minutes or under the grill to brown.

👑 BAKED CAULIFLOWER OMELETTE

Pre-heat oven to 180 °C/350 °F or gas mark 4
To serve 2:

1 small cauliflower	*1 tablespoon of chopped fresh*
salted water	*parsley*
1 onion	*4 eggs*
1 oz/30 g butter or bacon fat	*½ pint/30 cl milk*
	salt and pepper

Break cauliflower into sprigs, wash and boil in salted water until cooked but not over-cooked. Cut onion finely and fry gently until golden. Grease an ovenproof dish, half an inch (13 mm) in depth, and place the cauliflower in it. Sprinkle onion on the top. Whisk eggs with the milk, add parsley, season and pour over the cauliflower and bake in the oven at 180 °C/350 °F or gas mark 4 for twenty-five minutes.

👑 SPINACH AND ASPARAGUS IN MOUSSELINE SAUCE

To serve 4–6:

1 lb/500 g fresh spinach	*1 large tin of asparagus tips*
salt	*4 egg yolks*
4 tablespoons of asparagus	*½ tablespoon of finely chopped*
juice from the tin	*fresh parsley*
¼ lb/125 g butter	*grated Parmesan cheese*

This dish has all the lightness and brightness of early summer. The tenderness of the vegetables and the frothiness of the sauce recall at once a mild morning in May. In fact, this dish can be constructed at any time of the year with the help of canned and frozen produce – one of the nice things about modern cookery.

Wash spinach several times and remove coarse stalks and veins. Put spinach in a saucepan with salt, do not add water. Cover saucepan and place on gentle heat to cook for five minutes. Wrap the spinach leaves round the asparagus tips and place them in bundles in an ovenproof dish. Cover with well-buttered greaseproof paper and keep warm at a low temperature.

To make the sauce, put egg yolks in a saucepan and add the asparagus juice. Whisk over a low heat until frothy and add soft butter a little at a time. Keep whisking. When ready, remove the greaseproof paper from the vegetables and pour over the sauce. Sprinkle with a little finely chopped parsley and Parmesan cheese.

Serve either as an accompaniment to a grand dinner or as a dish on its own with small squares of toast.

STUFFED ARTICHOKE HEARTS ♔

To serve 4:

1 × 1 lb/500 g tin of artichoke hearts	1 tablespoon of mayonnaise
oil and vinegar dressing	1 tablespoon of grated Cheddar cheese
1 tin of sardines	chopped fresh parsley

Place the artichoke hearts on a dish and pour over some oil and vinegar dressing. Remove skin and bones from sardines, mash with a fork, add a tablespoon of mayonnaise and mix to a creamy consistency.

Stuff the artichoke hearts with the sardine cream and sprinkle some grated cheese and parsley on top.

CELERY AND BACON AU GRATIN ♔

To serve 4:

1 × 12 oz/350 g tin of celery hearts	1 teacup of grated cheese
1½ ozs/40 g butter	dash of cayenne pepper
½ pint/30 cl béchamel sauce made with the liquid from the tinned celery	salt and a pinch of sugar
	¼ lb/125 g bacon rashers, cut in strips free of fat and lightly fried

Drain the celery hearts of liquid. Butter an ovenproof dish with 1 oz/30 g of the butter and cover the bottom with a little of the béchamel sauce. Cut the celery hearts in half and place them across the dish on top of the sauce. Mix a tablespoon of the cheese into the remaining sauce, add a dash of cayenne pepper and season with salt and a pinch of sugar. Add remaining butter, mix well and cover the celery with the sauce. Sprinkle the remaining cheese on top. Put the dish under a grill or in a hot oven for five or ten minutes. When golden, sprinkle with crisp bacon on top.

♛ OEUFS SUR LE PLAT FLAMENCA

To serve 6:

6 eggs	*cayenne pepper*
2 lbs/1 kg tomatoes	*1 glass of port*
salt and pepper to taste	*1 tablespoon of double cream*
2 ozs/60 g butter	*tomato purée*
¼ lb/125 g peeled shrimps	*fried bread croûtons*

Poach the eggs. Slice tomatoes, season, and fry in butter. When the tomatoes are soft, put through a coarse sieve, add shrimps and bring to the boil. Add a dash of cayenne pepper and the port, simmer, remove from heat and stir in the cream. Pour into a dish two inches deep, dot the tomato purée around and place the poached eggs on top. Arrange the croûtons round the eggs and serve.

♛ BEANS AND BACON

To serve 6:

1 lb/500 g French beans, topped and tailed	*½ lb/250 g streaky bacon*
salt	*butter*

Boil the beans for ten minutes in a covered pan of salted water. Remove carefully with a spoon and tie in bundles like asparagus.

Place in a warm, buttered dish. Fry the bacon until golden-brown, cut in strips and sprinkle onto the beans.

CELERIAC IN CHEESE SAUCE 👑

To serve 2:

2 celeriac	*grated cheese*
salt	*½ pint/30 cl béchamel sauce (for recipe see page 201)*

Clean and peel the celeriac. Cut in half and boil in salted water for half an hour. When cooked, scoop out the centres and, adding some grated cheese to the béchamel sauce, pour over the celeriac, replacing the centres. Sprinkle with more grated cheese and put in a hot oven for five minutes.

RED PEPPERS WITH RISOTTO FILLING 👑

Pre-heat the oven to 180°C/350°F or gas mark 4
To serve 4:

4 red peppers	*1 large onion, chopped*
1 cup of rice, boiled	*2 ozs/60 g butter*
¼ lb/125 g back bacon, chopped small	*½ lb/250 g chickens' livers, chopped*
	seasoning

Blanch the peppers by bringing them to the boil in salted water. Slice off the tops and remove the seeds. Boil the rice in salted water and gently fry the chopped bacon, chopped chickens' livers and chopped onion in the butter for a few minutes. Fill the peppers with the mixture. Cover with greaseproof paper and cook in the oven set at 180°C/350°F or gas mark 4 for ten minutes.

♕ STUFFED CABBAGE

Pre-heat over to 180 °C/350 °F or gas mark 4
To serve 6:

½ lb/250 g minced beef
½ lb/250 g minced pork
½ lb/250 g bread panade (for
    recipe see page 213)
2 beaten eggs

½ pint/30 cl milk
1 large cabbage
butter for frying
½ pint/30 cl good beef stock
pepper, salt and a pinch of
    nutmeg and sugar

It seems odd to go back to wartime days to remember an outstanding dish; mostly then, one was at one's wits' end to find sufficient ingredients, let alone create new dishes. For a time during the Second World War, I was with ex-King Peter and ex-Queen Alexandra of Yugoslavia in a house they had in Egham. They were sad days for the King and Queen in exile; they were guarded night and day by security men and were not allowed outside the house at night. Small things mean a lot at times like that and, despite rationing and restrictions, I did my best to cheer them up with my food.

It was on one of these occasions that I first cooked stuffed cabbage, and it turned out to be a great success. King Peter said it reminded him strongly of a Yugoslavian dish whose name I cannot remember, and for an evening everyone forgot their troubles. This dish has, in fact, stood the test of time as there is something in the combination of ingredients which imparts a particularly appetizing flavour. The secret, I think, lies in careful handling and a really good beef stock.

Mix the finely-minced meat with the bread panade. Add the eggs and seasoning and stir in the milk. Mix until the consistency resembles sausage meat. Cut the hard part of the stalk out of the cabbage and boil in salted water for fifteen minutes. Separate the leaves and cut out any coarse veins. Fill the leaves with the forcemeat and fold round carefully and put in an ovenproof dish. Pour the stock into the frying pan, stir and bring to the boil. Strain the gravy over the cabbage and put the dish in the oven which has been pre-heated to 180 °C/350 °F or gas mark 4, to cook for half an hour.

TOMATES FARCIES 👑

To serve 5:

1 lb/500 g fresh or frozen peas	*pepper*
butter	*1 red pepper, chopped*
2 tablespoons of pickled onions	*1 jar of pickled pears, to*
10 firm tomatoes	*garnish*

Boil the peas in salted water for fifteen minutes. Strain and mix in a little butter and the pickled onions. Halve the tomatoes and remove the seeds, sprinkle with pepper and fill with the peas and onions. Sprinkle the chopped pepper on top.

This makes a delicious accompaniment to cold roast beef. Decorate with some small pickled pears.

POTATOES IN TOMATO COCOTTES 👑

To serve 10:

20 medium-sized tomatoes	*2 lbs/1 kg potatoes, boiled,*
salt and pepper	*mashed and creamed*
butter	*1 egg, beaten*
	grated Parmesan cheese

Skin tomatoes and cut in half, remove seeds and sprinkle with salt and pepper. Place a small piece of butter inside each and fill with the creamed potato. Brush the top with beaten egg, sprinkle with cheese and brown under the grill.

JANSSON'S FRESTELSE 👑

Pre-heat oven to 220°C/425°F or gas mark 7
To serve 4:

4 large potatoes	*¼ pint/15 cl cream*
2 ozs/60 g butter	*1 tin anchovies*
1 large onion	*2 ozs/60 g grated Parmesan or*
milk	*Gruyère cheese*

This is a favourite supper dish and every Swede worthy of the name has his own variation. We are very fond of our potatoes, you see, and are forever devising new ways of cooking them. Jansson's Frestelse are time-honoured and appear even at the grandest parties. I used to make them for Count Bonde who lived in feudal magnificence at Horningshom Castle in Sweden, surrounded by water, with his own private prison! The Frestelse used to be served at midnight when the Count had his wonderful crayfish parties that went on until the early hours. As a matter of fact, I always associate Jansson's Frestelse with ghosts, because I saw one once at one of these parties when everyone was eating Frestelse very late at night. It was a woman and she walked straight through a wall. It hasn't turned me against Frestelse, though.

Clean the potatoes well. Cut a ring round the top of each potato and bake in the oven. When cooked, cut off the lids and scoop out the inside of the potatoes into a basin and mash up until smooth and free from lumps. Add most of the butter and stir well. Keep hot. Chop the onion finely and boil in a little milk for five minutes. Add the cream to the onion and bring quickly to the boil. Remove at once from the heat and mix with the potato. Half-fill the potato jackets with the mixture, then add a layer of anchovies. Fill with the rest of the potato and top each one with one or two anchovies. Sprinkle the grated cheese on top and dot each potato with a knob of butter. Put the stuffed potatoes on a flat baking sheet in the oven set at 200 °C/425 °F or gas mark 7 for ten minutes.

♛ BOUCHÉES AUX EPINARD

To serve 6:

½ lb/250 g cooked spinach, fresh or frozen	salt and sugar, to taste
1 oz/30 g butter	6 pastry bouchée cases

Cook the spinach, sieve and mix in the butter, salt and sugar. Keep pastry cases hot and crisp, and fill them with the creamed spinach just before serving.

Serve very hot.

BAKED AVOCADO PEAR 👑

Pre-heat oven to 170°C/325°F or gas mark 3
To serve 6 as a first course:

> 3 avocado pears
> ¼ pint/15 cl Madeira wine
> salt and pepper
> 1 tablespoon of oil
>
> ½ tablespoon of tarragon
>   vinegar
> ½ tablespoon of finely-cut chives
> finely-chopped fresh parsley

Cut the avocado pears lengthwise in half, remove the stones, place on a baking sheet and fill the halves with the wine. Place in the oven set at 170°C/325°F or gas mark 3, to bake slowly for twenty minutes.

Mix the seasoning with the oil, vinegar, chives and parsley. Fill the baked pears with the mixture and serve.

ASPARAGUS IN MOUSSELINE SAUCE 👑

To serve 4:

> 2 bundles of fresh asparagus
> salt
>
> mousseline sauce (for recipe
>   see page 204)

Cut the asparagus tips three inches long. Peel, rinse and tie into four bundles. Boil in salted water for twenty minutes. Remove carefully from the water, drain in a cloth and place in an entrée dish. Remove string and cover with mousseline sauce.

👑 STUFFED ONIONS WITH KIDNEYS AND MUSHROOMS

Pre-heat oven to 180°C/350°F or gas mark 4
To serve 6:

2 lbs/1 kg potatoes	$\frac{1}{2}$ tablespoon of plain flour
$\frac{1}{4}$ pint/15 cl creamy milk	$\frac{1}{4}$ pint/15 cl beef stock
$\frac{1}{4}$ lb/125 g butter	$\frac{1}{4}$ pint/15 cl tomato purée
6 large onions	1 tablespoon of sherry (optional)
4 lambs' kidneys	$\frac{1}{4}$ lb/125 g bacon
$\frac{1}{4}$ lb/125 g mushrooms	salt and pepper to taste

Cook the potatoes, then mash them and beat in 3 ozs/90 g of the butter and the milk. Peel and rinse the onions, and boil in salted water until soft. Strain and drain on a cloth. Remove the centre of the onions and keep for use in the stuffing.

Cut the kidneys into slices and braise them in a little butter or bacon fat, add the cleaned and sliced mushrooms, and salt and pepper to taste. Stir over a low heat, add the flour and mix well. Pour in the stock and mix. Stir over the heat and bring to the boil, stirring all the while. When thickened, lower the heat and simmer for half an hour with the lid on, stirring once or twice.

When cooked, add the chopped-up onion centres, the tomato purée and the sherry. Bring to the boil slowly and simmer for two minutes. Stuff the onions with this mixture and place them in a flat ovenproof dish. Cut the bacon strips and fry until crisp. Strain the bacon fat over the stuffed onions and keep the bacon strips hot. Place the onions in the oven set at 180°C/350°F or gas mark 4 for ten to fifteen minutes.

Spread the creamed potatoes on a serving dish and place the stuffed onions on top. Sprinkle the bacon strips around the dish.

👑 SALADE VERONICA

To serve 4:

1 Cos lettuce	$\frac{1}{2}$ teaspoon of sugar
1 tablespoon of tomato purée	salt and pepper
juice of a lemon	

Rinse and quarter lettuce, mix the other ingredients together and pour over.

TOMATO AND GREEN PEPPER SALAD

To serve 4:

6 tomatoes
2 tablespoons of chives
1 green pepper, cut into strips
lettuce

1 tablespoon of oil
½ tablespoon of tarragon
   vinegar
salt, pepper and pinch of sugar

Peel tomatoes, cut into quarters, remove the seeds and cut into strips. Chop chives finely. Mix together with pepper strips and serve on a bed of crisp lettuce. Mix the oil, vinegar, salt, pepper and sugar together, and pour over the salad.

BEETROOT SALAD

To serve 4:

1 beetroot
1 cucumber
salt and pepper

equal parts of mayonnaise and
   double cream
lemon juice
lettuce

Cut beetroot into julienne strips and mix with the cucumber, also cut into strips. Add salt and pepper.

Make a mayonnaise sauce from equal parts of mayonnaise and double cream, mixed together with a little lemon juice and salt. Mix into the beetroot and cucumber and serve on a bed of shredded lettuce.

♛ APPLE SALAD

To serve 4:

> 2 Bramley apples
> ½ lemon
> ½ celery heart
> 2 medium-sized tomatoes
> ½ lb/250 g Cheddar cheese
> ¼ lb/125 g Danish blue cheese
>
> ½ green pepper
> 2 tablespoons of mayonnaise
>   diluted with 1 tablespoon of
>   double cream
> dash of cayenne pepper
> lettuce

Wash apples and cut them in half across, remove cores and scoop out enough of the flesh to make room for the salad filling. Cut up the scooped-out apple into small pieces and squeeze a little lemon juice over them to keep from discolouring.

Cut the white part of the celery into small pieces. Skin the tomatoes and cut into sections, remove seeds and cut into strips. Cut the Cheddar cheese into strips and crumble the Danish blue with a fork. Chop up the pepper and mix all the ingredients together with the mayonnaise, adding the cayenne pepper. Fill the apples with the mixture.

Serve the apples on the lettuce.

♛ SALADE CHARLOTTE

To serve 4:

> 1 lettuce
> 1 box of dates
> ¼ lb/125 g Danish blue cheese
>
> ½ red or green pepper
> ¼ lb/125 g walnuts
> 1 bunch of seedless grapes

Cut the head of lettuce into four parts, rinse and dry. Stone the dates, cream the cheese and stuff the dates with the cheese. Cut the pepper into strips, toast the walnuts in the oven and remove the skins. Skin the grapes and arrange the ingredients prettily in a glass bowl.

POTATO SALAD 👑

To serve 4:

4 large potatoes
1 tablespoon of oil
$\frac{1}{2}$ tablespoon of lemon juice
1 tablespoon of finely-cut
   chives

salt and sugar to taste
mayonnaise
1 tablespoon of double cream

Boil the potatoes, but do not overcook them. While the potatoes are still quite warm, mix up the oil, lemon juice, chives and seasoning and pour over the potatoes. Cut into cubes and when cooler, mix with mayonnaise and a little cream.

VEGETABLE SALAD 👑

To serve 4:

1 dessert apple
1 large cooked potato
1 raw celeriac
1 lb/500 g French beans
$\frac{1}{2}$ lb/250 g smoked ham

1 tin of mixed carrots and peas
2 onions, cut in thin rings
1 tablespoon of roughly
   chopped capers (bottled)

For the dressing:
1 tablespoon of oil
$\frac{1}{4}$ teaspoon of salt
$\frac{1}{4}$ teaspoon of white pepper

$1\frac{1}{2}$ tablespoons of tarragon
   vinegar

This is a hearty salad, which can be served as a separate course. It is delicious, too, with cold roast beef or steak.

Peel and cut the apple into strips, dice the potato, cut the celeriac into strips, cut the beans, and cut the ham into strips. Mix all together with the carrots, peas and onions. Mix the dressing ingredients together and pour over the salad.

👑 MOULDED SHRIMP SALAD

To serve 4:

For the aspic:
$\frac{1}{2}$ oz/15 g gelatine
$\frac{3}{4}$ pint/40 cl hot water

$\frac{1}{4}$ pint/15 cl white wine or dry
  sherry

For the salad:
$\frac{1}{2}$ lb/250 g frozen, peeled
  shrimps or prawns
1 lettuce, shredded
2 hard-boiled eggs, sliced

2 tomatoes, quartered and
  skinned
$\frac{1}{2}$ cucumber, sliced
watercress, to garnish

Make up the aspic jelly and line a mould when nearly at setting point. Allow to set and arrange half the shrimps or prawns at the bottom. Add a layer of shredded lettuce and sliced eggs, and a further layer of shrimps. Line the side of the mould with the remaining egg slices. Fill the centre with tomatoes and cucumber and cover with the rest of the aspic. Set in the fridge. Turn out on a dish and garnish with watercress.

👑 BUCKLING SALAD

To serve 6:

6 bucklings
3 hard-boiled eggs
2 small beetroots
2 dessert apples
2 boiled potatoes

1 dessertspoon of chopped
  onion
sliced cucumber and chopped
  parsley, to garnish

For the dressing:
$\frac{1}{2}$ tablespoon of vinegar
$\frac{1}{2}$ tablespoon of nut oil
1 tablespoon of tomato purée

1 teaspoon of French mustard
salt, pepper and pinch of sugar

Skin and bone the bucklings and keep in fillets. Chop the whites of the hard-boiled eggs roughly and sieve the yolks. Cut the beetroots, apples and boiled potatoes into cubes. Mix the onion, chopped egg whites, beetroot, apples and potatoes in a bowl.

Mix together the salad dressing ingredients and pour over the vegetable salad. Dish up on a flat serving dish and place the buckling on top. Place the sieved egg yolks in a line between the fish. Decorate the buckling fillets with a line of cucumber slices and sprinkle with chopped parsley.

MOULDED MELON SALAD WITH PARMA HAM 👑

To serve 2:

1 honeydew melon	1 packet of pineapple jelly
¼ lb/125 g Parma ham	1 glass of white wine

Cut the melon across, remove seeds and scoop out the fruit carefully with a teaspoon in a series of small egg shapes. Be sure to save the melon juice. Cut the ham into thin strips, mix with the scooped-out melon and return the mixture to the shell. Dissolve the jelly in ½ pint/30 cl of boiling water, add the juice from the melon and enough wine to make up to ¾ pint/45 cl. Let it cool until almost at setting point and then pour over the melon salad.

Keep in a cool place.

HOT GRAPEFRUIT SALAD 👑

To serve 6:

3 grapefruit	1 glass of dry white wine
6 teaspoons of caster sugar	dash of cayenne pepper
2 tablespoons of redcurrant jelly	6 black olives
	lettuce, to garnish

Cut grapefruits in half, remove inside skin and seeds and cut into sections. Place on a dish and sprinkle each half with a teaspoon of sugar. Place in a hot oven or under the grill until thoroughly heated.

Melt the redcurrant jelly with wine and a dash of cayenne

pepper, bring to the boil and glaze the grapefruit with the mixture. Put a black olive in the centre of each grapefruit half and serve on a bed of lettuce.

 SALADE PRINCESSE

To serve 4:

> 1 tablespoon of oil   salt and sugar
> 2 tablespoons of red wine   4 bunches watercress (picked
> 1 teaspoon of French mustard   over)
> dash of cayenne pepper

Stir oil, wine, mustard and seasoning well together and sprinkle over the watercress.

👑 CUCUMBER SALAD

To serve 4:

> 1 heart of lettuce   1 tablespoon of chopped fresh
> 1 cucumber   parsley
> salt, pepper and sugar to taste $\frac{1}{2}$ tablespoon of finely-cut
> 1 tablespoon of white vinegar   chives
> 1 tablespoon of water

Rinse the lettuce, dry and cut in four pieces. Place in the bottom of a salad dish. Peel and cut cucumber into thin slices, sprinkle with salt, pepper and sugar, and put in the middle of the dish. Mix the vinegar, water, parsley and chives together and pour over the cucumber.

LEEK AND BEETROOT SALAD 👑

To serve 4:

1 lettuce
1 beetroot
2 small leeks
1 tablespoon of water

1 tablespoon of tarragon
    vinegar
salt, pepper and sugar to taste

Separate the lettuce into leaves. Cut up the beetroot into Julienne strips and cut the white part of the leeks into thin rings. Sprinkle the rings on top of the lettuce and decorate with the beetroot. Mix together the water, vinegar, salt, pepper and sugar and pour over the salad.

AVOCADO PEAR SALAD 👑

To serve 4:

2 avocado pears
¼ pint/15 cl mayonnaise,
    diluted with whipped cream
1 tablespoon of tomato purée
6 ozs/175 g frozen or fresh
    peeled prawns

½ tablespoon of finely-cut
    chives
salt to taste
chopped red pepper
lemon slices
lettuce hearts

Cut the avocado pears in half lengthwise, remove the stones and scoop out a little of the fruit to make room for the filling. Cut up the fruit and add to the mayonnaise together with the purée, prawns and chives. Add some salt to taste. Fill the pears with the salad and sprinkle the chopped red pepper on top. Garnish with lemon twists.

Serve on a bed of lettuce hearts accompanied by melba toast.

♚ CUCUMBER AND DILL SALAD

1 large cucumber	*salt and pepper*
1 bunch fresh dill	*1 tablespoon white wine vinegar*

Slice the cucumber thinly, scissor over the dill and season with salt and pepper. Sprinkle with the vinegar. Very good with cold salmon or smoked salmon.

♚ JERUSALEM ARTICHOKE MOUSSE

2 lb/1 kg Jerusalem artichokes	*freshly ground nutmeg*
chicken stock	*salt and pepper*
2 oz/60 g gelatine	*½ pint/30 cl double cream*
6 tablespoons liquor from	*3 egg whites*
cooking the artichokes	*2 tablespoons dry vermouth*
juice of a lemon	*1 pint/60 cl mayonnaise*
	(for recipe see page 205)
	watercress to garnish

Clean the artichokes, placing them in a bowl of water with a slice of lemon as you do so (this prevents them turning brown). Drain and place in a large saucepan, covering them with well seasoned chicken stock. Bring to the boil and simmer until tender. Strain, reserving the stock for use in making soup. Sieve the artichokes and blend with the gelatine dissolved in six tablespoons of the reserved stock, and with the lemon juice. Season well with the nutmeg, salt and pepper and leave to cool.

Oil a large cake or jelly mould, preferably a ring shape with a hole in the centre. Whip the double cream until firm, stir into the cooled artichoke mixture. Beat the egg whites until stiff and carefully fold in. Spoon into the mould and refrigerate until set – at least four hours.

Stir the dry vermouth into the mayonnaise. Run a knife around the top of the mousse in the mould, plunge the sides of the mould into hot water for a few seconds, turn out onto serving dish. Coat the mousse with the mayonnaise and garnish with watercress.

Cakes and Puddings

I USED TO THINK THAT THE SWEET TOOTH WAS BECOMING EXTINCT. Apart from the Royal Family, who believed that something sweet 'balances a meal', people who spent hours preparing delicious and unusual dishes would finish the meal rather disappointingly by offering a bit of cheese instead of something sweet.

However, puddings and desserts have become popular once again. Often it is the simple ones that are most in demand. The big draw, for instance, at one of London's smartest restaurants is bread and butter pudding. Superbly prepared, of course, but with no frills. And only recently I heard a group of sophisticated young men discussing the best spot to find first-class treacle pudding.

Perhaps my happiest memories of Clarence House are of tea-time in the nursery, during those brief, unclouded years when the Queen was Princess Elizabeth. She would spend the afternoon playing on the lawn with Prince Charles and Princess Anne, carefully folding up the rug and taking in the toys when it was time for tea. Tea was always in the sun-filled nursery, informal and fun with sandwiches, sponge cake and home baked biscuits.

Tea-time with the Queen Mother and Princess Margaret was quite different; they took it at a small table laid with a white cloth in the drawing-room. Then they laid another tablecloth on the floor, on which the dogs were given their meal.

The Royal Family, particularly the Queen Mother, have always been appreciative of a good pudding and a number of their favourites are included in this chapter.

♔ RICE CROQUETTES WITH PINEAPPLE SAUCE

To serve 4–6:

½ lb/250 g pudding rice	2 ozs/60 g breadcrumbs
½ pint/30 cl water	oil for frying
½ pint/30 cl creamy milk	1 large tin of pineapple rings
pinch of salt	1 teaspoon of cornflour
2 ozs/60 g sugar	½ pint/30 cl pineapple juice
2 egg yolks	1 oz/30 g pistachio nuts,
½ pint/30 cl double cream	blanched
1 egg, beaten	

This dish was much-liked by Prince Charles when he was still in the nursery.

Boil rice for four minutes in water, add the milk, lower heat and bring slowly to the boil. Add salt and 1 oz/30 g of the sugar. Cover and let the rice simmer slowly until well cooked but the grains still separate. Remove from heat, mix the egg yolks with two tablespoons of the cream and add to the rice. Mix well and spread on a tray three inches deep to cool. When cold cut into slices with a pastry cutter. Dip the slices first into the beaten egg and then the breadcrumbs and fry in oil until golden-brown. Roll the croquettes in remaining sugar and place a ring of pineapple on top of each one. Keep hot.

To make the sauce, mix the cornflour and pineapple juice over a medium heat and whisk until thick and clear. Glaze the pineapple rings with some sauce and sprinkle pistachio nuts on top.

Serve the rest of the sauce separately with the remaining cream.

PINEAPPLE RICE WITH SABAYON SAUCE ♛

To serve 4–6:

½ lb/250 g pudding rice	pinch of salt
½ pint/30 cl water	2 egg yolks
½ pint/30 cl milk	½ pint/30 cl double cream
1 oz/30 g sugar	1 fresh pineapple
1 whole egg, beaten	oil
2 ozs/60 g breadcrumbs	caster sugar

For the sauce:

3 fl ozs/8 cl pineapple juice	4 egg yolks
3 fl ozs/8 cl white wine	angelica, for decoration
6 ozs/175 g sugar	

Boil rice for four minutes in the water, add the milk, lower the heat and bring slowly back to the boil. Add sugar and salt. Cover and let the rice simmer slowly until well cooked but the grains still separate. Remove from heat, mix two egg yolks with two tablespoons of the cream and add to the rice. Mix well. Beat the two remaining egg yolks.

Cut the top off the fresh pineapple and hollow out the flesh leaving a half-inch thickness round the shell. Save the juice. Cut away the core and cut the rest of the pineapple into small cubes. Mix the fruit with the hot rice and let the mixture cool. When cold, make into pear shapes and dip into the beaten egg and then the breadcrumbs, and fry in oil to a golden colour. Drain on kitchen roll, sprinkle with caster sugar and keep hot.

To make the sauce, put the pineapple juice, wine, sugar and egg yolks all together in a copper or stainless steel saucepan, whisk over a low heat until frothy and thick. Remove from heat and continue to whisk until the sauce is cold. Pour the sauce into the pineapple shell.

Place the pineapple in the centre of a dish and arrange the croquettes around it. Decorate the croquettes with stalks of angelica to resemble pears, and serve with remainder of the cream.

♛ VANILLA SOUFFLÉ

Pre-heat oven to 190 °C/375 °F or gas mark 5
To serve 4:

> *1 vanilla pod or essence to taste*   *5 eggs*
> *2½ tablespoons of butter*   *4 egg whites*
> *3 tablespoons of plain flour*   *a little icing sugar*
> *1 pint/60 cl creamy milk*

This smooth, creamy soufflé is fairly easy to make. And once up,
it does not go down.

Boil the vanilla pod in the milk, remove from the heat, cover the
pan and leave until the flavour becomes strong. Alternatively,
you can leave out this process and just use vanilla essence, though
the pod is preferable.

Melt the butter, add the flour and mix well over a low heat for
two or three minutes. Having removed the pod, add the milk a little
at a time, and cook, stirring continuously for a further two or three
minutes or until the mixture thickens. Pour the mixture into a bowl
and stir until nearly cold. Whip the whole eggs and sugar together
for fifteen minutes until pale and thick and add to the mixture a
little at a time, stirring for ten minutes. Lastly, whip the egg whites
until they form peaks and fold in gently. Pour into a buttered 2
pint/125 cl soufflé dish and bake in the oven at 190 °C/375 °F or gas
mark 5 for eighteen to twenty minutes. Remove from the oven and
dust with icing sugar.

Serve immediately with cream mixed with a little Curaçao or
Grand Marnier. Wonderful with fresh strawberries.

♛ PETIT CHOU SOUFFLÉ AU CARAMEL

Pre-heat oven to 180 °C/350 °F or gas mark 4
To serve 4–6:

> *3 tablespoons of golden syrup*   *grated rind and juice of*
> *2 tablespoons of butter*   *1 lemon*
> *5 tablespoons of plain flour*   *3 tablespoons of caster sugar*
> *¾ pint/40 cl milk*   *icing sugar*
> *5 eggs, separated*   *whipped cream*

Even at Clarence House the petit chou soufflé was always considered a great treat. It has a delicious lining of oozy caramel, which
must be tasted to be believed.

Start by lining a 2 pint/125 cl soufflé dish with caramel which
must cool and harden before the rest of the ingredients are added.
To make the caramel, bring the golden syrup to the boil over a
high heat, stirring to prevent burning, and boil until a dark, moist
brown. Watch for burning. Quickly pour the syrup into the
soufflé dish and swirl around so that it coats the dish evenly. The
caramel should stiffen straight away.

Melt butter in a saucepan, add flour and mix well over a low
heat for two minutes. Add the milk and stir until smooth and
thick. Simmer slowly for about five minutes or until the mixture
thickens and leaves the bottom of the pan. Remove and pour the
contents into a basin to cool, stirring all the time. When nearly
cold, stir in the beaten egg yolks, lemon juice, rind and the sugar,
spoon by spoon. Add these ingredients gradually, stirring continuously for about fifteen minutes.

Beat the egg whites into a stiff froth and continue beating for a
further five minutes and fold gently into the mixture. Pour into
the caramel-lined soufflé dish and place dish in a baking tin half-
filled with water. Bake in the oven at 180°C/350°F or gas mark 4
for forty minutes.

When cooked, dust with icing sugar and serve with whipped
cream.

SOUFFLÉ SALZBURG 👑

Pre-heat oven to 180°C/350°F or gas mark 4
To serve 6 or 8 according to method:

3 ozs/90 g cold butter	1 tablespoon of Cointreau
5 ozs/150 g caster sugar	5 eggs, separated
½ pint/30 cl double cream	icing sugar
grated rind and juice of	
1 orange	

Butter a 1 pint/60 cl soufflé dish. Beat egg yolks and sugar until
thick, add juice and rind of orange and the Cointreau. Beat egg

whites in a separate bowl and when peaked fold into the egg mixture. Pour into the soufflé dish and cook for about twenty-five minutes at 180°C/350°F or gas mark 4 until well risen.

Alternatively, use scooped out oranges (will do about eight oranges): cut off tops of oranges and scoop out flesh leaving the clean pith. Reduce the juice from the flesh in a small pan to about 2 fl oz (6 cl). Grate the discarded orange tops. Make mixture as above and place orange shells in baking tray. Fill to two-thirds with mixture. Cook at 230°C/450°F or gas mark 7 for eight to ten minutes.

♚ BANANES AU CARAMEL

To serve 4:

4 bananas	*½ pint/30 cl double cream*
caster sugar, to coat	*whipped*
2 ozs/60 g butter	*2 tablespoons of golden syrup*

Caramel is a most useful and delicious substance in sweet cooking. It is easy to make and a great asset to all sorts of puddings and sweets. It was certainly a great help to me on one occasion at Clarence House when I looked around and found that, due to an oversight, there was no pudding for lunch. The meat course had already gone up and I can remember that there was a certain amount of panic about what to do next. Apart from a few bananas there was nothing much in sight. I reached for the tin of golden syrup and hastily concocted this dish.

Cut the bananas through the middle and then in half. Sprinkle them with caster sugar. Fry gently in butter until they change colour. Cut up, mix with cream and put in individual sundae glasses.

Grease a metal sheet or slab of marble with butter and put the syrup in a frying pan. Melt until dark brown and pour over the greased surface thinly. When hardened, chip with a knife, then sprinkle over the banana cream.

I had a message of appreciation from the royal table for this simple dish and actually the slightly bitter-sweet flavour of the caramel mixed with the creaminess of fried bananas is very attractive. How close the royal table came to being bare, of course, was never disclosed.

BANANA-FILLED MERINGUES IN CANDIED SYRUP 👑

Pre-heat oven to 130°C/250°F or gas mark ½
To serve 6:

3 egg whites	*3 bananas*
6 level tablespoons of caster	*2 ozs/60 g butter*
sugar	*5 tablespoons of golden syrup*
½ pint/30 cl double cream	*juice of 1 lemon*

This is a dish that I have served at many royal dinner parties. It would probably find as much favour as a treat at a children's party.

First, make the meringues overnight. Whip the egg whites until the mixture is stiff enough to enable you to turn the bowl upside down. Whip for a further five minutes. Fold in the six tablespoons of caster sugar. Spoon or pipe the mixture onto a greased and floured baking tray (it will make twelve meringue shells) and put in a very low oven overnight. Alternatively, put in the oven pre-heated to 130°C/250°F or gas mark ½ for one to three hours, or until meringue is firm and dry to the touch. When the meringues have dried out, turn them over so that they dry out in the middle.

When the meringues are cooked and cooled, whip up the cream stiffly. Then stick the meringues together with the cream in the usual way, and place on a dish.

Halve and cut the bananas, dip in lemon juice, drain them and sprinkle with a little caster sugar. Fry lightly in butter. When cooled slightly, place on top of the cream between the meringues.

Put the golden syrup in a frying pan and melt until dark brown; be careful of burning. Remove from heat and taking a spoonful at a time, trail haphazardly over the meringues making a spider's web of candied syrup. Two spoons are useful as you can trail the caramel, scraping one against the other. Take care not to touch the caramel with your fingers as it retains its heat.

♔ APPLE SUET PUDDING

To serve 6–8:

> Suet pastry (for recipe see page   sugar to taste
>   216) $\frac{1}{4}$ pint/15 cl water
> 2 lbs/1 kg Bramley apples   2 or 3 cloves

This is the apple suet pudding which I served for lunch one day. 'Suet pudding!' said Bobo the Princess's maid, aghast, 'My lady will never touch it!'

The dish came back scraped clean. I had, of course, been making this particular pudding for many years, though mainly I admit, for the nursery.

Grease and line a 2 pint/125 cl pudding basin with suet pastry and let it overlap the rim. Peel, core and cut the apples and mix with sugar. Fill the basin with the apples, pour in the water and place the cloves on top. Fold over pastry and cover the basin with greaseproof paper and a cloth.

Place in a steamer with boiling water reaching three-quarters of the way up the basin.

Simmer continuously for four hours on a low heat, taking care that the water does not boil over onto the suet crust or boil dry. Turn out on a dish and sprinkle caster sugar on top.

Serve with cream.

♔ TREACLE PUDDING

To serve 6–8:

> 5 ozs/150 g golden syrup   8 ozs/250 g plain flour
> 6 ozs/175 g butter   2 level teaspoons of baking
> 4 ozs/125 g caster sugar   powder
> 4 eggs

Have a steamer ready with boiling water, then grease a 2 pint/ 125 cl pudding basin with a knob of butter, warm the syrup and add to the basin, swirling it around.

Cream the butter with the sugar, add the eggs one at a time, stirring continuously. Sift the flour with the baking powder and add to the mixture. Fill the basin, cover with greaseproof paper and a pudding cloth.

Place in boiling water in the steamer, the water reaching three-quarters of the way up the basin. Cover the steamer and boil for three-quarters of an hour, adding to the boiling water if necessary. See that the added water is also at boiling point.

Turn out and serve with cream and additional hot syrup if required.

PRINCESS PUDDING 👑

Pre-heat oven to 180 °C/350 °F or gas mark 4
To serve 6–8:

3 eggs, separated	*8 ozs/250 g fresh breadcrumbs*
7 ozs/200 g caster sugar	*2 tablespoons of melted*
1 pint/60 cl creamy milk	*redcurrant jelly*
vanilla essence	*grated rind of 1 lemon*

Whisk the yolks of the eggs with 4 ozs/110 g of the sugar. Heat the milk and add to the egg yolks whisking all the time. Add a drop of vanilla essence and the breadcrumbs and allow to stand for fifteen minutes.

Butter a 2 pint/125 cl soufflé dish and fill it with the mixture. Bake in the oven at 180 °C/350 °F or gas mark 4 for twenty to twenty-five minutes so that it is set but not brown. Spread the top with the melted redcurrant jelly. Whip the egg whites stiff, add the remainder of the sugar and the lemon rind and spread over the pudding. Bake in the oven at 170 °C/325 °F or gas mark 3 for ten to fifteen minutes till dry and light golden.

♛ APPLE PIE BANBURG

Pre-heat oven to 220°/425°F or gas mark 7
To serve 4–6:

1 lb/500 g cooking apples	juice and grated rind of
½ lb/250 g sultanas and currants	1 lemon
½ lb/250 g caster sugar	short pastry (for recipe see
½ teaspoon of cinnamon	page 214)

Peel and core the apples and cut in pieces, then add the sultanas and currants and the sugar mixed with cinnamon. Mix them all in a bowl and add the juice and rind of the lemon. Fill a 2 pint/ 125 cl pie dish with the fruit and cover with short pastry. Brush over with milk and sprinkle sugar on top.

Bake for three-quarters of an hour in the oven at 220°C/425°F or gas mark 7.

Serve with cream or vanilla sauce (for recipe see page 209).

♛ TREACLE TART

Pre-heat oven to 180°C/350°F or gas mark 4
To serve 6:

8 ozs/250 g plain flour	¼ pint/15 cl water
5 ozs/150 g butter	½ lb/250 g golden syrup
1 oz/30 g lard	¼ lb/125 g fresh breadcrumbs
½ oz/15 g caster sugar	1 tablespoon of melted butter.
1 egg	

Make the pastry by rubbing the flour with the butter and lard in a bowl until crumbly, add the sugar and the lightly beaten egg, and water. It should be fairly stiff. Cover with a cloth and allow to stand in a cold place for half an hour before use. Roll out the pastry to a thickness of a quarter of an inch, and then line a fairly deep baking sheet, approximately ten inches by eight inches.

Put the syrup into the pastry and sprinkle the breadcrumbs on top. Let the tart stand for half an hour. Spread the melted butter on top before placing it in the oven. Bake for twenty minutes in the oven at 180°C/350°F or gas mark 4.

Serve with cream.

BREAD AND BUTTER PUDDING 👑

Pre-heat oven to 170°C/325°F or gas mark 3
To serve 6–8:

1 white loaf, medium size	*1 pint/60 cl milk*
¼ lb/125 g currants	*2 tablespoons of caster sugar*
¼ lb/125 g sultanas	*1 tablespoon of golden syrup*
butter	*pinch of salt*
1 egg, beaten	

Cut loaf into fairly thin slices and remove crust. Rinse the currants and sultanas in hot water to soften. Butter the slices of bread and cut in triangles. Place the bread in a 2 pint/125 cl soufflé dish, layer upon layer, with two tablespoons of dried fruit between the layers. Finish with a layer of bread and butter. Beat the egg, milk, sugar, syrup and salt well together and pour over the bread and butter. Let it soak in for half an hour.

Bake in the oven at 170°C/325°F or gas mark 3 for one hour until the bread comes up, delicately browned on top, like a soufflé.

SUMMER PUDDING 👑

To serve 6–8:

2 lbs/1 kg redcurrants	*sugar to taste*
2 lbs/1 kg raspberries	*1 white loaf, medium size*

I used to make this dish for Lord Rothermere, whom I worked for after leaving Clarence House. He liked it served on a hot day after a tennis party.

Take half the amount of each fruit and stew in a little water with sugar to taste until soft. Meanwhile, line a 2 pint/125 cl pudding basin with bread slices, about a quarter of an inch thick. Great care must be taken to leave no gaps or the pudding will fall apart. It is really better to double-line the basin, placing the second layer over the seams. Pour the cooked fruit and juice into the pudding and cover the top with a double layer of sliced bread. Put a large plate or saucer over the top so that it is pressing on the bread, and leave overnight with a 1 lb/500 g weight on top.

Sieve the remaining fruit, add caster sugar to taste and mix into a thick purée. Keep cold.

Turn the pudding out and pour the purée on top.

Serve with plain cream or softened ice-cream.

♛ SWEDISH APPLE SPONGE

Pre-heat oven to 180°C/350°F or gas mark 4
To serve 6:

4 ozs/125 g butter	*4 ozs/125 g plain flour*
4 ozs/125 g sugar	*1 teaspoon of baking powder*
2 eggs	*2 or 3 cooking apples*

This is how we bake our sponge puddings in Sweden. It is a very simple process with a particularly pleasant result.

Cream the butter and sugar together, add the eggs, flour and baking powder and put in a 10 inch/25 cm sandwich tin. Peel and cut apples in slices and place them on top of the sponge mixture. Sprinkle with sugar and bake in the oven at 180°C/350°F or gas mark 4, for forty-five minutes or until the sponge shrinks slightly from the sides of the tin.

Serve with vanilla sauce (for recipe see page 209).

♛ BAKED ALASKA

To serve 6–8:

4 egg whites	*1 large block of vanilla*
8 ozs/250 g caster sugar	* ice-cream*

Beat egg whites very stiff indeed. Fold in the sugar and beat for a further two minutes. Take the ice-cream straight from the refrigerator, place in an ovenproof dish and cover or pipe with the meringue mixture. Put the platter on another tin containing crushed ice and put in a very hot oven for two or three minutes so that the meringue is just topped with a golden colour.

Serve immediately with fresh fruit such as raspberries or strawberries. The essence of baked Alaska is that it must be cooked and served at a cracking pace.

BROWN BREAD CREAM WITH BLACKCURRANT SAUCE 👑

To serve 4:

¼ pint/15 cl milk	vanilla flavouring, to taste,
¼ pint/15 cl double cream	or a little sherry
2 egg yolks	½ oz/15 g powdered gelatine
3 tablespoons of dry brown	10 ozs/300 g sugar
breadcrumbs	1 lb/500 g fresh blackcurrants

Put the milk, cream and egg yolks in a saucepan and whisk over a gentle heat until mixture reaches the consistency of a thin custard. Add most of the breadcrumbs, the flavouring and the dissolved gelatine and pour into a mould to set. Brown a few breadcrumbs with sugar in the oven and garnish the mould with them.

To make the sauce, pick and rinse the blackcurrants, put through a sieve and mix with the sugar. Serve separately.

CREAM CITRON 👑

To serve 10:

3 or 4 lemons	20 egg yolks
4–6 ozs/125–175 g loaf sugar	macaroons, to decorate
¾ pint/40 cl white wine	

Squeeze the juice of the lemons into a saucepan. Rub the lemon rinds hard with the loaf sugar so that the sugar absorbs the flavour and some particles of the rind, and then put into the saucepan. Add more sugar to taste. Add the wine and the yolks of eggs (yes, twenty). Whisk over a low heat until thickened, but do not boil.

When thick, remove from the heat and whisk until cold. Pour into individual glasses to set. Put little macaroons on top. Save the egg whites for meringue.

CRÈME À LA REINE

To serve 6:

3 egg yolks	*½ oz/15 g gelatine*
¼ pint/15 cl milk	*½ pint/30 cl double cream*
sugar, to taste	*3 oz/75 g bar of nougat*
vanilla essence	

Put the egg yolks and milk in a saucepan and whisk over a low heat to thicken. Do not boil. Add some sugar to taste, the vanilla essence and dissolved gelatine. Remove from heat and whisk until cold. When nearly set, whisk the cream to a froth and add to the mixture. Pour into a glass bowl to set.

When set, sprinkle chopped nougat over and serve with hot butterscotch sauce (for recipe see page 210).

PRUNE PUDDING

Pre-heat oven to 180°C/350°F or gas mark 4
To serve 6:

6 eggs, separated	*vanilla essence, to taste*
½ lb/250 g caster sugar	*1 lb/250 g tinned or soaked*
½ pint/30 cl double cream	*prunes*
2 tablespoons of plain flour	*whipping cream*
¼ lb/125 g butter	*1 oz/30 g chopped almonds*
1 lemon	

Mix egg yolks and sugar together for fifteen minutes (five minutes if using an electric beater). Add cream, flour and softened butter and whisk over heat until the mixture thickens. Move saucepan from heat and continue whisking until the mixture cools. Add juice of lemon, most of the grated rind and vanilla essence. Then add the beaten egg whites. Lay the prunes (stoned) and a little grated lemon rind on the bottom of a greased ovenproof dish, pour mixture on top and bake in the oven at 180°C/350°F or gas mark 4 for one hour. Turn the pudding out on to a dish so that the prunes are uppermost. Serve with whipped cream and sprinkle chopped almonds on top. This pudding can be eaten hot or cold.

BOMBE GLACÉE 👑

To serve 6:

> 4 egg yolks
> 2 tablespoons of sugar
> ½ pint/30 cl milk
>
> ½ pint/30 cl double cream
> vanilla essence, to taste

Put the egg yolks in a saucepan together with the sugar. Boil the milk separately and add it to the egg mixture, gradually, whisking all the time. Keep over a low heat but do not let the mixture boil. Whisk until it thickens like a custard. Remove from heat and whisk until cold. Add vanilla essence to taste. Whisk cream and add to the mixture, pour into an ice tray or bombe mould and put into the freezing compartment of the refrigerator until set.

CRÈME MARRON 👑

To serve 6–8:

> 1 lb/500 g chestnuts, or tinned
>   chestnut purée
> 2 ozs/60 g cold butter
> 4 ozs/125 g caster sugar
> 1 pint/60 cl double cream,
>   whipped
>
> ½ pint/30 cl vanilla ice-cream
>   (optional)
> a couple of drops of vanilla
>   essence or maraschino to
>   taste
> 1 orange

Peel the chestnuts and boil in ¼ pint/15 cl of water until dry and then sieve. Alternatively, you may used tinned chestnut purée. Add the butter and sugar and mix to a smooth cream. Put the mixture in a forcing bag and pipe with a medium fluted nozzle round and round the border of a silver dish, forming folds. Then whip the cream and mix with the vanilla ice-cream. Add the vanilla essence or maraschino, sweeten if necessary. Pile into the centre of the dish. If dispensing with the ice-cream, merely mix the flavouring into the whipped cream. Decorate with peeled and sweetened orange slices.

WHIPPED GOOSEBERRY SNOW

To serve 6–8:

1 packet lime jelly	4 egg whites
1 × 14 oz/450 g tin gooseberries	½ pint/30 cl whipped cream
	white grapes, to decorate

Dissolve the lime jelly in ½ pint/30 cl of hot water. Sieve the goose-berries, adding the juice, and mix in with the jelly. Add the beaten egg whites and allow to cool a little. While cooling, whip until frothy. Put into individual glasses. When set, pipe on the whipped cream and decorate with halved white grapes.

A popular dish in the nursery.

BAKED COMICE PEARS

Pre-heat oven to 220°C/425°F or gas mark 7
To serve 6:

6 comice pears	2 ozs/60 g caster sugar
juice of 1 lemon	vanilla ice-cream
3 bananas	

Peel the pears, leaving the stalks intact. Rub the surface of the pears with half the lemon juice, then remove cores from the bottom. Mash the bananas with remaining lemon juice and use to stuff the pears. Scratch the pears vertically with a fork. Sprinkle with sugar, place on a baking sheet and put in the oven pre-heated to 220°C/425°F or gas mark 7, for fifteen minutes. Baste once with their own juice to get a glazed effect. Serve hot, round a mound of cold vanilla ice-cream.

GOOD FRUIT SALAD 👑

To serve 8–10:

8 oranges   *3 bananas*
juice of 1 lemon   *1 bunch of grapes*
1 grapefruit   *sugar to taste*
2 or 3 mandarins or tangerines   *maraschino cherries*
2 pears   *pistachio nuts*
2 dessert apples

I am always surprised at the different ways in which people make fruit salad. The real point about fruit salad is that every drop of juice from the fruit should be saved and used. This means peeling the fruit over a bowl so that not a single drop is wasted. In one establishment where I once worked, the staff were in the habit of throwing away the fruit juice and dressing the salad with a watery sugar syrup.

Squeeze the juice of four oranges and add to the lemon juice in a large bowl. As you cut up the fruit, leave it in the juice to prevent browning.

Peel the other four oranges and free the segments from the skin. Do the same with the grapefruit and mandarins. Peel and core pears, cut into delicate wedges. Peel apples, cut in fairly thick sections and cut across. Pare the bananas into rings. Skin and pip the grapes, leaving as whole as possible. Sprinkle sugar over the fruit and toss.

Decorate with a few maraschino cherries and some pistachio nuts, blanched and skinned.

👑 RASPBERRY FOOL WITH ORANGE CURAÇAO

To serve 6:

2 lbs/1 kg raspberries, fresh or frozen	*2 tablespoons of orange Curaçao*
sugar to taste	*¾ pint/40 cl double cream*
	pistachio nuts, to decorate

Sieve the raspberries, add the sugar and orange Curaçao. If using frozen raspberries, defrost but do not add extra sugar. Whip the cream until stiff and mix in with the raspberries. Put in individual glasses or fill tartlets. Decorate with pistachio nuts. Serve within one hour.

👑 APRICOT MERINGUE

To serve 6:

1 lb/500 g dried apricots	*12 tablespoons of sugar*
¾ lb/350 g sugar (for the apricots)	*whipped cream*
6 egg whites (1 egg white makes two large meringues or three small ones)	*1 teaspoon of orange Curaçao (optional)*

Soak the apricots overnight. Cover with water, bring to the boil and simmer until cooked. Sieve with a nylon sieve, put back in saucepan, add sugar and mash with a fork. Never add sugar in the cooking stage as most of it is wasted when the fruit is sieved. Put the apricots in a glass dish to cool, adding more sugar if required.

Make the meringues overnight according to the following method. First, see that all the utensils, bowl, beaters, etc., are scrupulously clean and free from any trace of grease. Whip the egg whites until the mixture is stiff enough to enable you to turn the bowl upside down without disaster, then fold in the sugar. Spoon the mixture onto a greased and floured baking tray and put in a very, very low oven overnight. The meringues should turn a delicate pink in colour, never brown which means they have been cooked at too high a temperature. Alternatively, you can put the mixture into the oven set at 130 °C/250 °F or gas mark ½, for one to three hours, or until the meringues are firm and dry to the touch. When the meringues have dried out, turn them over so that they dry out in the middle.

Whip up the cream and orange Curaçao (optional) and stick the meringues together round the dish containing the apricot purée.

There can be no hitch with this dish; the apricots can be puréed the day before and the meringues ready for you on the morning of the day they are needed. Keep in a cool larder.

MUSCAT GRAPES EN GELÉE 👑

To serve 6–8:

> 1 packet of orange jelly
> ½ pint/30 cl boiling water
> ½ pint/30 cl white wine
> 1 lb/500 g Muscat grapes
>
> 2 egg whites
> whipped cream
> 1 orange
> pistachio nuts

Dissolve the jelly in the hot water, add the wine and cool. Skin and stone the grapes and put them in individual glasses, leaving aside a few for decoration. When the jelly is nearly set, whip it to a froth, add two beaten egg whites and fill the glasses. Leave to set and decorate with piped whipped cream, the orange cut in sections, and the rest of the grapes. Sprinkle pistachio nuts on top.

SWEET PANCAKES 👑

To make about 12 pancakes:

> 3 eggs
> 4 ozs/125 g plain flour
> ½ pint/30 cl milk
> ¼ pint/15 cl cold water
>
> ½ tablespoon of caster sugar
> pinch of salt
> ¼ pint/15 cl double cream
> unsalted butter

Beat the eggs with the water. Sift the flour, sugar and salt and add to the beaten egg. Mix well to a smooth paste. Then add the milk and cream. Allow the mixture to stand for half an hour.

Put a teaspoon of unsalted butter in a crêpe pan and melt until frothing. Add a ladle full of batter to coat crêpe pan and cook for two minutes until golden-brown on the bottom. Then turn pancake over and cook until golden-brown on reverse side. Fill with a soufflé mixture or ice-cream and serve immediately.

♔ CRÈME À LA DUCHESSE

To serve 6:

½ pint/30 cl milk	a few drops of vanilla or
½ pint/30 cl double cream	Curaçao
6 eggs, separated	almond flakes or pistachio
12 tablespoons of caster sugar	nuts, to decorate
grated rind of 1 orange and	
1 lemon	

Bring the milk and the cream to the boil and lower heat. Whisk the egg whites to a stiff froth. Add the sugar, a little at a time, and then the orange and lemon rind. Using a tablespoon, drop balls of the egg mixture into the simmering milk. The meringues will puff up to three times their original size and should be turned briefly during cooking. When set, remove carefully with a draining spoon and put into a sieve to drain thoroughly.

Put four yolks of eggs into another saucepan and add a little vanilla or Curaçao to taste. Whisk well and add the hot milk, whisking all the time over a low heat. Do not boil. Continue whisking until thickened. Remove from heat and carry on whisking until cold. Pour into a glass dish and then float the meringue balls on top.

Sprinkle with toasted almond flakes or chopped pistachio nuts.

Serve cold with strawberry sauce (for recipe see page 209).

CRÊPES SUZETTE À LA SUÉDOISE 👑

To make 12 crêpes:

3 eggs
¼ pint/15 cl water
1 teaspoon of sugar
½ teaspoon of salt

3 ozs/90 g plain flour
¼ pint/15 cl double cream
2 tablespoons of sunflower oil

For the sauce:
½ pint/30 cl double cream
2 tablespoons of caster sugar
rind and juice of 1 orange
a few drops of vanilla

2 tablespoons of orange
    Curaçao
lemon juice

Beat the eggs with water, add the sugar, salt and flour. Mix until very smooth, add the cream and mix well. Let the mixture rest for thirty minutes.

To cook the crêpes, have the pan greased with just enough oil so that the batter will not stick. Drop one tablespoon of the batter at a time into the heated pan and tip so that the mixture spreads as thinly as possible. Cook until golden-brown on each side. Repeat the process until all the batter is used up, fold the pancakes in quarters and stack one on top of another in a warm but not hot oven.

To make the sauce, bring cream and sugar to the boil, add orange juice, rind and vanilla essence. Boil for two minutes and then add the Curaçao slowly.

Serve pancakes by squeezing a little lemon juice over them, then sprinkle a little caster sugar on top and put under the grill for a minute to brown.

Serve the hot sauce separately.

♛ MELON SURPRISE

To serve 4:

1 large melon	*3 bananas*
1 lb/500 g fresh or frozen	*juice of ½ lemon*
strawberries	*crushed ice*
¼ lb/125 g sugar	*cream*

Cut the top off the melon, remove seeds, scoop out the fruit and cut into cubes. Sieve the strawberries and blend into the melon cubes, cut bananas into slices and toss in lemon juice. Add sugar to taste. Mix all together and fill the melon shell with the mixture.
Replace the lid and refrigerate until very cold.
Serve on crushed ice, with cream.

♛ PEACH MERINGUE WITH VANILLA CREAM

Pre-heat oven to 170 °C/325 °F or gas mark 3
To serve 6:

6 small round sponge cakes	*6 tablespoons of caster sugar*
1 tin of California peaches	*1 oz/30 g icing sugar*
1 tablespoon of Grand Marnier	*1 pint/60 cl vanilla sauce (for*
3 tablespoons of double cream	*recipe see page 209)*
4 egg whites	

Place the sponge cakes on a dish and put half a peach on each cake. Mix the Grand Marnier with the cream and spread on the cakes. Whip egg whites into a stiff froth, add sugar and pipe over the dish. Place in the oven pre-heated to 170 °C/315 °F or gas mark 3 until the meringue turns a very light brown.
Sprinkle with icing sugar and serve with vanilla sauce.

POIRES MARASCHINO AUX ANANAS 👑

To serve 6:

1 pint/60 cl water
6 ozs/175 g caster sugar
juice of 1 lemon
6 large comice pears
2 slices of lemon

1 × 14 oz/450 g tin of
  pineapple rings or
  1 small pineapple
6 fl ozs/20 cl maraschino
angelica, to decorate

Boil the water, sugar and lemon juice together to make a syrup. Peel pears and remove cores carefully leaving the pears intact. Drop the pears into the boiling syrup with the lemon slices. Boil for five minutes, remove from heat and let them cool in the syrup.

If using fresh pineapple, cut the slices half an inch thick and remove the core. Cut off skin with a corrugated cutting ring. Drop the pineapple rings in the syrup with the pears and leave until cold. Pour over ¼ pint/15 cl of maraschino.

Stand the pears upright on a flat crystal dish and place the pineapple rings on top of the pears like hats. Cut the stalk from the angelica and fix on top of each pear, so that it shows through the pineapple ring.

Serve with whipped cream flavoured with the rest of the maraschino.

GLACÉ SOUFFLÉ GRAND MARNIER 👑

To serve 6–8:

6 ozs/175 g sugar
¼ pint/15 cl water
8 egg yolks
¼ pint/15 cl Grand Marnier

½ teaspoon of vanilla essence
1¼ pints/75 cl double cream
oil

When cooking for the Queen Mother at Clarence House, I soon discovered that she was very appreciative of good home-made ice-cream. I was very happy indeed when I received kind messages for my efforts and I was soon spurred on to try new variations. This is a light and charming dish for a summer's day.

Boil the sugar and water together for one minute and then remove from heat. Whisk and allow to cool a little. Add the egg yolks, one at a time, whisking continuously over a gentle heat. Do not boil. Once the mixture is very thick, remove from heat and whisk until cold. When cold, add the Grand Marnier and the vanilla essence. Whip the cream and stir into the egg mixture. Line a soufflé dish with greaseproof paper brushed with oil and fill the dish with the parfait mixture.

Freeze for four to five hours in a freezer or the freezing compartment of a refrigerator. Remove fifteen minutes before serving. Turn out on a dish, remove the paper and serve with sieved fresh strawberry sauce (for recipe see page 209) and biscuits.

👑 GINGER SPONGE CAKE

Pre-heat oven to 190 °C/375 °F or gas mark 5
To make 1 × two-layer 8-inch/20-cm cake:

2 ozs/60 g butter	6 ozs/175 g self-raising flour
4 ozs/125 g sugar	1 teaspoon of cinnamon
2½ ozs/75 g golden syrup	1 teaspoon of ground ginger
2½ ozs/75 g black treacle	¼ teaspoon of ground cloves
¼ pint/15 cl milk	½ teaspoon of bicarbonate of
1 egg, well beaten	soda

For the filling:
2 dessertspoons of butter	
½ lb/250 g icing sugar	a few drops of hot water and vanilla essence, mixed

Beat butter and sugar to a cream, add the syrup, treacle, milk and egg. Sieve the flour, cinnamon, ginger, cloves and bicarbonate of soda into the mixture. Divide the mixture into two sandwich tins lined with greased paper. Bake in the oven at 190 °C/375 °F or gas mark 5 for twenty minutes, or until a skewer comes out clean. Allow to cool.

To make the filling, mix together all the ingredients and spread between the sandwich halves.

CURRANT CAKE ♔

Pre-heat oven to 140 °C/275 °F or gas mark 1
To make 1 × 9-inch/22-cm cake:

$\frac{3}{4}$ lb/350 g self-raising flour
$\frac{1}{2}$ lb/250 g butter
$\frac{1}{2}$ lb/250 g sugar
1$\frac{1}{4}$ lbs/600 g currants, cleaned
   and dried

$\frac{1}{4}$ lb/125 g almonds, blanched
   and finely chopped
2 tablespoons of milk
3 eggs, beaten
1 tablespoon of brandy

Put the flour in a bowl and rub the butter into the flour. Mix in the sugar, currants and the almonds. Mix milk with the beaten eggs. Add the brandy and mix with all the other ingredients, to form a firm dough. Roll out on a floured board until three-quarters of an inch thick. Bake in the oven at 140 °C/275 °F or gas mark 1 for two hours.

MADEIRA CAKE ♔

Pre-heat oven to 180 °C/350 °F or gas mark 4
To make 1 × 10-inch/25-cm cake

6$\frac{1}{2}$ ozs/185 g butter
6$\frac{1}{2}$ ozs/185 g sugar
6 eggs
12 ozs/350 g plain flour

$\frac{1}{4}$ pint/15 cl single cream
2 teaspoons of baking powder
candied peel

Cream the butter and the sugar together, whisk in the eggs one by one with a tablespoon of flour for each egg. Add the cream and mix in the baking powder, sieved, with the remaining flour.

Put the mixture in a greased and floured baking tin, place some slices of candied peel on top of the mixture. Bake in the oven at 180 °C/350 °F or gas mark 4 for one hour and twenty minutes.

👑 SPONGE SANDWICH CAKE

Pre-heat oven to 220 °C/425 °F or gas mark 7
To make 1 × two-layer 8-inch/20-cm cake:

4 *eggs*	2 *teaspoons of baking powder*
½ *lb/250 g caster sugar*	¼ *pint/15 cl whipped cream*
3 *ozs/90 g plain flour*	*jam*
2 *ozs/60 g potato or cornflour*	*icing sugar*

Break the eggs into a bowl, whisk lightly and add the sugar. Whisk for twenty minutes (ten minutes if you are using an electric whisk). Sieve the flour and potato or cornflour with the baking powder and add to the mixture. Mix well and pour into two buttered and floured sandwich tins. Bake on the middle shelf of the oven at 220 °C/425 °F or gas mark 7 for twenty-five minutes.

When cool, sandwich the cakes together with the cream and jam, and dust the top with sieved icing sugar.

👑 CHOCOLATE AND COFFEE CAKE

Pre-heat oven to 170 °C/325 °F or gas mark 3
To make 1 × 8-inch/20-cm cake:

8 *ozs/250 g butter*	6 *ozs/175 g cooking chocolate*
8 *ozs/250 g caster sugar*	8 *ozs/250 g plain flour*
5 *eggs, separated*	2 *teaspoons of baking powder*
1 *tablespoon of orange*	2 *ozs/60 g sweet ground*
marmalade	*almonds*

For the filling:

4 *ozs/125 g butter*	2 *tablespoons of coffee*
8 *ozs/250 g icing sugar*	*essence, or instant coffee*
	mixed with 2 tablespoons of
	warm water

This was my most popular cake with the Royal Family, made to my own recipe. Everyone seemed to like it and it went everywhere. By special request I have sent it off to Windsor, Balmoral and Sandringham, and the Queen Mother would request it for her birthday.

Beat butter and sugar to a light cream. Add egg yolks and marmalade. Stir in the melted chocolate. Add flour, baking powder and almonds. Whip egg whites until stiff and fold in lightly. Pour into a greased cake tin and bake in the oven at 170°C/325°F or gas mark 3 for one hour and fifteen minutes. When cool, cut in half.

To make the filling, cream together all the ingredients and warm slightly before spreading on the sandwich halves and the top of the cake.

CHILDREN'S BIRTHDAY CAKE ♔

Pre-heat oven to 200°C/400°F or gas mark 6
To make 1 × 9-inch/22-cm cake:

8 eggs	*4 ozs/125 g cornflour*
1 lb/500 g caster sugar	*redcurrant jelly*
4 teaspoons of baking powder	*½ pint/30 cl whipped cream*
6 ozs/175 g plain flour	

For the icing:
20 ozs/600 g icing sugar	*1 egg white*
1 dessertspoon of water	*colouring, if desired*

Break the eggs into a bowl, add the sugar and mix for fifteen to twenty minutes (ten minutes if you are using an electric whisk). Add the baking powder to the flour and sieve into the mixture. Mix well and fill a large cake tin lined with greased paper, and bake in the oven at 200°C/400°F or gas mark 6 for three-quarters of an hour. Remove from oven and cool on a wire tray. When cold, cut the cake in three layers. Spread one layer with redcurrant jelly and the other with cream.

To make the icing, mix together all the ingredients until thick and smooth. Beat until the mixture holds a peak. Cover the cake with the mixture, using a palette knife dipped frequently in boiling water and shaken dry.

♔ GINGERBREAD MEN

Pre-heat oven to 190°C/375°F or gas mark 5

2 ozs/60 g brown sugar
2 ozs/60 g butter
8 ozs/225 g plain flour
1 level teaspoon mixed spice
1 oz/25 g ground ginger
juice of ½ lemon

1 level teaspoon of bicarbonate
  of soda
1 tablespoon of tepid water
1 beaten egg
currants to decorate

Melt sugar and butter in a pan. Pour into a bowl and add two tablespoons of flour, the spices and lemon juice. Stir well. Dissolve the bicarbonate of soda in the tepid water, add to the mixture and continue stirring, gradually adding the rest of the flour. When thoroughly mixed, turn out on to a well-floured board. Shape a small ball for the head, flatten it and place on a greased baking tin, roll an oblong for the body and shape arms and legs. Join these together with a little of the beaten egg and place currants for eyes and buttons, making about six to eight men. Cook in moderate oven for about fifteen minutes. Cool and remove carefully to a wire tray.

♔ CHEESE CAKES

Pre-heat oven to 180°C/350°F or gas mark 4
To make 8–10 cheese cakes:

¼ lb/125 g Cheshire cheese,
  finely grated
¼ lb/125 g Parmesan cheese,
  grated
¼ lb/125 g plain flour

salt and pinch of cayenne
  pepper
2 egg yolks
1 egg white
cream cheese

Catering for savoury tastes at a children's party, you will find these cheese cakes popular. Good for grown-ups too.

Mix together the Cheshire cheese, Parmesan cheese, flour, salt, pepper and the egg yolks. Roll out and cut into round cakes a quarter of an inch thick with a pastry cutter. Brush with the egg white mixed with a little water. Bake in the oven at 180°C/350°F or gas mark 4, until golden-brown. When cold, make sandwiches of the cakes filled with cream cheese.

FUDGE TOFFEE 👑

To make 1 lb/500 g of toffee:

2 ozs/60 g butter	*¼ pint/15 cl condensed milk*
1 lb/500 g demerara sugar	*vanilla flavouring*

Some extra special fudge toffee is always popular for handing round at a children's party. It might also be an occasion for the young host or hostess to make their first attempt at cooking.

Melt the butter in a saucepan over a low heat, add the sugar and bring to the boil, stirring all the time. Then add the condensed milk mixed with 2 tablespoons of water. Stir and simmer for about twenty-five minutes. Remove from the heat and add a few drops of vanilla. Grease a baking sheet with butter and pour on the toffee to cool. Before it cools completely, mark with a knife into squares which can be separated when cold.

CHILEAN BUNS 👑

Pre-heat oven to 220°C/425°F or gas mark 7
To make 8 small buns:

6 ozs/175 g plain flour	*½ teaspoon of salt*
1 tablespoon of butter	*¼ pint/15 cl milk*
1 teaspoon of baking powder	*½ teaspoon of ground cinnamon*

Here are some light buns suitable for a children's tea. I call them Chilean buns because I was given the recipe by the Chilean Embassy after a member of the Royal Family had enjoyed them there for tea.

Mix all the ingredients together into a hard dough and roll into a long sausage. Cut into small bun shapes, place on a greased baking sheet and cross them with the back of a knife. Place in the oven which has been pre-heated to 220 °C/425 °F or gas mark 7, for five to ten minutes.

👑 APPLE MERINGUE SPONGE

Pre-heat oven to 230 °C/450 °F or gas mark 8
To make 1 × two-layer 8-inch/20-cm cake:

For the sponge:
4 eggs
equal weight of the eggs in
   caster sugar

half the weight of the eggs in
   plain flour
1 teaspoon of baking powder

For the filling:
4 cooking apples
sugar to taste
juice of $\frac{1}{2}$ lemon

$\frac{1}{4}$ pint/15 cl single cream
$\frac{1}{2}$ teaspoon of vanilla essence

For the meringue:
3 egg whites
3 tablespoons of caster sugar

grated rind of $\frac{1}{2}$ lemon

This is an apple meringue sponge with a difference. The difference, I think, lies mainly in the lightness of the sponge and the cream filling which flavours the cake if left to soak overnight.

To make the sponge, whip the whole eggs and sugar together for twenty-five minutes with a whisk (ten minutes if you are using an electric whisk). Mix the flour and baking powder together and sieve, mix with the sugar and eggs. Put into two flat, greased tins and bake in the oven at 220 °C/425 °F or gas mark 7 for twenty minutes. Remove and turn out, and when cold place in a flat ovenproof dish.

Peel and core the apples, cut into thin slices and poach with a little sugar and squeeze of lemon until tender. Drain. Mix cream with vanilla essence and spread over each cake. Arrange slices of apple on top of one of the cakes and place the other on top as a lid. Arrange the rest of the apple on top and leave to soak into the sponge for a few hours.

Whip up the egg whites and then fold in the sugar and the

lemon rind. Pile it up on top of the apple and place in a very hot oven (230°C/450°F or gas mark 8) for four or five minutes or until tips of peaks are golden-brown. Serve immediately.

ALMOND BISCUITS 👑

Pre-heat oven to 220°C/425°F or gas mark 7
To serve 6:

$\frac{1}{2}$ *lb/250 g unblanched almonds*	*butter*
2 egg whites	*plain flour*
4 tablespoons of caster sugar	

Chop the almonds roughly. Whip whites of egg with the sugar for two or three minutes and add the almonds.

Spread on a well-buttered and floured tin and bake in the oven at 220°C/425°F or gas mark 7 for five to seven minutes or until light brown. When ready, remove, cool a little and cut while still warm into sections four inches long and two inches wide. Return to the oven to heat and then quickly remove the biscuits with a knife. Bend them, while still warm, over a rolling pin. Leave to cool and become crispy.

MRS MCKEE'S CHRISTMAS CAKE 👑

Pre-heat oven to 150°C/300°F or gas mark 2
To make 1 × 12-inch/30-cm cake:

1 lb/500 g butter	*1 lb/500 g sultanas*
1 lb/500 g caster sugar	$\frac{1}{2}$ *lb/250 g stoned raisins*
2 tablespoons of orange	$\frac{1}{4}$ *lb/125 g candied peel*
marmalade	$\frac{1}{2}$ *teaspoon of nutmeg*
1 tablespoon of black treacle	*pinch of salt*
10 eggs, separated	*1 teaspoon of vanilla essence*
$1\frac{1}{2}$ *lbs/750 g plain flour*	$\frac{1}{2}$ *teaspoon of almond essence*
1 lb/500 g currants	*2 tablespoons of rum*

If you like dark, stodgy Christmas cake, this recipe is not for you. This cake is lighter in appearance and texture than the traditional kind but will keep equally well for a year or more. It is the cake that the Royal Family enjoyed. I would bake it on the 13th of November when all the royal puddings were prepared, keep it and send it off to Sandringham for Christmas Day.

Stir butter and sugar together until creamy. Add marmalade and treacle. Drop in the egg yolks one at a time and a tablespoon of flour to each yolk, stirring continuously. Mix all the fruit in with the flour. Add nutmeg and pinch of salt, the essences and the rum. Beat the egg whites to a stiff snow and fold in.

Line a tin with paper, grease it well, fill it with the mixture and bake in the oven at 150°C/300°F or gas mark 2 for two to three hours.

♔ PINEAPPLE CAKE

Pre-heat oven to 180°C/350°F or gas mark 4
To make 1 × 9-inch/22-cm cake:

1 fresh pineapple	*6 ozs/175 g plain flour*
8 ozs/250 g sugar	*2 ozs/60 g cornflour*
8 ozs/250 g butter	*1 heaped teaspoon of baking*
3 eggs	*powder*

Pulp the fresh pineapple by grating or putting in a food processor. Add just a little of the sugar to taste. Put in a greased ovenproof dish and keep warm. Cream together the butter, sugar, eggs, flour, cornflour and baking powder. Put the cake mixture on top of the pineapple pulp and bake in the oven at 180°C/350°F or gas mark 4 for three-quarters of an hour. Loosen carefully. Turn out and serve with cream.

Special Occasions

═══════

IN THIS COUNTRY MOST OF THE OCCASIONS THAT PEOPLE RATE AS special seem to have some connection with sport. This is quite logical, of course, since healthy exercise produces healthy appetites. There may, too, be feelings of guilt that one should not really be indulging oneself unless a lot of hard work has been put in beforehand. I can't help thinking, for instance, that the thunderous exercise that takes place in the hunting season, also has something to do with the wild abandon that goes on at some hunt balls and horse show festivities. One cannot exactly say that the tennis parties in English country gardens are the scene of mad revels, but the China tea and cucumber sandwiches doubtless taste all the better for a bit of activity.

At any rate, to my mind, all these sporting occasions compare quite favourably with the sterility of so many London cocktail parties, where the chief purpose seems to be to deaden palate, appetite and senses.

I have chosen the recipes in this chapter to go with a particular type of sport, but they will, of course, go equally well with any number of different activities.

THE SHOOTING LUNCH

lobster salad   *curried eggs*

cold minced veal cutlets
roast lamb cutlets in aspic with glazed onions

potato salad   *tomato and pepper salad*

apple turnovers
cheese selection

👑 LOBSTER SALAD

To serve 4:

1 large cooked lobster
¼ pint/15 cl double cream
½ pint/30 cl mayonnaise
juice of ½ lemon

salt and cayenne pepper to
   taste
cucumber slices and chopped
   fresh parsley, to garnish

Cut the lobster in half lengthways and remove the meat. Save the red coral part of the lobster and the green creamy bit inside. Break the claws and remove the meat. Cut the lobster meat into large pieces. Sieve the red coral and keep for decoration. Mix in the greenish cream with the lobster meat in a bowl. Whip the cream to a froth and add to the mayonnaise, together with the lemon juice, salt and cayenne pepper. Mix half of the mayonnaise mixture with the lobster. Put the lobster in a dish on a bed of lettuce and cover with the rest of the mayonnaise. Garnish with the sieved red coral in a pattern on top and slices of unpeeled cucumber. Sprinkle chopped parsley over the cucumber.

👑 CURRIED EGGS

To make up to 12 eggs:

1 large onion
1 apple
2 ozs/60 g butter
2 tablespoons of plain flour
2 tablespoons of curry powder
1 tablespoon of Escoffier
   chutney
1 tablespoon of Worcestershire
   sauce

dash of paprika
1 pint/60 cl hot chicken stock
1 tablespoon of sultanas
1 tablespoon of grated coconut
3 fl ozs/8 cl double cream
juice of ½ lemon
2 hard-boiled eggs per person
mustard and cress
¼ lb/125 g Patna rice

Peel and chop the onion, core and chop the apple. Melt the butter in a saucepan, add the onion and braise gently to a golden colour. Add the flour and curry powder and stir well. Add the apple, chutney, Worcestershire sauce and paprika. Pour in the hot stock and mix well. Lastly, add the sultanas and coconut and bring to the boil. Cook for twenty minutes. Strain and add the cream and the lemon juice. Cover the eggs with the sauce.

Allow to cool and garnish with mustard and cress. Boil rice in salted water and serve with the curried eggs.

COLD MINCED VEAL CUTLETS ♔

To serve 6–8:

1 lb/500 g minced veal	*salt and pepper to taste*
1 lb/500 g bread panade (for	*½ pint/30 cl creamy milk*
* recipe see page 213)*	*1 teaspoon of sugar*
1 egg	*butter*

Mix the veal and bread panade in a bowl. Stir in the egg and the seasoning. Add the milk gradually and stir for five or ten minutes. Add the sugar and mix well. Shape into half-inch thick cutlets and fry in butter until golden-brown on both sides. When fried put in a baking tin with a few knobs of butter and place in a hot oven for ten minutes.

Allow to cool.

ROAST LAMB CUTLETS IN ASPIC WITH GLAZED ONIONS ♔

Pre-heat oven to 220 °C/425 °F or gas mark 7
To serve 6–8:

3 lbs/1.5 kg best end of neck of	*½ pint/30 cl good stock*
* lamb*	*1 teaspoon of Bovril*
salt and pepper	*dash of Worcestershire sauce*
1 clove of garlic, sliced	*1 pint/60 cl aspic*

For the glazed onions:
12 button onions	*a knob of butter*
1 tablespoon of tomato purée	*1 teaspoon of sugar*

See that the backbone is chined and trim off unwanted fat. Trim the end of the bones of meat and fat, up to about an inch. Rub in some salt and pepper and insert small pieces of garlic. Roast in the oven at 220°C/425°F or gas mark 7 for one hour, basting frequently. When cooked, place the meat on a dish and remove the garlic. Drain off all the fat from the gravy and stir in the stock. Add the Bovril and a dash of Worcestershire sauce and bring to the boil over a brisk heat. Reduce to a glazed sauce. Strain and cover the meat with the sauce.

When the meat is cold, divide into cutlets and cover with aspic.

To make the glazed onions, peel then cook the onions in salted water until soft. Lift out with a straining spoon and keep warm. Then add one tablespoon of tomato purée, a knob of butter and one teaspoon of sugar to the onion water. Boil down to a glaze and pour over the onions. When cool, place in the dish with the lamb cutlets.

♛ POTATO SALAD

(For recipe see page 145)

♛ TOMATO AND GREEN PEPPER SALAD

(For recipe see page 143)

♛ APPLE TURNOVERS

Pre-heat oven to 220°C/425°F or gas mark 7
To make 18–20:

1 lb/500 g puff pastry (for   *icing sugar*
recipe see page 216)   *½ pint/30 cl thick apple purée*

Make the puff pastry according to the method on page 216. Roll out a quarter of an inch thick and cut out rounds about four inches across with a fancy pastry cutter. Place some thick apple purée in the middle of the pastry rounds. Moisten the edges of the pastry with a little water. Fold over to a half circle and press the edges together.

Place on a baking sheet and bake in the oven at 220 °C/425 °F or gas mark 7 for fifteen minutes, then lower the heat and bake for another five or ten minutes. When ready, dust some icing sugar on top.

Jam or fruit of any kind can be used instead of the apple purée.

CHEESE SELECTION 👑

Boursin – a very pleasant French dessert cheese
Chantilly – delicious with fruit
Port Salut – mild and pleasing
Swedish Herrgurds Ost – mild, but sharp when ripe

* * *

THE TENNIS PARTY

cucumber sandwiches
biscuit crunchies with ice-cream   *gooey chocolate cake*
iced tea   *iced coffee*

CUCUMBER SANDWICHES 👑

It is most important that the bread and cucumber are very thinly sliced. Add a sprinkling of salt and a drop of tarragon vinegar to each sandwich.

♔ BISCUIT CRUNCHIES

Pre-heat oven to 180 °C/350 °F or gas mark 4
To make 18–20 biscuits:

$\frac{1}{4}$ lb/125 g butter	2 teaspoons of ground ginger
2 ozs/60 g sugar	2 egg whites
2$\frac{1}{2}$ ozs/75 g plain flour	

Beat butter and sugar until fluffy. Mix the flour and ginger together and add to the mixture. Whip egg whites until stiff. Fold in carefully. Shape into slabs, three inches wide by four inches, and place on a greased tin. Bake in the oven at 180 °C/350 °F or gas mark 4 until lightly browned.
Serve with ice-cream.

♔ GOOEY CHOCOLATE CAKE

Pre-heat oven to 170 °C/325 °F or gas mark 2
To make 1 × 8-inch/20-cm cake:

8 ozs/250 g butter	5 ozs/150 g cooking chocolate
8 ozs/250 g sugar	8 ozs/250 g plain flour
5 eggs, separated	2 teaspoons of baking powder
1 tablespoon of orange marmalade	2 ozs/60 g sweet ground almonds

For the chocolate butter icing:

$\frac{1}{4}$ lb/125 g unsweetened plain chocolate	1 egg, beaten
$\frac{1}{2}$ lb/250 g icing sugar	a few drops of vanilla and almond essence
4 ozs/125 g butter, softened	

Beat the butter and sugar to a light cream. Add the egg yolks and marmalade. Stir in the chocolate, previously melted over a low heat. Add the flour, baking powder and almonds. Whip egg whites and fold in lightly. Pour into a greased tin and bake in the oven at 170 °C/325 °F or gas mark 2, for one hour and fifteen minutes.

When cool, cut into three layers.

To make the icing, melt the chocolate over a low heat. Sieve the icing sugar into a bowl, stir in the soft butter, add the chocolate and beaten egg and stir until smooth and light. Add the flavouring and spread immediately between the layers of chocolate cake and on the top with a palette knife. Some of the icing can be piped on top with a forcing bag.

ICED TEA

2 teaspoons of China tea (Earl Grey)
2 teaspoons of Indian tea
1½ pints/90 cl boiling water

½ pint/30 cl fresh orange juice, strained
juice of 1 lemon, strained
demerara sugar, to taste
ice

Make the tea in the usual way and brew for five to eight minutes. Strain and add the orange and lemon juice. Add demerara sugar (or serve separately). Allow to cool in tall glasses with ice.

ICED COFFEE

1½ ozs/40 g good-quality coffee
1 pint/60 cl boiling water

1 block of vanilla ice-cream

Place the coffee in a jug or percolator and add the boiling water at intervals. Keep the pot hot but do not boil. Leave to cool. When cold, pour into tall glasses and scoop a tablespoon of ice-cream into each one.

*   *   *

THE HUNTING BREAKFAST

fruit and vegetable juices
cold ham
egg, bacon, sausages, mushrooms
fried egg balls (morning only treat)
toast, marmalade, honey
coffee and cream

Catering for a hunting party is ideally simple. You send the guests out with a big, hearty breakfast under their belts, with perhaps one treat. They are then gone for the rest of the day when the time is your own. On their return, give them more breakfast – without the morning treat, but with whisky.

♛ COLD HAM

1 ham or gammon, size according to numbers	a little beer
a couple of wisps of hay	2 tablespoons of demerara sugar
2 teaspoons of mustard powder	1 teaspoon of ground cinnamon

Soak the ham for twenty-four hours. Scrub and wash with water. Place in a big saucepan and cover with water. Bring to the boil and add the wisps of hay. Cover and simmer at the rate of twenty-five minutes to the pound (500 g). When cooked, remove the pan from the heat, turn the ham upside down and leave to cool in its own juice. Remove the skin and any surplus fat. Put in a roasting tin.

Mix the mustard powder with a little beer and spread evenly over the ham. Mix the demerara sugar with the cinnamon and press firmly into the ham. Place in a hot oven to glaze for a few minutes. Remove and allow to cool before serving.

FRIED EGG BALLS ♛

4 hard-boiled eggs
½ pint/30 cl thick English
    butter sauce (for recipe see
    page 207)
pinch of sugar and nutmeg

plain flour
egg
breadcrumbs
oil

Chop up the hard-boiled eggs fairly coarsely in a bowl and add the thick butter sauce. Season to taste. Shape into balls and dip in flour, the beaten egg and then coat in breadcrumbs.

Fry in deep oil until golden-brown. Drain on kitchen paper and serve with crisp, grilled bacon rashers.

* * *

THE CHILDREN'S BIRTHDAY PARTY

sandwiches
cream horns   jam canapés
sponge tea cakes   meringue gateau birthday cake
                    mousse of lychees

Children's parties may not be a recognized form of sport but they certainly provide masses of exercise; in comparison, preparing a four-course dinner for ten is a rest cure.

I have been told that, nowadays, children prefer their parties to be as much like adult occasions as possible – bar the drinks. Personally, I think it is a mistake to cut out sweet food entirely – there is plenty of time for cocktail parties when the children are grown-up.

👑 SANDWICH SUGGESTIONS

Hard-boiled egg, chopped and seasoned with peeled, thinly-sliced tomato; grated cheese and shredded lettuce; minced ham and mayonnaise, mixed to a smooth cream, with sliced tomato and watercress; thinly-sliced cucumber rolled up in brown bread and butter.

👑 CREAM HORNS

Pre-heat oven to 220 °C/425 °F or gas mark 7
To make 18 cream horns:

> 1 lb/500 g puff pastry (for   2 ozs/60 g jam
>   recipe see page 216)   1 pint/60 cl double cream
> 1 egg yolk, beaten   vanilla flavouring
> 1 oz/30 g caster sugar

Roll out the puff pastry to one-fifth of an inch thick, then cut into strips ten inches long and one inch wide. Moisten the edges and fold round individual moulds, ensuring the edges overlap. Brush with egg yolk mixed with a little water and roll in caster sugar. Rinse a tin in cold water, fill with the horns and bake in the oven set at 220 °C/425 °F or gas mark 7 for twenty to twenty-five minutes. Leave to cool. When cold, remove the moulds and fill with jam and whipped cream, flavoured with vanilla.

👑 JAM CANAPÉS

Pre-heat oven to 190 °C/375 °F or gas mark 5
To make 12 jam canapés:

> ½ lb/250 g puff pastry (for   raspberry jam
>   recipe see page 216)   double cream
> caster sugar   icing sugar

Roll out the puff pastry to one-fifth of an inch thick and sprinkle with caster sugar. Fold the square of pastry edge to edge. Press lightly with the rolling pin. Sprinkle with caster sugar and fold again. Fold again in half and press gently. Allow to stand for fifteen minutes in a cold place. Then cut the folded pastry in half-inch strips across. Stand the pastry strips on a greased tin, resting on the cut side, allowing a couple of inches between each cake. Bake for eight to ten minutes in the oven at 190°C/375°F or gas mark 5 until light brown. Reduce heat and bake for a further three or four minutes. When cold, sandwich the halves with seedless raspberry jam and cream, and sprinkle with icing sugar.

SPONGE TEA CAKES ♛

Pre-heat oven to 190°C/375°F or gas mark 5
To make 12–18 tea cakes:

2 eggs	*4 fl ozs/12 cl milk*
4 ozs/125 g caster sugar	*4–5 ozs/125–150 g plain flour*
2½ ozs/75 g butter	*a few drops of vanilla essence*

For the icing:
½ lb/250 g sieved icing sugar	*1 tablespoon of lemon juice*
1 tablespoon of orange juice	*1 tablespoon of butter*

Grease bun tin, dust with just a light sprinkling of the flour. Whip the eggs and sugar until fluffy. Boil butter and milk together and whip into beaten egg mixture. Fold in the flour and add vanilla essence. Stir until smooth. Bake in the oven at 190°C/375°F or gas mark 5 for ten to fifteen minutes. Allow to cool.

To make the icing, mix with the sieved icing sugar the orange and lemon juice until all lumps have vanished. Add the butter and heat mixture very gently, stirring quickly, until the butter is absorbed. Spread mixture over the cakes with a palette knife.

👑 MERINGUE GÂTEAU BIRTHDAY CAKE

Pre-heat oven to 190 °C/375 °F or gas mark 5
To make 1 × 12-inch/30-cm cake

4 eggs	*2 egg whites*
8 ozs/250 g caster sugar	*4 ozs/125 g caster sugar*
4 ozs/125 g plain flour	*½ pint/30 cl whipped cream*
1 oz/30 g cornflour	*redcurrant jelly*
2 teaspoons of baking powder	*cherries*

Beat the eggs and sugar for twenty minutes, or ten with an electric mixer. Add the flour and cornflour, sieved with the baking powder, and stir well. Fill a large cake tin with the mixture and bake for twenty to thirty minutes in the oven at 190 °C/375 °F or gas mark 5. Turn onto a wire tray to cool.

To make the meringues, whip the egg whites stiffly and fold in the sugar. With a tablespoon, set out neat blobs of the mixture on to a greased and floured tin. Bake the meringues in a very low oven for two or three hours or until a very pale fawn colour.

Cut the cooled cake in half and spread with a layer of redcurrant jelly and cream. Put the two halves together and cover the top with another layer of redcurrant jelly and cream. Decorate by piping on the rest of the cream and distributing the meringues and some cherries.

👑 MOUSSE OF LYCHEES

1 large tin of lychees	*½ pint/30 cl double cream*
vanilla essence	*whipped cream and pistachio*
1 tablespoon of gelatine	*nuts, to garnish*
2 tablespoons of caster sugar	

Drain and chop the fruit, removing the stones. Place in individual glasses. Heat the syrup from the tin, add the vanilla and dissolve the gelatine and sugar. When cold, whip the double cream and fold in. Pour over the fruit and allow to set. Garnish with whipped cream and chopped nuts.

Menu Suggestions

DINNER AT EIGHT ... AND YOU COULD SET YOUR CLOCK BY THE QUEEN'S appearance at the dinner table with her guests. This punctuality, I am sure, was dictated by a natural consideration for the people who worked for her. Dinner at eight meant that on a good day I could be finished in the kitchen by 10 p.m. I always saw the dinner through, right down to the serving of the coffee, although I did not, of course, have to wash up. After this I would go to my room and write out the menus for the following day. Oddly enough, this was often my greatest headache. The menus had to be in French and being no scholar of languages I used to struggle for hours with the language of haute cuisine. Eventually I found a wonderful, but very expensive, book which contained all the terms I needed, though I was still conscious of the odd mistake. However, the Queen, who speaks excellent French, was very kind about this and tactfully ignored any errors.

The tick-tocking punctuality that typified the Queen's household was replaced by a more elastic routine when the Queen Mother came to Clarence House.

The gong would often ring several times before the Queen Mother was ready to come into dinner. As she once explained to me very charmingly, 'I spend most of my life being hurried from one place to another and when I am with friends, I really enjoy not having to rush. I'm sure you understand'.

Well, I did. I have been in households where the chefs become very dominating over time-keeping and it doesn't make for a happy atmosphere. That time before dinner when the Queen Mother was relaxing with guests over drinks was important to her. Bennett told me that she was never able to do it before. The late King was a stickler for punctuality but hers was a more unhurried temperament. I just had to adjust the menus, choosing dishes that would wait without being spoiled and getting a footman to report on progress. He would run down to the kitchen saying 'five minutes', 'ten minutes' or on occasions, 'half an hour'.

On special occasions I would make a list of initial suggestions and the Queen or Queen Mother would select the final dishes very carefully. We had some fairly simple menus at Clarence House but also some very grand ones. I enjoyed doing both.

The Queen Mother would often remember dishes she had enjoyed in the past and ones that had been a disaster such as soufflés which had sunk before reaching the table on their long journey from the kitchens at Buckingham Palace. But at Clarence House we prided ourselves on getting food to the dining room within three minutes.

People often ask me if I was made nervous by the illustrious names on the guest lists when I was cooking at Clarence House. Well, I would have been of course if I had known beforehand who was to be there. But often the Comptroller's guest list, issued a fortnight in advance, simply stated the number of guests to a particular meal. Once there were four Queens to lunch! Luckily, I did not know until afterwards when I received a message that the royal ladies had thoroughly enjoyed my sole. Had I known, I might have been influenced to try something grander. Yet sole at its best, is certainly a dish to set before a Queen.

Cooking for royalty is an honour and it would be easy if all one had to do was to produce inspired menus for the family and bask in the glory of it all. But with staff to feed as well there could be as many as three different menus going at once. During my time at Clarence House I only had one assistant and numbers doubled with the arrival of the Queen Mother and Princess Margaret. Staff would eat from a different menu before the Royal Family in the evening and after them at lunchtime. When the Royal Family were away at Sandringham, Windsor or Balmoral – 'We migrate like the birds,' the Queen Mother once said – there were usually staff left behind to be catered for. It was then I enjoyed practising new dishes.

This chapter contains the dinner party menus I have designed and cooked over the years and which have received the most favourable comment. Some of these may suit you; some of course may not. They are not, after all, meant to be strictly adhered to. My aim is for them to inspire you with ideas of your own.

Use the menus according to your own taste, means and entertaining needs. The one thing the dishes have in common is that not only do they taste exceptionally delicious but they *look* so very attractive too. Small details like the way vegetables are served are, I think, extremely important when entertaining. Creamed spinach in little puff pastry cases, for example, is probably something you would not dream of serving up for the family, but what a difference it makes to any dinner party menu.

All of the recipes are given elsewhere in the book under the relevant chapter heading. These dinner party menus have happy memories for me. I hope you will enjoy using them, too.

MENU ONE (*serves 6*)

Consommé en Gelée aux Sherry

*

Filet de Sole Meunière
Roast Duckling
Bouchées aux Epinard
New Potatoes

*

Hot Grapefruit Salad
Poires Maraschino aux Ananas
Almond Biscuits

MENU TWO (*serves 6*)

Cold Cherry Soup Chantilly

*

Filet de Boeuf with Sauce Piquant
Potatoes Suédoise
Tomates Farcies
Salade Princesse

*

Peach Meringue with Vanilla Cream

MENU THREE (*serves 4*)

Consommé Contessa

*

Saumon Court Bouillon
Sauce Hollandaise
New Potatoes with Dill
Cucumber Salad

*

Lamb Noisettes
Champignons
Petits Pois à la Français

*

Melon Surprise

MENU FOUR (*serves 6*)

Potage Alexandra

*

Chicken Sauté Provençale
Braised Celery
Potatoes in Tomato Cocottes

*

Salade Alma

*

Crêpes Suzettes à la Suédoise

MENU FIVE (*serves 6*)

Baked Avocado Pear

*

Schnitzel de Veau au Diplomat
Brussels Sprouts
Macrée Potatoes
Tomato Salad with Chives

*

Crème à la Duchesse with Strawberry Sauce

MENU SIX (*serves 6*)

Asparagus in Mousseline Sauce

*

Turbot Café de Paris

*

Glazed Bacon
Boiled Rice
French Beans
Watercress
Orange Sauce

*

Muscat Grapes en Gelée

Sauces and Essential Mixtures

THERE IS ONLY ONE WAY TO MAKE A GOOD SAUCE AND THAT IS WITH love and care. All sauces should have one thing in common, and that is that they should look good enough to eat by themselves.

Sauces are a versatile accompaniment to so many dishes. They can be used to harmonize with or enhance the flavour of a certain food, or they can provide a pleasant contrast. However, never try disguising indifferent food with a highly-flavoured sauce.

Of all the members of the Royal Family, the Queen Mother was perhaps the most appreciative of a good sauce, frequently sending messages of thanks and mentioning the sauce by name. In fact, I think it was my sauces that won her over, for when I first started cooking for Her Majesty at Clarence House, after Princess Elizabeth became Queen and moved to Buckingham Palace, I was naturally employed on a temporary basis only, to see how we would get along together. I understood perfectly the reasons for this since in those days all the really big kitchens were run by men, as it was thought that the administrative work of a large kitchen with a big staff was probably better handled by a man. The Queen Mother and Princess Margaret had a larger staff than that of the Queen and her family. The Queen Mother and Princess Margaret also frequently entertained separately, sometimes on the same day.

So if the Queen Mother was doubtful, I was certainly extremely apprehensive, but I am pleased to say that rapport was soon established – in no small way, I am sure, due to the quality and range of my sauces.

BASIC BÉCHAMEL SAUCE ♕

1 oz/30 g butter
1 oz/30 g plain flour
¾ pint/40 cl warm milk

pepper, salt and sugar to taste
pinch of nutmeg

This is the sauce that no cook can do without for long; it is one that never changes and that, at the same time, no two people ever make in quite the same way. The order in which the ingredients are added, the small variations of quantity, the heat of the stove, and the amount of time spent in cooking it, plus the mood of the cook, are the factors which make the classic béchamel sauce what it is. 'Thick and lumpy – hot and grumpy,' I always think to myself when tasting the wrong sort of béchamel, made, I am sure, in the wrong frame of mind. The right sort of béchamel must be made smoothly and sweetly, as though without a care in the world. If the telephone rings – one does not answer it.

This is how I like to make my béchamel – with a little cold butter added at the end to give a smooth consistency.

Melt half the butter, add the flour and stir over a low heat. Do not allow to brown. Add the warmed milk gradually, whisking all the time until smooth and creamy. Boil for about five or six minutes. Add the seasoning, a pinch of nutmeg and simmer for a couple of minutes. Remove from heat and stir in the rest of the butter.

♔ MORNAY SAUCE

½ *pint/30 cl béchamel sauce*   1 *tablespoon of grated*
1 *tablespoon of grated Gruyère*   *Parmesan cheese*
     cheese   *knob of butter*

Heat the béchamel sauce and stir in the grated cheese. Remove from heat and stir in the knob of butter.

♔ SUPRÉME SAUCE (FOR POACHED CHICKEN)

½ *pint/30 cl béchamel sauce*   *pepper, salt and sugar to taste*
1 *glass of dry white wine or*   1 *egg yolk*
     ¼ *pint/15 cl chicken stock*   1 *tablespoon of double cream*
pinch of garlic salt

Bring béchamel sauce to the boil, add the wine or stock and seasonings and simmer for five minutes. Stir in the egg yolk, remove from heat and stir in the cream.

When using with boiled chicken, first remove the skin of the chicken and allow the sauce to settle in the pan for a few minutes away from the heat. Then coat the chicken with the sauce.

EGG SAUCE 👑

¾ pint/40 cl béchamel sauce	2 tablespoons of butter
3 hard-boiled eggs	salt and pepper

Make the béchamel sauce rather thin. Separate the hard-boiled egg yolks from the whites. Cut the whites into strips and sieve the yolks. Add sieved yolks and butter to the béchamel sauce and stir well over a low heat. Season to taste and add the egg whites. Serve hot.

HOLLANDAISE SAUCE 👑

4 tablespoons of dry white wine or 3 tablespoons of white vinegar	½ teaspoon of white pepper
	3 egg yolks
½ teaspoon of salt	½ lb/250 g butter
	juice of ½ lemon

Hollandaise sauce, simplified here as much as possible, likes a regular low heat. Sauces made from butter and thickened with egg yolks are not designed to be served piping hot.

Put the wine or vinegar into a saucepan with five tablespoons of water and seasoning, and reduce to half the amount by boiling down. Whisk the egg yolks in a basin with three tablespoons of water and add to the sauce. Stir over a low heat until thickened. Remove from heat and add the slightly softened butter a little at a time with a small amount of water, then add the lemon juice.

Serve with vegetables – delicious with asparagus – and fish.

👑 BÉARNAISE SAUCE

3 tablespoons of dry white
   wine or 2 tablespoons of
   malt vinegar
2 tablespoons of water
sprig of parsley
2½ tablespoons of chopped
   onion

½ teaspoon of white pepper
1 tablespoon of tomato purée
salt and cayenne pepper
1 level tablespoon of finely-
   chopped fresh parsley
3 egg yolks
6–7 ozs/175–200 g soft butter

Put the white wine (or vinegar), 2 tablespoons of water, the sprig of parsley, onion and white pepper into a saucepan and boil down to a third of the quantity. Strain and allow to cool a little.

Return to a low heat and add the tomato purée, salt, cayenne pepper and chopped parsley. Add the egg yolks one at a time, whisking continuously. Be very careful at this stage not to boil the mixture. Whisk until it becomes frothy. Remove the saucepan from the heat and add the soft butter a little at a time, still whisking. Sample the sauce for seasoning, return to a low heat and when warm, remove to a bain-marie or double boiler. Very, very gradually, drop by drop, add 1 tablespoon of cold water.

Serve with steaks and grills.

👑 MOUSSELINE SAUCE

3 egg yolks
pinch of salt

¼ lb/125 g soft butter

Whisk the egg yolks, 2 tablespoons of water and a pinch of salt together over a low heat until frothy. Remove from the heat and add the butter in small portions. Serve at once.

This is a light and delicate sauce, delicious with asparagus, artichokes or broccoli.

MAYONNAISE 👑

4 egg yolks
½ teaspoon (or more, according
  to taste) of mustard powder
½ teaspoon of salt
1½ pints/90 cl olive or
  sunflower oil
1 tablespoon of vinegar (best
  malt wine or tarragon)

juice of ½ lemon
boiling water ready to drip in if
  necessary
dash of cayenne pepper
½ teaspoon of sugar

Mayonnaise is the basis of many sauces. You will find it very useful to have some home-made mayonnaise in stock to which you can add other ingredients to make a variety of delicious sauces. Remember when making the mayonnaise that all the ingredients must be the same temperature, so stand them all together in the same place for several hours before mixing.

Mix egg yolks, mustard and salt together into a thick paste. Add the oil, drop by drop, ensuring that each drop is whisked in and emulsifies with the paste. When the mixture is good and thick, add the vinegar drop by drop. Continue whisking all the time, alternating drops of vinegar and lemon juice with the oil. If the mixture gets stiffer than desired, soften with a few drops of boiling water. If it curdles, i.e. separates, put an extra egg yolk in another bowl and gradually whisk the curdled mixture into the new egg yolk. Finish off by adding the cayenne pepper and sugar and give a final whisk.

GREEN TARTARE SAUCE 👑

small bunch of parsley
½ pint/30 cl mayonnaise
1 tablespoon of chopped celery
1 tablespoon of chopped
  chives

1 tablespoon of chopped
  capers
1 tablespoon of chopped
  dessert apple

Rinse the parsley and chop very finely. Put into a muslin bag and wring out the juice into the mayonnaise. Add all the other ingredients and mix well together. Keep the parsley for decorating.

♛ HERB BUTTER SAUCE

2 large shallots, finely chopped	salt and white pepper
2 tablespoons of tarragon or	8 ozs/225 g cold unsalted
white wine vinegar	butter cut into pieces
3 tablespoons of dry white wine	1 tablespoon of chopped chives
2 tablespoons of double cream	1 tablespoon of chopped tarragon
	1 tablespoon of chopped parsley

Served with baby vegetables such as beetroot, carrots, turnips with green tops or tiny artichokes, Herb Butter Sauce makes a wonderfully spring-like first course.

Simmer shallots in the vinegar and wine over a medium heat until reduced to about two tablespoons. Reduce heat, add herbs, stir in cream and simmer, whisking until the mixture is reduced to about three or four tablespoons. Stir in the butter. Season lightly. Serve spooned onto a plate with the vegetables arranged attractively on top.

If using beetroot, steam for about fifteen minutes or until just tender. Allow to cool for a few minutes and slip off skins.

♛ VINAIGRETTE SALAD SAUCE WITH EGGS

½ teaspoon of mustard powder	4 hard-boiled eggs
2 tablespoons of vinegar	2 egg yolks
pepper, salt and sugar to taste	4 fl ozs/10 cl double cream

Mix the mustard with the vinegar, pepper, salt and sugar to a smooth paste. Sieve the hard-boiled egg yolks into a bowl, blend in the raw egg yolks, and stir well. Add the vinaigrette sauce to the egg mixture gradually, stirring all the time. Finish with the cream.

COOKED SALAD CREAM ♔

4 tablespoons of plain flour
1 dessertspoon of mustard
1 pint/60 cl water
½ teaspoon of salt
dash of cayenne pepper

½ teaspoon of sugar
2 egg yolks
4 tablespoons of oil

Mix the flour and mustard with 1 pint/60 cl of water to a smooth consistency and bring to the boil. Whisk and add seasoning. Remove from heat and allow to cool a little, then add beaten egg yolks and finally stir in the oil.

BREAD SAUCE ♔

¼ pint/15 cl milk
1 medium-size onion, finely-
    chopped
2 or 3 cloves

6 ozs/175 g fresh white
    breadcrumbs
½ oz/15 g butter
¼ pint/15 cl single cream
pepper, salt and nutmeg

Boil the milk with the onion and cloves for five or six minutes. Remove the cloves and add the breadcrumbs. Simmer for five minutes. Then stir in the butter, cream, salt, pepper and nutmeg.
    Serve with poultry and game.

ENGLISH BUTTER SAUCE ♔

¼ lb/125 g butter
1 oz/30 g plain flour
¾ pint/40 cl milk

salt and pepper
pinch of nutmeg and sugar

Melt half the butter in a saucepan, add the flour and mix well over a gentle heat. Add the milk and seasoning and whisk until smooth. Simmer on a low heat for five or six minutes. Remove from the heat and add the remaining butter in small portions, stirring all the time.
    The sauce should be thick and shiny and is served mainly with vegetables or fish.

 HORSERADISH BUTTER SAUCE

4 ozs/125 g butter   1 tablespoon of grated
                                                    horseradish

Cream the butter and mix with the grated horseradish. Do not melt the butter as this will produce the wrong sort of flavour and texture. Serve with fish.

 TOMATO SAUCE

2 onions, coarsely cut $\frac{1}{4}$ pint/15 cl water
1 oz/30 g butter   dash of Tabasco
6–8 tomatoes, cut up   salt
$\frac{1}{4}$ pint/15 cl sherry

Braise the onions in the butter and add the tomatoes. When soft add the sherry, water and a dash of Tabasco. Sample and add salt to taste. Bring to the boil and simmer for one hour with the lid on. Sieve and bring back to the boil before serving.

 APPLE SAUCE

6 cooking apples   2 tablespoons of redcurrant
3 cloves   jelly
                                                    pinch of salt

Peel, quarter and core apples and put into a saucepan with a small amount of water and the cloves. Cook for ten minutes with the lid on over a gentle heat until soft. Add the redcurrant jelly and stir well. When the apples are well pulped, sieve, put back in the saucepan and add a pinch of salt to bring out the fullness of the taste. Keep hot.

ORANGE SAUCE ♛

juice of 3 oranges
1 tablespoon of marmalade
1 dessertspoon of tomato sauce

pinch of cayenne pepper
1 teaspoon of French mustard
1 teaspoon of cornflour

Put the orange juice, marmalade, tomato sauce, pepper and mustard into a saucepan and bring to the boil. Mix the cornflour with a little water and add, stirring all the time. Boil for one minute. Serve hot.

VANILLA SAUCE ♛

¾ pint/40 cl single cream
1 vanilla pod or ½ teaspoon of vanilla essence

5 egg yolks
3 ozs/90 g caster sugar

Boil the cream with the vanilla pod for half a minute (or add vanilla essence), remove from heat, cover with a lid and stand for fifteen minutes.

Beat the egg yolks and sugar together for fifteen minutes, five minutes if you are using an electric beater. Remove the vanilla pod and add the cream to the egg mixture, whisking very hard. Pour the mixture back into the saucepan and whisk over a gentle heat until thick and frothy. Do not boil. Pour into a bowl and whisk till cold.

Serve with fruit dishes, puddings, gateaux and tarts.

STRAWBERRY SAUCE ♛

½ lb/250 g fresh or frozen strawberries

sugar to taste
orange Curaçao

Sieve the strawberries, add sugar to taste and flavour with a little orange Curaçao. Serve with vanilla ice-cream.

👑 BUTTERSCOTCH SAUCE

2 ozs/60 g butter
¼ lb/125 g brown sugar
2 tablespoons of golden syrup

¼ pint/15 cl single cream
½ lb/250 g caster sugar
½ teaspoon of vanilla essence

Mix all the ingredients together and cook slowly in the top section of a double boiler for ten minutes.

👑 SAUCE VELOUTÉ AU CHAMPAGNE

2 ozs/60 g butter
2 ozs/60 g plain flour
2 pints/60 cl good chicken or
    veal stock
salt and pepper

1 bouquet garni
1 large onion
½ lb/250 g mushrooms
¼ pint/15 cl champagne or
    white wine

This is a very grand sauce that makes a banquet out of boiled chicken. The sauce can be served either separately with the chicken or the chicken meat can be flaked into the sauce to make an excellent blanquette of chicken.

Melt the butter in a saucepan, add the flour and mix well. Add the hot stock a little at a time and stir until smooth. When all the stock has been absorbed, bring to the boil. Reduce the heat and add seasoning, bouquet garni, chopped onion and mushrooms. Add the champagne and allow to simmer for half an hour. Sieve and strain the sauce.

👑 CHAUD-FROID SAUCE

½ pint/30 cl double cream
½ pint/30 cl velouté au
    champagne sauce
    (see recipe above)

¼ oz/8 g powdered gelatine,
    diluted in a little hot water
    or stock

Simmer the cream and velouté au champagne sauce over a gentle heat and mix in the diluted gelatine. Let the sauce cool so that it is nearly, but not quite, at setting point. Use to coat cold chicken.

THE STOCKPOT ♔

There is some doubt these days as to whether the ever-simmering stockpot on the kitchen stove is still an essential part of the contemporary scene. Certainly it makes for a steamy kitchen and you may get fed up with the smell. Also, there is competition in the form of so many good manufactured bouillon cubes which you can buy in the specific flavour you want. However, the good cubes are quite expensive and nobody, I hope, would think of throwing away chicken and beef bones with all the goodness there waiting to be extracted. The ingredients of your stockpot will depend on what is available in your kitchen, and the season of the year.

MEAT STOCK ♔

shin of beef	*peppercorns*
veal and beef bones	*chicken or game carcasses*
carrots	*onions*
parsley	*thyme*
bay leaf	*swede*
celery	*1 beetroot*

This is a recipe for a meat stock that leans on the side of perfection, but shows the basic method. No exact quantities can be given.

Brown the shin of beef and the bones in the oven or pan, put in a large saucepan and cover with water. Bring slowly to the boil and skim. Simmer slowly for several hours. Then strain off the bones, clean the pan and add the vegetables and herbs to the meat stock. Simmer for a further hour. Strain before using.

No salt is added until the stock is used in conjunction with a specific dish. The object is not to have a highly-flavoured liquid, but a basic stock full of goodness yet flexible enough to combine with other ingredients. To strengthen the flavour, simply reduce by boiling down in an open pan. This stock can be kept in a cold larder for anything up to a week.

♛ FISH STOCK

> to every 1 lb/500 g of fish or   ½ bay leaf
>   fish trimmings take   2 cloves
>   1½ pints/90 cl water   1 onion
> ½ teaspoon of pepper   1 stick of celery
> 1 bouquet of parsley   1 carrot

Fish stock is the essential basis of all fish soups. The fish used for making the stock must be fresh and of good quality. Cod or haddock will do; a mixture of mussels, oysters and flat fish (sole or whiting are best) makes a stock fit for a Queen. Cooking time should be as short as possible, as the stock may take on a bitter flavour if overcooked.

Rinse and clean the fish, cut in thick slices and add the water, seasoning, herbs and vegetables to the pan. Place on a low heat and bring to the boil. Simmer until the fish is broken up. Remove at once and strain through a fine sieve, lined with dampened muslin.

You now have a good fish stock. It can be thickened by adding whipped egg or grated Gruyère or Parmesan cheese, or purée of vegetables. Flavour by adding white wine, or lobsters, oysters, shrimps etc.

♛ ASPIC

Now that all the hard work has been taken out of aspic preparations – you used to have to boil calves' feet for hours or soak leaves of gelatine – it has once again become very popular for cold food preparation. Nobody can go wrong with the packets of easily-dissolved powdered gelatine. You simply follow the directions, using ½ oz/15 g of gelatine powder to 1 pint/60 cl of liquid. But as the aspic must taste as good as it looks, it is advisable to add your own flavouring to the mixture. For meat or fish aspic, a glass of wine can be added. For fruit jellies, first dissolve the powder in a cup of boiling water then make up to the required quantity with fruit juice.

Here are a few do's and don'ts concerning the use of aspic jelly:

1. Never boil an aspic mixture. Always dissolve the gelatine in a cupful or more of boiling liquid first, adding afterwards the rest of the liquid which can be cold. Stir well.
2. When making a fruit, vegetable or meat mould, let the gelatine mixture thicken to the consistency of an unbeaten egg, then add the ingredients and gelatine in alternate layers.
3. To line a mould pour in some cool aspic and turn the mould round and round with smooth, steady movements so that the sides are coated first. Continue this process so that the sides and then the bottom are coated with a good layer of gelatine.
4. To decorate a mould with appropriate garnishes, like sliced, hard-boiled egg, truffle or artistic bits of flower-shaped vegetables, arrange the garnishes on top of the turned-out mould and spoon a little nearly-set aspic on top of them to hold the shape.
5. To turn out a mould, dip quickly into hot water several times, taking care that the water does not come over the top; put a plate on top of the mould, turn it upside down and shake gently. If the mould does not slide out, dip it quickly into hot water once again.

PANADE

This is a thick paste of bread and milk to which minced meat or fish is added to make a forcemeat.

Cut white bread into cubes and soak in warm milk to soften. Work with a wooden spoon until the bread has absorbed the liquid. Add salt and pepper and put the mixture over a low heat to get hot. Work with a spoon until it leaves the side of the pan. Allow it to cool before using.

FARCE (OR FORCEMEAT)

This is a stuffing of finely-minced or sieved ingredients bound with egg and well seasoned. It should have a creamy consistency and lends flavour and bulk to other foods. Here is a recipe for fish farcie, which is normally used for stuffing salmon and trout or is rolled up inside fillets of white fish.

♛ FISH FARCE (OR FISH CREAM)

1 lb/500 g fillets of lemon sole,   *½ pint/30 cl single cream*
    haddock or pike   *3 eggs, separated*
3 ozs/90 g butter   *salt and pepper*
1 oz/30 g plain flour   *pinch of sugar*

Pass the fish, together with the butter, through the mincer three times. In another bowl stir the flour into the cream and mix in the yolks of eggs. Season and add to the fish in small quantities, stirring to a smooth cream. Whip the whites of eggs and fold into the farcie. Use for stuffing fish. Freeze surplus in small packets.

♛ PASTRY

One of the basic mixtures in the kitchen is pastry. Some people find it difficult to make a good, light, crunchy pastry crust, whereas others produce the most delicious pastry every time. However, don't despair. The important thing is to hit upon a good formula and once you have achieved that, go on using it until it becomes second nature.

If you have not already discovered your secret formula, the following methods for pastry may suit you. Cool hands help pastry to turn out very well – here's hoping my recipes will do the same for you too.

♛ SHORT PASTRY

Sweet pastry for flans
To make 1 lb/500 g pastry, enough for two × 8-inch/20-cm flans:

4 ozs/125 g butter   *1 tablespoon of sugar*
8 ozs/250 g plain flour   *pinch of salt*
rind and juice of ½ lemon   *1 tablespoon of iced water*

Rub the fat into the flour until the mixture has a coarse, crumbly texture, and add the grated rind, the lemon juice, the sugar and the salt. Stir in the water, mix to a firm dough and let it stand for half an hour. Grease two 8-inch/20-cm flan tins, roll out the pastry to about the thickness of $\frac{1}{4}$ inch/5 mm and line the tins. Prick the pastry at the bottom of the tins, cover with rice paper to keep from rising and bake in the oven at 180°C/350°F or gas mark 4 for fifteen to twenty minutes.

Sweet pastry for fruit pies
To make 1 lb/500 g pastry, enough for two × 8-inch/20-cm flans:

4 ozs/125 g butter   *2 ozs/60 g ground almonds*
2 ozs/60 g sugar   *8 ozs/250 g plain flour*
1 egg

Cream the butter for three minutes with 1 oz/30 g of the sugar until light and fluffy. Add the egg and mix well. Add the almonds and flour and make into a firm paste on a floured board. Allow to stand for half an hour. Roll out and sprinkle with sugar. Fold the dough into a ball, then roll again and bake in the oven at 180°C/350°F or gas mark 4 for about twenty to thirty minutes.

Short pastry for meat pies
To make 12 oz/350 g pastry, enough for two × 8-inch/20-cm pie lids:

3 ozs/90 g butter   *pinch of salt*
1 oz/30 g lard   *1 tablespoon of water*
8 ozs/250 g plain flour   *1 egg*

Rub the butter and lard into the flour and salt, stir in the water and egg and mix to a thin dough. Cover a dish of cooked meat and bake in the oven at 180°C/350°F or gas mark 4 for thirty to thirty-five minutes.

👑 PUFF PASTRY

To make 2 lbs/1 kg of pastry:

1 lb/500 g plain flour	*1 lb/500 g butter*
pinch of salt	*½ pint/30 cl cold water*

Sieve flour and salt into a large bowl. Rub in 4 ozs/125 g of butter and mix until fine and crumbly. Make a well in the centre and pour in the water a little at a time, mixing gently until the mixture becomes a stiff dough. Form into a ball and allow to stand for fifteen minutes in a cool place. Knead remaining butter until soft and make into a flat, round cake. Roll out the pastry so that it is a little thicker in the middle than at the sides and place the butter in the middle. Fold the pastry over the pat of butter like a parcel and put in a cold place for ten minutes. Roll out the pastry into a square about ¾ inch/20 mm thick and fold the two sides to meet in the middle, then fold in half. Roll out into a square again and repeat the folding process four times. Rest the pastry for twenty minutes and again roll out and repeat the folding process. Again roll four times and rest the pastry. Repeat twice more and rest the pastry for one hour before rolling out for use in pies or bouchées. Bake in the oven at 220°C/425°F or gas mark 7 for the first ten minutes. For pies that need a full half an hour's cooking, reduce the heat for the remainder of the time.

👑 SUET CRUST

1½ lb/750 g plain flour	*5 ozs/150 g shredded beef suet*
½ teaspoon of salt	*¼ pint/15 cl water*
1 teaspoon of baking powder	

Sieve the flour, salt and baking powder into a bowl, mix in the suet, make a well and pour in warm water. Mix to a fairly stiff dough. Grease a 2 pint/125 cl pudding basin and roll out the dough. First of all, line the basin with the dough, leaving some of the paste hanging over the sides of the basin. Put in the filling. Cover the top with the extra paste rolled out in a circle to fit. Press the top firmly into position and trim off the edges close to the basin. Cover the pudding with a cloth, greaseproof paper or foil, fasten with string and put in a saucepan with boiling water to come half way up the pudding basin. Steam according to the time given in the particular recipe you are using – usually from four to six hours.

Note If making a sweet pudding instead of savoury, substitute one teaspoon of sugar for the half teaspoon of salt in the above list of quantities.

Table of Measurements

WEIGHT

15g	1/2oz	350g	12oz
20g	3/4oz	500g	1lb
30g	1oz	750g	1 1/2lb
60g	2oz	1kg	2 1/4lb
90g	3oz	1.25kg	2lb 12oz
125g	4oz	1.5kg	3lb 5oz
150g	5oz	2kg	4 1/2lb
175g	6oz	2.25kg	5lb
200g	7oz	2.5kg	5lb 8oz
250g	8oz	3kg	6lb 8oz

VOLUME

1.25ml	1/4 tsp	
2.5ml	1/2 tsp	
5ml	1 level tsp	
15ml	1 level tbsp	
30ml	1fl oz	
50ml	2fl oz	
15 cl	5fl oz	1/4 pint
20 cl	7fl oz	1/3 pint
30 cl	10fl oz	1/2 pint
40 cl	15fl oz	3/4 pint
60 cl	20fl oz	1 pint
75 cl		1 1/4 pints
90 cl		1 1/2 pints
1 litre		1 3/4 pints
1.25 litres		2 pints
2 litres		3 1/2 pints

AMERICAN MEASUREMENTS

Butter, margarine, lard
	25g	2tbsp 1/4 stick
	100g	8tbsp 1 stick

Breadcrumbs
Fresh	50g	1 cup
Dried	115g	1 cup

Cheese
Grated cheddar	115g	1 cup
Diced cheddar	170g	1 cup
Parmesan	150g	1 cup
Cream cheese	225g	1 cup

Cornflour 25g 1/4 cup

Dried fruit
Currants, sultanas	150g	1 cup
Apricots	150–175g	1 cup
Prunes	175g	1 cup
Glacé cherries	125g	1 cup

Fish
Prawns, peeled	175g	1 cup
Fish, cooked & flaked, firmly packed	225g	1 cup

Flour 115g 1 cup

Golden syrup, treacle, clear honey 350g 1 cup

Liquids 225ml 1 cup

Meat, minced, firmly packed 225g 1 cup

Nuts
Almonds, whole, shelled	150g	1 cup
Almonds, flaked	115g	1 cup
Hazelnuts	150g	1 cup
Walnuts & pecans	115g	1 cup

Almonds, ground & other ground nuts	115g	1 cup
Chopped nuts	115g	1 cup

Oats
Rolled oats	100g	1 cup
Oatmeal	175g	1 cup

Pulses
Split peas, lentils	225g	1 cup
Haricot beans	200g	1 cup
Kidney beans	300g	1 cup

Rice
Uncooked	200g	1 cup
Cooked & well drained	165g	1 cup
Semolina, ground rice and couscous	75g	1 cup

Sugar
Caster & granulated	225g	1 cup
Moist brown	200g	1 cup
Icing sugar	125g	1 cup

Vegetables
Onions, chopped	115g	1 cup
Cabbage, shredded	75g	1 cup
Peas, shelled	150g	1 cup
Beansprouts	50g	1 cup
Potatoes, peeled and diced	170g	1 cup
Potatoes, mashed	225g	1 cup
Spinach, cooked, purée	200–225g	1 cup
Tomatoes	225g	1 cup

MEASUREMENT

3mm	1/8in	10cm	4in
5mm	1/4in	11.5cm	4 1/2in
1cm	1/2in	12.5cm	5in
2cm	3/4in	15cm	6in
2.5cm	1in	17cm	6 1/2in
3cm	1 1/4in	18cm	7in
4cm	1 1/2in	20.5cm	8in
5cm	2in	23cm	9in
6cm	2 1/2in	24cm	9 1/2in
7.5cm	2 3/4in	25.5cm	10in
9cm	3 1/2in	30.5cm	12in

OVEN TEMPERATURES

Celsius	Fahrenheit	Gas mark	Description
110°C	225°F	1/4	cool
130°C	250°F	1/2	cool
140°C	275°F	1	very low
150°C	300°F	2	very low
170°C	325°F	3	low
180°C	350°F	4	moderate
190°C	375°F	5	mod/hot
200°C	400°F	6	hot
220°C	425°F	7	hot
230°C	450°F	8	very hot

For fan-assisted ovens reduce temperatures by 10°C

Index